Revolutionary Fights
& Fighters

The capture of the *Philadelphia*

AMERICAN FIGHTS & FIGHTERS SERIES

Revolutionary Fights & Fighters

Battles on Land and Sea from the American War of Independence, the North West Indian War, the Wars with France & Tripoli, and the War of 1812

Cyrus Townsend Brady

LEONAUR

Revolutionary Fights & Fighters
Battles on Land and Sea from the American War of Independence,
the North West Indian War, the Wars with France & Tripoli, and the War of 1812
by Cyrus Townsend Brady

First published under the title
Revolutionary Fights & Fighters

Leonaur is an imprint of Oakpast Ltd

Copyright in this form © 2011 Oakpast Ltd

ISBN: 978-0-85706-529-2 (hardcover)
ISBN: 978-0-85706-530-8 (softcover)

http://www.leonaur.com

Contents

Prefatory Note   9

PART 1 THE WAR OF THE REVOLUTION 1775–1783

The Defence of Fort Sullivan   11

Washington's Greatest Campaign   21

Paul Jones' Greatest Battle   38

The Saratoga Campaign: The Defeat of the Detachments   51

The Saratoga Campaign: The End of the Main Army   61

Greene's Campaign in the Carolinas   71

Storm and Surprise   95

Some Minor Sea-Fights of the Revolution   103

Yorktown   113

PART 2 THE INDIAN WAR IN THE NORTHWEST 1791–1794

St. Clair's Defeat   126

PART 3 THE WAR WITH FRANCE 1798–1800

Truxtun and the "Constellation"   136

PART 4 WAR WITH TRIPOLI 1802–1805

Decatur and the "Philadelphia"   149

PART 5 THE SECOND WAR WITH ENGLAND 1812–1815

The "Constitution's" Hardest Fight   158

The Niagara Campaign   167

The American "Wasps" and Their Victims   181

Macdonough at Lake Champlain   192

Reid and the "General Armstrong"   203

The Defence of Louisiana—The Last Battle
With England   213

The "Constitution's" Last Battle   226

To the Memory
of My Sister,
Cora Townsend Brady

Prefatory Note

This book is designed to call to the attention of those interested in our early struggles, some of the most remarkable of the great battles, heroic achievements and desperate undertakings through which we became a nation. No attempt has been made to cover all the events in the wars referred to. The author has chosen such as would serve to present a variety of incident, to illustrate the period and to exhibit the leaders and men. In the compiling of this book he has freely used every available source of information to which he had access, including the numerous printed volumes on the subject, and much material in manuscript form. Although the sketches are intended for popular reading, it is believed that they are accurate and reliable. Other volumes of the same character, covering the history of the wars and adventures in which we have been interested, from the voyages of Columbus to the capture of Manila, are in contemplation and preparation. That the stories may serve to stimulate patriotism and love of country, and to encourage men to consecrate themselves, with the devotion of their forefathers, to the civic battles for freedom and honour which are still to be waged, is the hope of the author.

C. T. B.

Philadelphia, Pa., 1900.

PART 1
THE WAR OF THE REVOLUTION
1775-1783

The Defence of Fort Sullivan

HOW THE SOUTH WAS SAVED TO THE REVOLUTION

While Washington's masterly strategy held Howe's army cooped up in Boston, the British government determined to send an expedition to the southern colonies in the hope of alienating them from the American cause. It was a foolish expedition and an unnecessary one. Sir Henry Clinton with seven regiments left Boston early in January, 1776, for the Cape Fear River, where he was to meet a large auxiliary force of war vessels and transports early in the spring. Meanwhile Martin, the royal Governor of North Carolina—the fourth in population and importance among the colonies—had organized a Tory force of some sixteen hundred men, mainly Scots, former adherents of the Stuarts, who had come to the colony after the futile rebellion in 1745.

This force was led by Donald Macdonald and his kinsman, Allan Macdonald, the husband of the noted and romantic Flora Macdonald, who had secured the escape of the Pretender, Charles Edward, after Culloden. They were now become loyal adherents of the British crown. At the Battle of Moore's Creek, February 27, 1776, this force was defeated by Colonel Richard Caswell with one thousand men strongly posted at a bridge over the creek, which Macdonald attempted to storm. The rout of the highlanders was complete; they lost nine hundred prisoners, two thousand stand of arms and seventy-five thousand dollars in gold. That settled the fate of North Carolina. In the face of the militia force, now amounting to ten thousand men, Sir Henry Clinton decided not to land, but cruised to and fro off the coast waiting for Parker and the expedition from Ireland, and a lonesome time they had of it.

In England preparations to carry on the expedition were allowed to drag in a most unmilitary manner, and it was not until February,

11

1776, that the force which had rendezvoused at Cork, in Ireland, set sail for the Cape Fear River, where they were to meet the weary and impatient Sir Henry Clinton with the seven regiments aforesaid. When they did start, misfortune attended them from the beginning. A succession of fierce westerly gales and head winds so far delayed their progress that it was not until May that they reached America. Commodore Sir Peter Parker, the early friend and patron of Nelson and Collingwood, a distinguished veteran, then sixty years old, and who afterward rose to the very high rank of Admiral-of-the-fleet in the British service, commanded the expedition. The troops he convoyed were led by Lord Cornwallis, who was, however, junior to Sir Henry Clinton, who assumed command of all the land forces at their junction.

There were divided counsels between the army and the navy in this ill-organized expedition, but at the earnest solicitation of Lord William Campbell, the deposed royalist Governor of South Carolina, it was finally decided to attack Charleston first; it was then, as now, the most important city in the South, and, as always, quite spoiling for a fight! Early in June, the British fleet of some fifty vessels appeared off the bar of Charleston Harbor. Unaccountable delays prevented the attack until the twenty-eighth of June. The Americans were not idle during this period. The South Carolinians, under the energetic leadership of Governor Rutledge, had been busily engaged in putting the harbour, the city and the province in a state of defence. The militia had been called out and the erection of a rude fort had been commenced on the southern extremity of Sullivan's Island, which commanded the channel some three miles from the town. The Island was low, sandy, and in parts thickly wooded with palmetto trees. Adjoining the Island on the seaward side and separated from it by a small inlet was another body of land, known as Long Island, which was a bare strip of sand, dotted here and there with a few bushes.

To the second regiment of the North Carolina militia, Colonel William Moultrie, had been entrusted the construction of the works, for the defence of the Island and the protection of the channel. Out of the *palmetto* logs on the Island, they built a square fort with bastions at each angle called Fort Sullivan. Two rows of logs notched and bolted together with wooden tree-nails and placed about eighteen feet apart, with the interspace solidly filled with sand, formed the enclosure. General Charles Lee, who had been sent to take charge of the defences of the province, sneered at it as being absolutely untenable, characterizing it as a probable slaughter-pen, and predicted that one British frigate would knock it to pieces in an hour! All the British frigates present seemed to have entertained the same opinion. The only other contributions that Lee made to the defence of the place were to withdraw about eight hundred of Moultrie's men, to endeavour to relieve him of the command of the post, and to abandon it. These last attempts were prevented by the determined resistance of Governor Rutledge, who had faith in Moultrie and in the work. The governor asked Moultrie if he could defend the fort. "I think I can," replied the phlegmatic soldier; whereupon Rutledge wrote him as follows:

> General Lee wishes you to evacuate the fort. You are not to do so without an order from me; I will sooner cut off my right hand than write one!

Brave words! When Lee could do no more, he wearied Moultrie to death with orders and instructions for him to build a bridge by which to retreat. The idea of a retreat absolutely never even presented itself as a possible contingency to the imperturbable American, who built no bridges!

The fort was armed with twenty-six guns of assorted sizes, long eighteen and twenty-four pounders being in the majority. On the day of the battle, it was garrisoned by some four hundred and fifty men, only thirty of whom were artillerists. The rest, however, were expert riflemen; it was found that their training with small arms was of great value in enabling them to sight the great guns. Next to Moultrie in command was Lieutenant-Colonel Isaac Motte, and the major of the regiment was the subsequently famous partisan leader Francis Marion. Moultrie and his officers had served in the Indian wars of the province, and were cool, resolute soldiers. The English plan of attack seems to have been for the troops to land upon Long Island, pass the inlet which separated them from Sullivan's Island, and which they had been informed was easily fordable; and then, in conjunction with the ships which would silence the American guns, they would storm the position, which would leave the channel free and open the way for their attack on the town. It never seems to have occurred to them that the ships could have passed the fort without difficulty, as indeed was done several years later, and by capturing the city render the outworks untenable.

However, in spite of his contempt for American arms, Sir Peter Parker seems to have made his dispositions wisely. He purposed that the *Bristol* and the *Experiment*, two small line-of-battle ships of fifty guns each, and the frigates *Active* and *Solebay*, of twenty-eight guns each, should assault the fort at close range directly in front of it. The frigates *Actaeon* and *Syren*, of twenty-eight guns each, the sloop-of-war *Sphynx*, of twenty-two guns, with the *Friendship*, the *Ranger* and the *St. Lawrence*, small armed ships, were ordered to take a position on the west flank of the fort, which was there still unfinished, the wall rising only seven feet; though the parapet had been strengthened by heavy planking as a protection against possible or probable assault this defence would avail little against heavy guns. These latter ships were to enfilade the works and render them untenable. On the other flank, a bomb vessel, the *Thunder*, was stationed to shell the works.

Unfortunately for the British, the shallowness of the water did not permit them to bring the heavy ships of the main attacking column nearer than three hundred and fifty yards, which of course prevented the effective use of grape-shot, a main resource for clearing an enemy's works in such a contingency. At half past ten o'clock in the morning the ships got under way with the flood tide; at a quarter after eleven the first four had anchored at their stations, the *Active* off the east bastion, the *Experiment* and the *Solebay* off the west bastion, and the *Bristol*, carrying Sir Peter Parker's flag, off the curtain, or wall between the two bastions. The *Sphynx, Actaeon* and *Syren* owing to mismanagement on the part of the pilots, fouled each other disastrously and got aground on a shoal in the middle ground. The bomb vessel broke down after throwing a few shell into the fort, which produced no material effect, as they mainly alighted in a morass where their fuses were quenched; and the three smaller vessels, not liking the look of things, and deprived of the assistance of the frigates, withdrew without going into action at all. This left the two small ships-of-the-line and the two light frigates to do the fighting.

A little after eleven o'clock they poured their heavy broadsides of solid shot into the fort, and on the part of the British thereafter the firing was fast and furious. The shot of the British guns made little or no impression upon the soft, spongy *palmetto* logs into which they sank, or through which they penetrated without splintering them, only to bury themselves harmlessly in the sandy banking between the log walls. On the other hand the firing of the Americans was slow but dreadfully destructive. At the beginning of the battle Moultrie actually had but twenty-eight charges of powder per gun! He sent to General Lee for more and received word that if he had exhausted his powder without driving off the ships he should retire! Governor Rutledge, however, sent him a small supply and the intrepid Marion volunteered with a small party of heroic men to get some from a small schooner nearby which was fully exposed to the British fire. Altogether the supply did not amount to more than forty rounds. It was enough, however.

Rutledge had given orders to Moultrie to throw away no shot, and these instructions were in consonance with the cool, deliberate spirit of the American commander. The riflemen of the fort exhibited wonderful marksmanship and scarcely a shot was lost. The officers themselves sighted the guns, and their bullets nearly always sped to their mark. The heavy shot ripped up the planking of the ships in every direction. "Mind the commodore, look out for the fifty-gunships!" was the word Moultrie gave to be passed among his men, and the execution on these ships was dreadful. About noon, when he looked for the co-operation of the army, Sir Peter Parker was informed by a message from Clinton that he had found that the passage between the islands was some seven feet deep at low tide and utterly impracticable. Only the grossest indifference on the part of the British had prevented this fact from being known for days before.

Sir Henry Clinton had marched some troops down to the inlet, where he was met by a smart fire from the American militia, encamped on Sullivan's Island, for the purpose of disputing the passage of the inlet and supporting the fort; and after a brief artillery duel between his batteries and a single American eighteen pounder, under Thompson, which was ineffective on both sides, the English marched back again. Later in the day, Clinton also embarked a number of troops in boats and sailed down the coast with a view to effecting a landing on the same Island; but a number of Thompson's militia who took advantage of the cover afforded by the sandhills and bushes and poured in a hot fire, rendered the operation impracticable—Sir Henry at least had not forgotten Bunker Hill and its lessons—so he took his men back to Long Island, where they continued their battle with the hot sun, the bad water, and the active mosquito, and watched Parker banging away furiously at the fort for the rest of the day. His excursion had been a notable diversion indeed.

The wharves and buildings along the shore of Charleston were covered with people listening to the roar of the guns, watching the attack on the fort, upon whose resistance their own future so largely depended. There had been flying from a staff the flag of the regiment,

Sergeant Jasper raising the flag at Fort Moultrie

which had been designed by Moultrie himself—it was a blue flag with a white crescent in the dexter corner, with the word "*Liberty*" emblazoned upon it—when, to the horror of the spectators, they observed through a rift in the smoke that the flag was down! It had been shot away, and had fallen on the sand outside of the fort. Their emotions can be imagined. That little fort alone stood between them and disaster, its capture meant the destruction of their homes, their captivity, possible dangers worse than death to their wives and children from savages against whom they would be unable to protect themselves subsequently. Every hope was wrapped up in Moultrie and his gallant men—a fact, by the way, of which the latter were fully sensible—and it was that which nerved their arms and sustained their spirits, it was that which made them determine that not a single precious charge of powder should be wasted.

Sergeant William Jasper, an heroic soldier, instantly climbed through an embrasure, leaped over the parapet, seized the flag, tore it from its broken staff and affixed it to a halberd; and untouched by the storm of shot which was poured upon him, planted it as he said "in the bastion nearest the enemy," where it flew unharmed during the remainder of the battle. Sergeant Mcdaniel was mortally wounded by a shot which came through an embrasure. As he was carried away from the gun platform the brave fellow cried out to his brother soldiers, "I am dying, but don't let the cause of liberty die with me this day." But there was equal heroism on the other side as well. The British had expected an easy victory, but they took the dreadful punishment they received like the heroes they were.

As the tide began to ebb, one of the springs on the cable of the *Bristol* was shot away, and the ship swung with the tide, presenting her stern to the fort. Her condition at once became critical, not to say desperate. She was raked again and again; every man on her quarter-deck was either killed or wounded. The brave old commodore covered with blood, his clothing torn from him by splinters, remained alone at his station, on the exposed quarter-deck on which all of the other officers stationed there had been killed or wounded, calmly refusing to retire to a safer spot while he gave directions for extricating the ship from her terrible position. Captain John Morris, the commander of the ship, lost his right arm, and when the stump had been dressed insisted on resuming his station by the commodore, and it was not until he received several other severe wounds from the effects of which he very soon died, that he allowed himself to be taken below. The *Ex-*

periment was in little better case than the *Bristol*. The carnage on both ships was appalling, amounting to nearly thirty-five *per cent,* of their total force. Through the energy of Midshipman Saumarez, afterward a famous admiral, a new spring was bent to the cable and the broadside of the *Bristol* was again turned to the fort. Sir Peter in all his wars had never stood under a hotter fire.

During the action General Lee came over to the fort to see how matters were getting along, and finding everything was going well, he returned to his position in the city. The officers, who had been coolly smoking their pipes, received him with all military honours, and Moultrie of course said nothing about the bridge, though I imagine he wished to do so. The men, most of them half-naked, in the fierce sun and heat, deliberately fought on, refreshed by copious draughts from large buckets of grog, which Moultrie mixed with his own hand. As the shades of evening descended, Parker made a last desperate effort to batter down the defences. The firing was by broadsides simultaneously, and as the heavy shot from the tremendous discharges of over one hundred guns smashed upon the fort, the walls quivered and trembled so that Moultrie thought several times that the merlons between the embrasures would be beaten in.

However, they still held, and after continuing a fierce fire, to which the Americans kept up their slow, persistent, annoying, galling reply, until most of their ammunition was expended, they gave over the attempt. A little after nine o'clock in the evening, the British withdrew, all, that is, except the frigate *Actaeon*, which had not yet succeeded in getting off the shoal. By Parker's orders, next morning she was set on fire by her crew and abandoned. The Americans took possession of her, discharged her battery at the retiring Englishmen, captured her colours, and several boatloads of arms and supplies, before she blew up.

The loss on the *Bristol* amounted to forty killed and seventy-two wounded, including Captain Morris, mortally. The *Experiment* had twenty-three killed and forty-five wounded, her captain losing his right arm; on the *Active* and *Solebay*, fifteen men were killed and wounded; and the American loss was ten killed and twenty-six wounded! Lord William Campbell, the quondam royal Governor of South Carolina, served on the *Bristol* as a volunteer and took charge of a division on the lower gun deck during the action. He was severely injured by a spent ball and after suffering for two years, died from the effects of the blow. The *Bristol* and the *Experiment* were nearly dismantled, the main and mizzenmasts of the former were tottering, the foremast badly wounded. The mizzenmast fell over the side early the next day before it could be secured, the mainmast was cut away fifteen feet below the hounds, the ship was completely unrigged, and several of her guns had been dismounted. The *Experiment* was in a scarcely better condition. The *Active* and *Solebay* could with difficulty be kept afloat. The *Sphynx* and the *Syren* had suffered somewhat from the American fire and much more from the effects of their collision and grounding.

Sir Henry Clinton loaded his troops back on the transports and, convoyed by a single frigate, the only war vessel left seaworthy after the action, sailed away and joined Howe's expedition at New York. Parker took three weeks to refit his ships when he also departed. South Carolina and the Southern States generally, were free from invasion for at least two years and the story of this splendid victory helped to encourage and inspirit the remainder of the Americans in the critical period attending the beginning of their great struggle for liberty. The greatest praise was given Moultrie and his gallant comrades for their brave defence of the fort, which in his honour was renamed Fort Moultrie, and the commander was made a brigadier-general in the regular Continental service.

He rose to the rank of major-general thereafter, and on one occasion saved Charleston a second time from being captured, by the spirited defence he made against Prevost's attack. He was unfortunately made prisoner when Charleston was captured by Cornwallis, several years later, and remained in captivity during the balance of the war. But he resisted every attempt which was made by the British to seduce him from the American cause, with the same determination that he had defended his position. He was several times made governor of his native state after independence had been achieved, and died early in the present century full of years and honours. The heroism of Sergeant Jasper was rewarded by the present of an elegant sword and the proffer of a lieutenant's commission. He accepted the former, but modestly declined the latter on the ground that neither by birth, education nor fortune, was he a fit person for the command. One of the most beautiful women of Charleston presented a pair of colours to Moultrie's regiment with the following little speech:

> Your gallant behaviour in defence of liberty and your country entitles you to the highest honours; accept these two standards as a reward justly due your regiment; and I make not the least

doubt, under heaven's protection, you will stand by them as long as they can wave in the air of liberty.

The regiment accepted the colours in the spirit of the generous donor. When the ill-fated attempt by Howe and d'Estaing was made to storm the British lines at Savannah during the war, the flags were planted upon the entrenchments by their bearers, Lieutenants Bush and Hume, who were both immediately shot down. Lieutenant Gray while making an effort to advance them met the same fate. Sergeant Jasper successfully bore them away finally in the repulse, but in so doing received his death wound—faithful to the last. The colours were captured when Charleston was finally surrendered and they are now among the most cherished mementoes of British prowess kept in the trophy room in the Tower of London. Certainly no flag ever flew over better men than that under which Moultrie and Marion commanded and Jasper and Macdaniel fought!

Washington's Greatest Campaign

1. TRENTON

There are three things which determine the relative values of military enterprises—the idea, the method and the result. From these points of view, Washington's Trenton and Princeton campaign ranks among the most brilliant in history, and its conception and the manner of its prosecution stamp him as a soldier of the first order. The importance of the end aimed at, and attained in large measure, can hardly be overstated. Although neither of the engagements which took place in carrying out the great idea of it rose to the dignity of a battle but must rather be classed as heavy skirmishes, I regard it as one of those decisive operations which are turning points in history. Had the results been other than they were, the whole course of the world would have been altered. In spite of the apparent insignificance of the operations, the incidents of the campaign, when the material with which it was worked out is considered, are as fraught with interest, as full of value to the soldier, and evidence as much greatness in the leader, as if Washington had held under his command a hundred thousand men, and the little combats had been as great and as sanguinary as the gigantic battles of larger wars and later days. It is not numbers, but strategy, tactics, personal courage, and things achieved, by which we judge the soldier.

In these operations, which certainly represented the culminating period of his career, Washington displayed a dash and daring like that of Napoleon in his early Italian campaigns, an inflexible capacity of resistance and recuperation which suggests the great Frederick in his days of adversity, and a determined, dogged, not-to-be-denied persistence which calls to mind the indomitable Grant. The fate of the Revolution was determined right then and there. More than at any other given period of that great conflict, the cause of human liberty hung in the trembling balance on that wild December night.

The American army had been consistently beaten since the ruinous battle of Long Island, six months before. Their manoeuvres had been one long series of retrograde movements in the face of a superior enemy, which, though conducted with great courage and masterly skill (any fool can lead a charge, it takes a soldier to retreat without the disorganization and destruction of his army), had as yet proven most disastrous to our arms. Post after post had been lost, and finally the whole Province of New Jersey had been abandoned. The moral effect of the continued retreat was exceedingly discouraging to army and nation. Washington's army had been reduced by capture, the casualties of battle, desertion, straggling and expiration of terms of enlistment, to a little handful of less than two thousand men, the term of service of the major part of whom expired with the beginning of the year.

This little handful had wearily straggled across the Delaware River. Taking the precaution, by Washington's orders, to gather up and take with them to the west bank of that broad stream every boat for sixty miles up and down the river, they gained a little respite from the slow but persistent pursuit which had forced them on. In the absence of transportation, the advance of the English was temporarily checked, and the hunted Americans had time to breathe. That was all Washington wanted. They were yet to learn, these red-coats, what manner of man this was whom they were driving so relentlessly ahead of them. So, with fatal supineness, they made no attempt to build boats—they waited. Delays in warfare and in love are always dangerous and the subsequent results proved the maxim.

The British absolutely despising their oft-beaten, always-retreating enemy, were cantoned in several scattered detachments on the east bank of the Delaware; going into winter quarters for the time being, to wait for the freezing of the river, when it was Howe's intention to cross on the ice, brush aside the last remnants of armed resistance under Washington, occupy Philadelphia, and end the war. Man proposes, but—Washington had contemplated the possibility of such action and had resolved, if unable to prevent it, to retreat to the mountains of Virginia and keep up a partisan warfare to an end. This was only a last alternative, however, and he had another plan in view.

The British headquarters and general supply depot had been located at New Brunswick. General Grant had been left in command. Howe and Cornwallis returned to New York, and Cornwallis made preparations for a trip to England. As soon as Washington discovered the separation of the British army into different groups, he conceived the idea of recrossing the river, assuming the offensive, falling upon the scattered detachments, beating them in detail, moving on for New Brunswick to capture the supplies and clear the country, and take a position in the hills about Morristown, where he could threaten New York and protect Philadelphia.

His attack on Trenton was no mere return snarl of a goaded animal—it was part of this brilliant plan. He had the nucleus for offensive action in his own little army, tried by summer's burning heat, by fire and water, steel and lead, and now to show themselves impervious to winter's biting cold. They had been pursued until their spirits were absolutely upon an edge, and the great American felt that he had under his command an army of baited lions. It is sometimes a bad thing for the conquerors when they press the conquered up against the wall, till the beaten face about with nothing behind them but destruction and nothing before them but the foe. Men have ever found the last ditch an easy place in which to die. That was the situation of this patriot army. They literally had no clothes, no blankets, no shoes, no provisions, no anything but arms and souls, but they were not born to die like hunted foxes. Washington *knew* that he could depend upon them.

He decided to break through the English line at Trenton, where there was a large detachment of Hessian troops commanded by Colonel Rall, comprising three regiments. Rall, Lossburg and Anspach, with some artillery and cavalry, amounting to about sixteen hundred men. Colonel Rall was a dashing soldier who had distinguished himself in the storming of Fort Washington, and as negligent and confident as he was brave. Washington's plan was that Putnam, who had been appointed military governor of the city, should send out a large force from Philadelphia to skirmish and engage the attention of Von Donop, who had command of a large detachment of English and Germans at Bordentown and vicinity. General Ewing, in the centre, with a portion of the militia of New Jersey and Pennsylvania, which had been called out by the most desperate appeals, was to cross two miles below Trenton at Bond's Ferry to interpose between Von Donop and Rall, to prevent any junction and to intercept any fugitives from Washington's attack.

On the right, Gates and Cadwalader, with a larger body of Pennsylvania militia, was to cross at Bristol and advance upon the posts at Mt. Holly and vicinity; Washington, on the left with the Continental line, was to cross above the town, and deliver the main attack in person. Thus Von Donop would be kept off, Rall overwhelmed, and the dash made for New Brunswick, after the divisions had united. Before the campaign began, General Charles Lee, who was as great a traitor as Benedict Arnold, without any of Arnold's redeeming qualities, had been captured by the British, fortunately for the American cause, and General Sullivan had brought to Washington's aid the remnants of the northern army. This increased his available force to about twenty-five hundred men.

The night of Christmas day, Wednesday, December 25, 1776, was chosen for the attempt. The surprise was to take place in the early morning of the day after. Washington counted upon the well known convivial habits of the Germans and the relaxation attendant upon the Christmas festivities, to facilitate his operations. The army had been divided into two divisions. General Greene was to command the first division, General Sullivan, the second. Washington was to go with the first. About six o'clock in the evening his own detachment, which he was to lead, was paraded on the Pennsylvania side at McKonkey's Ferry, nine miles above Trenton, and immediately thereafter the passage of the river began. It was a clear moonlight night. There was a light snow upon the ground which had fallen during the day, but it was very cold and growing colder with each succeeding moment.

The river, the current of which flowed swiftly by the place of crossing, where the width of the stream was about twelve hundred feet, was filled with huge cakes of ice, which made the attempt to pass it both difficult and dangerous. Large *scows*, *bateaux*, and a kind of trading vessels called Durham boats, sharp-bowed, double-ended affairs, thirty or forty feet long, had been provided; and under the skilful charge of Glover's regiment of Gloucester and Marblehead fishermen, who had already done such signal service in the retreat at Long Island, the passage was effected. Washington had hoped to begin his march to Trenton by midnight, but it could not be. It was eleven o'clock before the infantry had all crossed. The cold had grown more intense with every passing moment. The sky was now deeply overcast, and a few flakes of snow gave ominous presage of an approaching storm.

The little army was compelled to wait for five hours on the low bleak hills, unsheltered from the tempest of snow and sleet which raged with ever increasing fury, until the artillery under the indefatigable Knox could get over, which was not until after three o'clock in the morning. All hope of an early surprise was of necessity abandoned.

24

While they waited, two men arrived with messages for Washington. The first apprised him that the miserable Gates, upon whom he had depended, had left Cadwalader's detachment, and gone to Congress, which had fled precipitately to Baltimore. Cadwalader had made desperate and heroic attempts to get over, but that owing to the ice which banked up against the shore at the side of the river, he had been unable to land a single piece of artillery or horse, and had therefore given over the attempt and would be unable to cooperate. The second message was from Ewing to the effect that he had not even attempted to cross in view of the conditions. The messengers had found Washington by following the bloody footprints of the barefooted men in the drifting snow!

Suggestions were made that they recross and try it again some other time, but Washington had retreated just as long as he was going to, and he resolved—momentous decision that it was—to push on with his own force and after he had done what he could, recross and then prepare to try it again. The watchword given by the commander himself was "victory or death" and that represented his state of mind perfectly. It was four o'clock in the morning when they started for Trenton. There were two roads which led from McKonkey's Ferry to Trenton, one near the river, the other further inland. They strike the town at different ends. The lower, or river road, enters the village of Trenton, which then contained upward of a hundred houses, near the stone bridge, which crossed the Assunpink Creek which bounds the southern side of the village. The upper, called the Pennington road, enters the town at the junction of the two broad streets which ran together at a sharp angle. Washington and Greene took the upper road, Sullivan, the lower.

What were the thoughts of those men of desperate purpose as they toiled through the drifts on those frozen roads, cut to pieces by the pitiless sleet, torn by the fierce wind which searched out every rent in their flimsy, tattered garments? They were making a way for liberty, blazing the path of freedom with their own bleeding feet—marking the trail as it has ever been marked, by the blood of man—staggering, fainting, freezing, pressing on, and the genius of Independence walking by their side. A *via dolorosa* of suffering, this, in that bitter Nativity night, and those who followed worthy subjects of that great Master, who ever fought the battle of human freedom, even to the awful Cross!

About seven o'clock a message came up from Sullivan on the river road to Washington on the inland road. The snow had wet the priming of their firearms, and they could not be used. What was to be done? "Tell him to push on with the bayonet," said the grim commander, "the town must be taken and I am resolved to take it." When Sullivan's men heard this reply delivered by the officer, in their impetuosity they began slipping the bayonets over the gun-barrels without order, and gaily resumed the advance. It was eight in the morning when the head of the upper column struck the Hessian advance picket on the Pennington road. All of the men comprising the guard had sought shelter in a hut from the driving snow and the furious sleet.

Without a moment's hesitation the Americans went forward at a double-quick; at the same time the other column on the river road came in contact with the picket there. The sharp rattle of musketry broke the stillness of the wintry morning at both ends of the little town. In the midst of the drifting snow, the startled Hessians retreated rapidly upon the main guard. The Americans came forward with determination and soon all of the advance parties of the enemy were in the full retreat toward the town. There the drums were beating the assembly wildly, and the terrified Hessians were running through the streets half-dressed toward the rallying points, so far as they had been designated. Rall, whose indulgences the previous day and night had been long and deep, had awakened and hastily dressed himself and descended to the street.

The whirling snow and sleet prevented the Hessians from discovering the force of their opponents even at this juncture. The alert Americans were soon extending along the upper road past the village to encircle the town from the left. Other regiments started down toward the river to meet the advance of Sullivan's division. The artillery was massed at the head of King and Queen Streets, under Washington's direction, and a steady fire raked the two main avenues of the village. Several hasty and entirely ineffective shots were fired in return by two guns of the regiment Rall in King Street, but before they became dangerous, they were captured by a spirited charge led by Captain William Washington and Lieutenant James Monroe, afterward President of the United States. These officers were both wounded before the guns were taken and turned upon the Hessians.

Meanwhile Sullivan's men had seized the stone bridge over the Assunpink on the right, routing the cavalry picket; Stark's regiment had extended to the left, parallel to the main streets, and the other regiments were led out beyond the town to encircle it from below;

their artillery meanwhile played upon the huddled enemy attempting to escape through the wood, and by a ford, to pass the creek. The American troops took cover behind fences, walls and houses, and poured a withering fire upon the already demoralized Hessians who finally retreated outside of the town to an apple orchard on the east where they re-formed. Under the orders of Rall himself, they bravely attempted to retake the town, which was full of their plunder, and charged forward with the bayonet. The Americans met this charge by a volley and countercharge. It is interesting to note that as the Continentals rushed forward determinedly upon the wavering Dutchmen, they shouted with a grim humour which savours marvellously of the present, the opening-words of Thomas Paine's famous tract, written at this period, "*These are the times that try men's souls!*"

Certainly the words were apposite to the Hessians' situation. Rall, their commander, had fallen mortally wounded. Von Dechow, the second in command, likewise. Many other officers who had gallantly exposed themselves in the attempt to rally and lead the men forward had been killed or wounded. Forrest's battery was pouring in a withering fire of grape. Greene's men were pressing them from the north, Stark's from the west, Sullivan's from the south. Gun after gun was being brought up on their flanks and in their rear. The Assunpink bridge and ford had been secured after several hundred had escaped. There was no salvation for the rest. In panic terror they lowered their flags and threw down their arms. The actual fighting had lasted about half an hour. The battle was over. "*This is a glorious day for our country,*" said Washington.

The killed and wounded of the enemy numbered over one hundred, the captured nearly nine hundred and over five hundred escaped. One thousand stand of arms, six field pieces, and a large quantity of supplies and munitions of war came into the hands of the Americans, who had only two killed and two wounded!

So far everything had gone well. The failure of the other divisions to cross, however, had rendered Washington's position, in spite of his success, most precarious; so with a prudence as great as his courage, he at once decided to cross to the west bank of the river once more. Allowing his troops until the afternoon to recuperate, as the shades of night advanced they retraced their steps, but in what different spirits. They had demonstrated their right to be. They were an army, their leader a soldier. No one would ever doubt it again, certainly not the British. That road which in the morning had been the path of freezing despair, was now the way of the conquerors. Accompanied by all of their prisoners—and what a contrast there was between the well fed and well clothed Hessians and their ragged captors—they recrossed the river, and occupied their old camps. Two of the men froze to death, and over one thousand were prostrated by the exposure incident to the fearful hardships they had undergone. More determined than ever, Washington despatched letters and couriers in every direction to assemble his forces and move upon New Brunswick, which was still the goal of his endeavour.

> The successful issue of his daring adventure entailed yet further responsibilities, and the campaign was only just begun. As for himself, the world now knew him for a soldier. And a withered old man in the palace of the Sans Souci, in Berlin, who had himself known victories and defeats, who had himself stood at bay, facing a world in arms so successfully that men called him 'The Great,' called this and the subsequent campaign the finest military exploit of the age![1]

2 PRINCETON

There was mounting in hot haste on the Jersey side of the river when the astonishing news of the fell swoop on the Hessians at Trenton was carried back to the negligent and over-confident British commanders in New York. Washington was still to be reckoned with, it appeared, and with an energy utterly foreign to their previous movements, the various advanced posts to the south were abandoned, the troops in the northern part of the state were concentrated at New Brunswick and marched thence to Princeton, to which place the lower division had repaired. Lord Cornwallis, the ablest of the British soldiers in America, was put in command with orders to catch and crush the pestilent American who never knew when he was beaten, or who refused to stay so if he knew it—a harder task, this, than either Howe or his gallant subordinate had ever set themselves to accomplish before, and one they found quite impossible after all. All that they desired, however, was an opportunity to get at him, they thought, and this opportunity Washington, with his eyes still fixed on the main plan, of which the engagement at Trenton had only been a detail, was quite willing to afford them.

Fired by the splendid success of the Continentals, the Pennsylvania

---

1 From the author's book *For Love of Country*.

Surrender of Colonel Rall at the Battle of Princeton

and New Jersey militia under Cadwalader, Ewing and Mifflin, at last got across the river and established themselves in the vicinity of Burlington, and on the twenty-ninth of December, Washington followed with his staff and escort and took up his headquarters upon the scene of his successful battle. It took two days for his victorious Continental troops to get across, however, on account of the heavy ice in the river, but by the evening of the last day of the year they were all assembled at Trenton. It was a fateful hour for the Revolution—all the hours of this campaign were fateful—and a mischance at any time or place would have ended it. The period of enlistment of most of the men expired that night; if they left him, Washington would find himself on the morrow abandoned by the veteran and heroic soldiery who had enabled him to inaugurate his great campaign, and would be forced to rely entirely upon the raw and untried militia.

He was equal to the emergency, however, for he had the men paraded, and rode along the lines, addressing the several regiments in the brief soldierly style in which he was a master, imploring them to remain with him until he could complete his campaign, telling them of the importance of their action, firing their hearts with his own determined resolution and patriotic devotion, pledging his private fortune—in which glorious example he was followed by many of his officers, gentlemen of condition and means—for their long arrears of pay, and promising them a small bounty besides. He was seconded in his appeal by all of his officers, and the results were most happy. The men unanimously elected to stay with him for at least six weeks, or until the campaign was terminated one way or the other. We, today, can scarcely imagine what this decision involved. It was the expression of willingness on the part of the naked, barefoot, hungry, frozen men, to stay and fight against overwhelming odds through the dreary winter, when they could have gone back home to a situation so superior to their present condition, that it might have been called luxury; and the glory of the men should not be lost sight of in the glory of the man. To that army of patriots our eternal gratitude, nay, the gratitude of all those who love and cherish and would fain fight for human liberty, is surely due.

Stout old Robert Morris now sent up to his friend George Washington the money he had raised by going from door to door with extended hand among his friends in Philadelphia. To such desperate straits had they been reduced in the field, that the first instalment of less than five hundred dollars had been most gratefully received; and when a day or so later he made a further glorious remittance of fifty thousand dollars, the faithful troops, for the first time in many months, were paid in part.

By Washington's orders there were skirmishing parties of horse and light infantry scattered all through the country between Trenton and Princeton, where it was soon learned that Cornwallis had assembled some eight thousand men preparatory to the dash for Trenton. Much valuable information was gathered and some prisoners made, besides great annoyance, inflicted upon the British. The English and Hessians had behaved with frightful barbarity in their march through, and occupation of, the country; there had been murder, pillage, rapine, and outraging of women, and now the enraged country people hung upon their flanks, aided the American skirmishers, and cut off unwary stragglers without mercy. Washington had ordered Cadwalader from the Cross Wicks and Mifflin from Bordentown to join him at Trenton. After a hard night march in the bitter cold, sleet and rain, over frightful roads, they reached Trenton on the second day of the year about noon. These reinforcements raised his little force to a total of about five thousand men, three-fifths of them being militia who had probably never heard a shot fired in anger.

Cornwallis leaving Grant's brigade, three regiments of British, about thirteen hundred men, under Lieutenant Colonel Mawhood at Princeton, as a reserve and to protect his rear, advanced early on the morning of January 2, 1777, in great haste toward Trenton. All day long he was compelled to fight his way forward against a heavy skirmishing fire from the riflemen under Greene, who took advantage of their opportunity to pour a galling fire upon the regular troops. Washington needed one more day to assemble and unite his force, and Greene agreed to give it to him. The delay gave Washington time to withdraw his army across the Assunpink, swollen with the winter rains, and post them on the high ground south of it in a strong and advantageous position, for two miles along the bank. The artillery was massed at the famous stone bridge.

In the gray of the evening, the van of Cornwallis' wearied troops, the American riflemen having been cleared out of the northern side of the creek, after severe fighting and heavy loss on the part of the British, advanced to take Washington's position. Three separate charges were made upon the bridge, and were repulsed with loss. But the British subordinate commanders urged Cornwallis to push the attack and end the matter then and there. The creek was fordable in half a dozen places, and all that would be necessary would be to make a simultaneous attack upon the bridge and the fords with their superior forces, place themselves upon the other bank, turn the flank of the rebel army, drive Washington into the *cul de sac* formed by the creek and the river and hammer him to pieces at leisure and at pleasure.

The British were tired out, however; they had marched and fought in the mud all day; there was no escape for the "old fox" now; they had him cornered at last and there was no need for hurry—so they reasoned. Cornwallis resolved to wait until morning. This is where he made the mistake of his life. Washington was as keenly appreciative of the exigencies of the situation of his army as Cornwallis and his officers. He had no mind to be caught in that trap, he had not put himself in that position for nothing, and his plan for extricating himself had been already matured. He would try an offensive defence.

As the night fell and the British went into camp, he caused tremendous fires to be built all along his lines next to the river bank, which were to be continuously fed by a small body of men detailed for the purpose, who were to act as sentries and to move about, make a great deal of noise and expose themselves as much as possible with safety, to convey the idea that they were in great force and very actively preparing for the morrow. The rest of the army muffled the wheels of the guns, and sent the heavier baggage down toward Philadelphia, where Putnam had sent a detachment to meet and protect it, and then about eleven o'clock at night, in little detachments in rapid succession, they silently stole away.

Whispering their orders, making no sound, giving no alarm, they followed a long roundabout road called the Quaker road which passed through the village of Sand Town, and for several miles led away from the river toward the southeast before it made an abrupt turn to the north. The weather had changed, the wind came from the north and the wet, muddy, impassable roads froze as hard as iron; it grew bitter cold once more, as it had before the attack on Trenton. They crept cautiously around the left flank of Cornwallis' sleeping army, and headed for Princeton, to that goal for which the indomitable American had been making since Christmas day—the stores at New Brunswick. To extricate an army safely from a desperate situation has ever been accounted a work of great generalship; no army was ever moved more quickly, dexterously and ably than this one. The British never dreamed they had gone until morning.

It was another desperate march over the badly cleared, stump encumbered roads. When the morning came, clear, very cold, the ground covered with hoar frost, the advance under General Mercer reached the lower bridge over Stony Brook Creek and, crossing the bridge, went up the river bank toward another bridge which crosses it on the direct road to Trenton, which they had intended to hold as long as possible and then destroy, to check the advance of Cornwallis; while the rest of the army under Washington continued by another road through the trees and, sheltered by the hills, on toward the College and village of Princeton. A part of the British detachment at Princeton had crossed the Stony Brook bridge already on the march to join Cornwallis, when this advance regiment, the seventeenth under Mawhood in person, caught sight of Mercer's men, the sunlight gleaming on the gun-barrels through the trees betraying them. The English retraced their steps and recrossed the bridge at once.

To deploy on both sides was the work of a few moments. There was a little rise of ground off to the right which would make a strong defensive position. Both parties rushed headlong for it immediately. The Americans were the quicker and lined up on it pouring a heavy fire into the advancing British, which did great execution. The redcoats were most gallantly led, however, and proved themselves soldiers of the highest class. In spite of the withering rifle fire, they poured in a return volley and covered by the smoke, they desperately charged the American position at the point of the bayonet. General Mercer on a white horse was in front of his men, by his side Colonel Haslet of the Delaware regiment was standing dismounted.

The first volley killed Mercer's horse. throwing him heavily; he rose to his feet at once, however, to encourage his men. The same volley sent a bullet crashing into Haslet's brain. Many others were killed and wounded. The Continentals were thrown into some confusion by this fierce discharge, delivered scarcely a hundred feet away, and as this brigade was most unfortunately unprovided with bayonets, they resisted stubbornly for a few minutes with clubbed muskets, and then gave way, retreating back toward the main body on the lower road.

Mercer, sword in hand, threw himself before the fugitives, rallied a few of his officers and men and fiercely attacked the oncoming British. He was beaten to the ground, called a rebel, asked to surrender, and when he answered in indignation with a sword cut, was thrust through and through with the bayonets, and left for dead on the field. He died a few days after the battle in great agony, leaving behind him a stainless and honoured name.

At this juncture, when the British were sweeping everything before them, the Pennsylvania militia dashed out of the wood. They had been sent up on the double-quick to the rescue by Washington, who had heard the noise of the conflict. Undaunted by this new enemy, the British, with admirable precision, which won Washington's admiration and commendation, faced quickly about and began to move forward to apply the deadly cold steel again, and to try to take Moulder's Philadelphia battery. The militia hastily returned the fire of the enemy, but as the smoke blew away, they saw that the British were unchecked, and as the red-coats came fiercely on, the American line began to waver. They had never been in action before, and a hand to hand conflict was more than they bargained for; only a veteran could meet the British bayonet after all. An incipient panic was there. One more moment and they too had been in retreat, but the hour brought the man.

Attended by one or two staff officers, Washington galloped recklessly on the field; one glance put him in possession of the situation. The Americans were being routed; he could not fight a long drawn out battle here; whatever was to be done must be done at once. Cornwallis had already heard the roar of the guns at Trenton, and awaking to find himself outgeneraled at once discovered Washington's escape, and had pushed his army forward at the double-quick. If the British could hold the Americans in play for a short space of time, the veterans of Cornwallis would be upon them. Without a second's hesitation, Washington rode by Mercer's shattered brigade and called upon them to advance, and then dashed down the wavering Pennsylvania line, turning his horse as he came before the main body of the advancing British, and by the very force of his splendid personality led the erstwhile hesitating militia down upon their enemies in a surprising charge, both parties firing before they met.

There was a sharp hand to hand struggle, with Washington in the midst of it. At the same moment, the other regiments of the Americans came up and took up a position on the flank of the British, and poured into them a deadly fire. Moulder's Philadelphia battery raked the valley with grape. Washington was in the thick of it all. He was lost sight of by his aides in the smoke for the moment, and when it cleared away he was discovered mad with the excitement of the battle leading on the men. A born fighter, he! He bore a charmed life, for amid the hail of bullets, not one had touched him. The British now were in full retreat; a few broke away and ran toward Trenton, but the greater part made for Princeton. Washington pressed his advantage to the fullest limit.

The Americans were sent forward to attack the other two British regiments coming to the rescue. They dashed at them before they had time to form and irresistibly overwhelmed them, capturing large numbers and utterly putting the rest to flight in a wild rout. Some of them, to the number of about two hundred, took refuge in Nassau Hall, the college building, whence they were at once dislodged and captured. After following the thoroughly terrorised British who had escaped, for a short time, Washington, having no cavalry, gave over the pursuit.

The British lost about five hundred, including killed, wounded and captured, no less than one hundred being left dead upon the field, which shows the fierceness of the hand to hand fighting; the total American loss was about one hundred, including many valuable officers. The three British regiments had been utterly defeated and turned into a disorganized mob; their retreat was a pell-mell rout.

But now when the goal of his endeavour—the stores, material and treasure at New Brunswick—was almost within his grasp, he was compelled to abandon it. Suffering humanity absolutely could do no more. The troops were completely exhausted by their fight of the day before, their night march, their desperate battle, their long fast and the intense cold. For more than thirty hours they had been in action or on the march; most of them had received nothing to eat.

"If I could have had eight hundred fresh troops I could have done it," said Washington. Alas, there were no fresh troops to be had. They fell out of the ranks asleep whenever they halted. Even these iron men must have rest. Within reaching distance, these untoward circumstances compelled him to refrain from New Brunswick. Reluctantly Washington headed his men toward the heights of Morristown.

The British army under Cornwallis had been moved with incredible celerity. A little party of Americans with a heavy field piece delayed the advance somewhat, a broken bridge delayed it still further, and though the British, unable to repair it, had waded breast-high through the icy stream in their endeavours to catch him, Washington effected his escape. Cornwallis, in alarm for his stores, pushed on to New Brunswick to save them, and battle and campaign were over.

The Revolution was saved. Washington, with his weak, inferior army, had so manoeuvred that he had, in spite of his disadvantages, twice struck the enemy with superior force at the point of contact, and routed him. His movements were an early illustration of the modern phrasing of an old maxim, to the effect that the art of war consists in "getting there first with the most men!" In addition to his soldierly ability he had shown his capacity as a statesman. His enterprise was undertaken at that precise moment when victory was vital to the success of the struggle, not merely from a military standpoint, but in order to maintain the drooping spirits of the nation then "borning," and to demonstrate to the world that the birth was not to be a still one. There never was any doubt of the ultimate success of the Revolution after that, and it was settled right then and there.

[1]To complete this brief *résumé* of one of the remarkable campaigns of history, Washington strongly fortified himself on Cornwallis's flank at Morristown, menacing each of the three depots held by the British outside New York; Putnam advanced from Philadelphia to Trenton, with the militia; and Heath moved down to the highlands of the Hudson. The country people of New Jersey rose and cut off scattered detachments of the British in every direction, until the whole of the field was eventually abandoned by them, except Amboy, Newark and New Brunswick. The world witnessed the singular spectacle of a large, well-appointed army of veteran soldiery, under able leaders, shut up in practically one spot, New York and a few nearby villages, and held there inexorably by a phantom army which was never more than half the size of that it held in check.

The results of the six months' campaign were to be seen in the possession of the city of New York by the British army. That army which had won, except the last two, all the battles in which it had engaged, which had followed the Americans through six months of disastrous defeat and retreat, and had overrun two colonies, now had nothing to show for all its efforts but the ground upon which it stood. And this was the result of the genius, the courage, the audacity of one man—George Washington. The world was astounded, and he took an assured place thenceforward among the first soldiers of that or any age.

Even the English themselves could not withhold their admiration. The gallant and brave Cornwallis, a soldier of no mean ability himself, and well able to estimate what could be done with a small and feeble force, never forgot his surprise at the

---

1. Taken from the author's novel *For Love of Country*.

Assunpink; and when he congratulated Washington, at the surrender of Yorktown years after, upon the brilliant combination which had resulted in the capture of the army, he added these words:

But, after all, your Excellency's achievements in the Jerseys were such that nothing could surpass them!'

And the witty and wise old cynic, Mr. Horace Walpole, with his usual discrimination, wrote to a friend. Sir Horace Mann, when he heard of the affair at Trenton, the night march to Princeton, and the successful attack there:

Washington, the dictator, has shown himself both a Fabius and a Camillus. His march through our lines is allowed to have been a prodigy of generalship.

Paul Jones' Greatest Battle

On the evening of Thursday, September 30, 1779, a rather small, brown faced, dark haired man, about thirty-two years of age, and of a melancholy, poetic and even scholarly cast of countenance, clad in a blue naval uniform, stood on the weather-side of the high poop deck of a large war-ship, looking keenly about him with his bright, brilliant black eyes. Sometimes his glance fell meditatively upon two gallant white ships under full sail, men-of-war evidently, which were slowly crossing his course at a right angle a mile or two ahead of him, and making in toward the not distant land the while. *Anon*, with thoughtful vision, he surveyed the crowded decks before and beneath him; the rude, motley men, half-naked and armed with cutlass or pike and pistol, who were grouped about the grim great guns protruding menacingly through the open ports; the old gun captains squinting along the breech and blowing their smoking matches while looking to the priming of the guns; the little groups of pig-tailed veterans, sail trimmers, assembled about the masts; the brilliantly uniformed soldiers, or marines, in the scarlet and white of France; the agile topmen hanging in great human clusters over the broad tops above his head. Sometimes he turned about and swept the sea behind him with his eager gaze, frowning in high displeasure at what he saw.

The soft light of the setting sun streamed over the larboard quarter, and threw into high relief the lonely officer on the weather-side of the ship. Seamanship spoke in the careless yet confident poise of the well-knit muscular figure, as he unconsciously balanced himself and easily met the roll of the ship in the sea; intelligence and kindness sparkled in his eyes; power and force were instinct in every line of his aggressive person; and determination evidenced itself in the compressed lip, the firm, resolute mouth, and the tightly closed hand which hung easily by his side. The gentle breeze of the evening tenderly and softly fell on the worn sails of the ancient ship, swelling the soiled and weather- beaten cloths of canvas out in graceful, tremulous curves as if in caress, as she swept slowly toward the enemy. The ripple of the waves clinging about her cut- water alone broke the silence. The scene was as peaceful and as quiet as if the loud calling of the drum which had so lately re-echoed along the decks had been an invitation to church service, instead of a stern summons to quarters for action. A faint smell of balm and spicery which clung about the ship, a reminder of her distant voyages in Eastern seas, was like incense to the soul.

Off toward the side of the sinking sun rose the bold shore of England. Flamborough headland, crowned by a lofty tower already sending a broad beam of warning light to voyaging mariners out over the waters, thrust out a salient wedge of massive rock-bound coast in rude, wave piercing angle through the tossing sea. To the east the full moon, already some hours high, shot the soft silver of her rays, mingled with the fading gold of the dying day, over the pallid ocean. At this moment the mellow tones of the ship's bell forward striking three couplets in quick succession awakened the commander from the reveries in which he had been indulging, and he turned to find his first lieutenant mounting the poop deck ladder to report the ship clear for action. The dark expressive eye of the captain lingered affectionately upon the form of the lithe, bright-eyed, honest and able young subordinate who had yet to see his twenty-fourth birthday. Between the two officers subsisted the fullest confidence and the deepest affection.

Who was the lonely captain? The greatest novelist of England calls him a traitor. One of the most prominent naval authorities of today, from the same proud nation, describes him as a blackguard. Popular feeling among his contemporary enemies considered him as neither more nor less than a bloodthirsty, murdering pirate. The captain of the ship which he was about to conquer is reputed to have most ungraciously expressed his regret at having been compelled "to surrender to a man who fought with a halter around his neck." But the people who made and loved the flag, the Stars and Stripes, which fluttered above his head, and gave it a high place in the glorious blazonry of nations, told a different tale. The admiration of Washington, the incorruptible soldier and leader; the beloved of Franklin, the discerning statesman and philosopher; the friend of Robert Morris, the brilliant financier and patriot; John Paul Jones, the son of a poor Scotch gardener, who had left his native land in infancy, and who had been brought up with the scanty advantages afforded by life from childhood passed upon the sea, rose, against every sort of discouragement by sheer merit alone, to be the greatest figure in the naval history of his adopted country for nearly a hundred years.

By his indefatigable resolution and unsurpassable valour, his wonderful technical skill and fascinating personality, he became a *Chevalier* of France, an Admiral of Russia, the friend at once of two queens, one the most beautiful and unfortunate, the other the greatest and most splendid, of his age. He was an honoured associate of the king of a great country, and yet never renounced that which he considered his proudest title to honour, and by which in that final end of things in which the truth that is in a man speaks out, he loved to describe himself, "a citizen of the United States."

This was a man who had been an apprentice boy at twelve, a sea officer at fifteen, a captain at twenty-one; who, in a slight inconsiderable vessel, a small war-brig, had rendered most notable service to his chosen country in the face of war vessels of overwhelming force; who, in a crank lightly built sloop-of-war, the *Ranger*, a year ago, had swept the Irish Channel, terrified the whole western seaboard of England, captured in fair fight a regularly commissioned English sloop-of-war of equal force with and more heavily manned than his own; and all this with a crew of mutineers, refusing to obey his orders and even threatening his life at the last moment before the action.

His hands had hoisted the first American flag that ever fluttered from a masthead, the pine tree rattlesnake flag, with its motto *"Don't tread on me,"* which seems somehow significant of the man himself; the same hand later on had thrown to the breeze the first banner of the Stars and Stripes that was ever seen upon the ocean; his address and resolution had elicited, in the way of a naval salute, the first official and public recognition of the new figure among the nations of the world from the authorized representative of a recognized government. As a fighter, as a lover, as a diplomat, he was among the first men of his time. He loved glory and fame and duty with a passionate devotion, and as he stated, "ever looked out for the Honour of the American flag." He was afterward thanked by Congress, made the head of the American Navy, and especially commended in a public letter to the King of France, his friend, an unique honour in our history. Before he died he had participated in "twenty-three battles and solemn *rencontres* by sea."

A pirate, a traitor, a blackguard, this? Nay, as true a man as ever fought for human freedom, as brave an officer as ever overcame heartbreaking adversity, as gallant a sailor as ever trod a heaving deck, and as sweet a lover as ever kissed a lady's hand. In the hundreds of letters written by and to him still extant, many of them on *affaires du cœur*, there is not a single coarse or rude expression to be found. I sum him up the hero and the gentleman. Not without his faults, of course, which I cheerfully refrain from cataloguing—always a poor business—but they were not great and were easily counterbalanced by his many virtues.

Look at him now as he approaches the culmination of his career. After his brilliant cruise in the *Ranger*, unable to obtain a decent war vessel, forced to put up with a nondescript antique, a worn out East Indiaman, the *Duc de Duras*, now renamed the *Bonhomme Richard*, which had been filled with old and makeshift guns; a ship so rotten that it was impossible to make the necessary alterations to properly fit her for her new service. Attended by a squadron under his nominal command, one of the ships of which, and the best one, was manned largely by British seamen, and commanded by an insane coward; at this very moment previous acts of mutiny were culminating in a flagrant disobedience of orders to follow the *Richard* into the action. The *Alliance*, fighting shy of the English warships, was sweeping toward the frightened convoy huddling off for shelter under the lee of Scarborough Castle. Another vessel, the *Vengeance*, French *in toto*, was fleeing with all speed from the action, and the third, the *Pallas*, another Frenchman, the only thing American about her being the flag flying above her, hung quivering in the wind in frightful indecision as to whether she should engage the weaker of the two English ships before them.

At this moment the total crew on the *Bonhomme Richard* (so called from the *nom de plume* of Benjamin Franklin) was about three hundred, of which only one fourth were Americans, about one half French soldiers, and the balance the riff-raff of all nations, Portuguese preponderating; among their number being some Malays, perhaps Filipinos, thus early fighting for freedom. Two hundred desperate English prisoners were confined below in the hold. Beside the captain, not a single deck officer was left, through a series of mishaps, save Richard Dale, the first lieutenant, than whom no man ever was a better, by the way. Commodore Dale, who has been justly honoured subsequently in the United States Navy, loved and venerated Jones above all other men, always speaking of him to the last day of his life with his eyes filled with tears of affection and regret as "Paul," which was his captain's birth name. Why John Paul assumed the name Jones has never been discovered; certainly for no disgraceful reason, for whatever name he might have taken he would have honoured.

The armament of the *Richard* consisted of twenty-eight twelve pounders on the gun deck; on the quarter deck and forecastle were eight nine pounders. In desperation, Jones had cut three ports on each side on the berth deck below the main battery and mounted six old condemned eighteen pounders therein. His ship had in all, therefore, forty-two guns, twenty-one in the broadside, discharging a total weight of two hundred and fifty-eight pounds of shot. The larger ship of the enemy was the brand new double-banked frigate *Serapis*, mounting three tiers of guns on two covered and one uncovered deck; twenty eighteens, twenty nines, and ten six pounders, making a total of fifty guns, twenty-five in broadside, throwing three hundred pounds. As a further advantage the destructive power of an eighteen pound gun is immensely greater than that of a twelve. The crew of the *Serapis* was about three hundred and fifty trained and disciplined men. Her captain, Pearson, was a brave and determined sailor of reputation in the service.

There appeared to be no uncertainty in the mind of either commanding officer as to the character and force of his opponent. Pearson confidently expected an easy victory, which he certainly should have won, and Paul Jones determined to make him fight as no English ship had ever fought before, for all he got. About half after seven in the evening the two ships drew within gunshot distance of each other, the *Richard* rounding to off the port bow of the *Serapis*. The thirty-two-gun ship *Pallas* at last gathered sufficient resolution to engage the *Scarborough*, a twenty-gun sloop, and thus eliminated her from Paul Jones' calculations.

The *Vengeance* had fled, and Captain Landais, in the *Alliance*, was hovering after the convoy out of range.

For some reason, as the Richard approached, Captain Pearson withheld his fire and hailed. The answer, which was indistinguishable, was followed by a shot from the *Richard*, and the two ships immediately exchanged terrific broadsides. Of the three eighteen pounders down on the berth deck near the water-line of the *Richard*, two burst at the first discharge, killing and wounding a large part of their crews, and blowing up a part of the deck. The other gun was of course abandoned. Side by side in the bright moonlight of the autumn night, the two ships slowly sailed together for nearly an hour. The roar of one discharge answered the other, cheer met cheer, as the iron hailed bullets wove a hideous net of death about the two ships.

Fearful that he might be raked astern by the *Serapis* (which some accounts say was done), Jones, who had kept slightly in the lead, finally threw his ship aback, checking her onward motion so that the *Serapis* passed slowly ahead of him. As Pearson drew ahead, Jones attempted to throw his vessel across the rear of the English ship to rake and board, which of course would be his best plan, as in that case he could make good use of the soldiers on his decks. The attempt was a failure on account of the sluggish motion of the unwieldy *Richard*, which only swung in aft of, and in line with, the Englishman. No guns now bearing on either ship, except for the continuous small-arm fire there was a slight lull in the action. As soon as the *Serapis*, which had drawn further ahead, swung up into the wind and partially raked the *Richard*, Jones filled away again and the battle was at once resumed with determined energy.

Pearson now checked the speed of his own ship by throwing all aback, or else wore short around to cross the *Richard's* bows and rake, and the two vessels slowly drew together again. The fire from both ships had been kept up with unremitting fury from every gun as they bore, but the *Serapis'* heavier metal had played havoc with the lighter American. The carnage and slaughter upon the Richard had been simply frightful. The rotten old ship was being beaten to pieces beneath the feet of her crew by the terrific battery of the *Serapis*. Gun after gun in the main battery had been dismounted. At this moment the *Richard* fortunately drew ahead of the *Serapis* once more in the game of seesaw they had been playing, and Jones, with a last desperate attempt to close, put his helm hard over, and this time the Richard paid off in front of and athwart the hawse of the *Serapis*.

The jib-boom of the English ship caught in the mizzen rigging of the American. The wind upon the after sail forced the stern of the *Serapis* round broadside to the Richard, and they lay locked together; the bow of one by the stern of the other, the starboard batteries of both in contact. Pearson had, unknown to Jones, dropped his port bower anchor at the moment of contact in an endeavour to drag clear of the *Richard*, which he determined to knock to pieces at long range with his heavy guns; but as Benjamin Franklin said in a word or two which well describes the man, "*Paul Jones ever loved close fighting*," and he saw his opportunity and rose to it then and there; as the two ships fouled each other, with his own hands he passed the lashing which bound them together. He found time at this critical moment to reprove one of his officers for profanity.

"Don't swear, Mr. Stacy," he said reprovingly to his excited subordinate, "in another moment we may all be in eternity, but let us do our duty."

Fine language from a "pirate," was it not?

As the *Serapis* swung in board, the starboard anchor of the *Richard* caught in the mizzen chains of the former and the two ships were bound together in an embrace which nothing but death and destruction could sever. The Englishman's ports on the starboard side had been closed, and he worked his batteries by firing through them, thus blowing off the port lids. The vessels were so close together that the rammers and sponges of the great guns in one ship had to be extended through the ports of the other; they were so close in fact, that, as they ground and chafed together in the waves, the men on the lower decks were actually fighting a hand to hand conflict with great guns. But the heavier fire of the *Serapis* was too strong for the endurance of the half-breed crew of the *Richard*. The guns below were burst, silenced and dismounted, and from the mainmast aft the timbers were beaten in and out until both sides of the American ship were literally blown away and disappeared, so that at last the *Serapis* actually fired her batteries through the open air without meeting any obstruction to their shot.

There was really imminent danger that the upper decks aft on the *Richard* would collapse and sink down into the ruins below; why they did not was a mystery. Dale and a French colonel of infantry had toiled like heroes in the battery to the last, but the carpenter now reported six feet of water in the hold and the ship making water fast, and the frightened master-at-arms at once released the prisoners, crying that the ship was sinking, and the whole assemblage rushed headlong to the main-deck, the carpenter and other petty officers in the lead crying for quarter.

Things had gone better above, however. The heavy mass of men, including the riflemen in the tops of the *Richard* and the marines under De Chamillard, had simply swept the crowded decks of the *Serapis* with a searching rain of bullets from their small arms since the moment of contact and before. Nearly every man upon her, with the exception of the undaunted Pearson, had been driven below or disabled, the decks were covered with dead and wounded, groaning and shrieking, unheeded. Some bold, undaunted spirits on the *Richard* had run along the interlacing yard-arms, and after a dizzy hand to hand conflict in mid-air, upon their precarious footholds, had driven the English from the tops of the *Serapis*, and gained possession, whence they poured a bitter musketry fire down the hatchways.

When the ships had come together, the English made an attempt to board. Jones seized a pike and, followed by a few men, resolutely sprang to the point of attack, whence the British immediately retired. A like attempt of the Americans also failed. As the prisoners and crew came springing up from the useless guns and the decks below, several young American officers implored Jones to strike. He was not the striking kind. The doctor ran from the cock-pit below, crying that the water was gaining so that it floated the wounded there, and they must surrender.

"What, doctor," cried Jones, smiling, "would you have me strike to a drop of water? Help me to get this gun over."

The doctor concluded that the cock-pit was a safer place than the quarter-deck and went below again to his ghastly station. The master-at-arms, not seeing Jones, now ran aft to lower the flag; finding it had been shot away and was dragging in the water, he sprang on the rail repeating his cry for quarter. Dale and a few determined men were busy below with the pumps desperately trying to keep the ship from sinking beneath their feet. Jones first braining with the butt of his pistol the carpenter who was shrieking that the ship was sinking and also crying for quarter, with infinite presence of mind and an address and resourcefulness which alone would write his name among the great commanders if there was nothing else, succeeded with the assistance of the gallant Dale in quieting his alarmed crew, and then compelling the confused prisoners to go to the pumps on the plea that the English ship was sinking and their own would soon follow, if not kept afloat by their exertions. By this means he relieved a number of his own crew, and for the rest of the battle the singular spectacle was presented of a vessel being kept afloat by the people of the very nation against whom he fought, and whose heroic exertions in the heart-breaking work of continuous pumping—the hardest labour that falls to a sailor's life—contributed not a little to the final success of their captors. In a lull of the fire as they came together, Pearson, probably hearing the carpenter or others crying for quarter, shouted:

"Have you struck?"

To him Jones returned that immortal answer upon which Americans love to dwell:

"I have not yet begun to fight."

Think of it! On a beaten ship, sinking beneath his feet, kept afloat by the exertions of bewildered prisoners who outnumbered his own wavering and slaughtered crew, any other man would have struck his colours long since, but Jones had not yet begun to fight! Things proved that he had not. The battle recommenced at once, the English having their own way with their big guns below decks, the Americans equally successful above. With his own hands, assisted by some others, the captain, who had already acted as sail trimmer, pikeman, and in nearly every other capacity as well, dragged another nine pound gun across the deck with great difficulty, and concentrated the fire of the three small guns loaded with double-headed and grape shot upon the mainmast of the *Serapis*. During the contact both ships had caught fire repeatedly from the burning gun-wads, or the flame of the close discharges, the *Serapis* no less than twelve times and the *Richard* almost continuously. Dale now took charge below, and fought the fire as gallantly as he had fought the British.

After the two ships had first grappled, about eight o'clock, the *Alliance* made her appearance on the scene. Landais sailed slowly across the stern of the two combatants, delivering a raking fire upon both from his starboard guns which had been heavily charged with grape. More men were killed and wounded on the *Richard* by this discharge than on the *Serapis*. Disregarding the warning shouts and signals of the *Richard*, the *Alliance* then sailed away and repeated her performances upon the two other ships. A few moments before ten o'clock, the battle between the *Serapis* and the *Richard* having continued with the utmost fury during the intervening period, she again crossed athwart the interlocked combatants. Once and again her broadside did more damage to her consort than to her enemy. That was her contribution to the fight.

A little before the last onslaught of the *Alliance*, by Tones' orders, one of his seamen ran out on the main-yard with a bucket of hand grenades which he deliberately proceeded to light and throw down the main hatch of the *Serapis*. A number of powder charges had been carelessly allowed to accumulate upon the main-deck by the too confident English, and a fearful explosion took place which killed and wounded over forty of the crew. About the same time the battered mainmast of the Englishman upon which Jones had been persistently playing with his small guns, fell over the side, carrying with it the mizzen top-mast as well. That was the end. With his own hand Captain Pearson tore down the colours which had been nailed to the mast by his orders, at half after ten o'clock, and surrendered his ship to his thrice beaten enemy.

Dale, in spite of a severe wound which he had received, but of which he was not yet conscious so great was the excitement of the battle, at once leaped upon the rail and followed by a party of boarders swung himself aboard the *Serapis*. As they landed upon the deck of the English ship, one of her crew, not knowing of the surrender, dangerously wounded Midshipman Mayrant, Dale's second, with a pike. From beneath their feet still came the roar of the *Serapis'* guns, her crew ignorant of the fact that she struck, had been cheered to renewed exertions by an English shipmaster among the prisoners on the *Richard*, who had escaped from the pumps and made his way to the lower decks of the *Serapis*, revealing the desperate condition of their antagonist and encouraging them to persevere when success would be both speedy and certain. So the English in spite of their captain fought on. However, as the fire of the *Richard* was at once stopped when Pearson tore down the colours, an English lieutenant came up on deck to see if she had struck. When he learned from his commander that his own ship had surrendered he was astounded. He turned to go below intending to notify the others, but Dale, fearing that he would resume the combat, compelled him to follow his reluctant captain to the deck of the *Richard*.

There stood the indomitable Paul Jones in the midst of the dead and dying, wounded himself, and covered with blood and the soil of the battle, the *Richard* sinking beneath him, flames from his burning ship mingling with the moonlight and throwing an uncertain ghastly illumination upon the scene of ineffable horror presented. Still locked in the deadly embrace of the *Richard* lay the beaten *Serapis*, her white decks covered with the mangled bodies of her crew, her lofty masts broken and wrecked, her rigging tangled in inextricable confusion, flames breaking forth from her as well; the sullen English filing up from below and laying down their arms at the behest of their blood-covered, battle-stained conquerors, completed the picture. To such a pass had the once stately ships been brought by the passions which had raged, nay, which still burned, in the bosoms of the men who manned them. It was at this moment that Pearson, handing his sword to Jones, is reported to have made the ungracious remark about the halter referred to. To him, with a magnanimity as sweet to think on as was his valour, Jones replied:

The *Alliance* firing on the *Bon Homme Richard* and the *Serapis*

"Sir, you have fought like a hero; and I make no doubt your sovereign will reward you in the most ample manner."

His words were prophetic, for Pearson, though he had lost his ship, was knighted for his gallant defence and received pieces of plate, etc., for his efficient protection of his convoy. The *Scarborough* after a most gallant defence had struck to the *Pallas*, and Captain Piercy of the English ship was also substantially rewarded. When Jones heard of Pearson's advancement, he characteristically made this remark:

"He deserves it, and if he get another ship, and I fall in with him, I'll make a duke of him."

The English government put a price upon the head of Paul Jones, dead or alive, of ten thousand pounds—an immense sum and certainly equivalent to one hundred thousand dollars today. Considering his quality, they rated him cheaply after all.

What of the fate of the *Serapis* and the *Richard* and her captain? It was impossible to save the American ship, though the most strenuous efforts were made to that end. On the twenty-fifth of September, therefore, Jones transferred his flag to the *Serapis*, upon which jury masts had been rigged, and at ten o'clock in the morning, the brave old *Richard*, still flying the great flag under which she had fought, sank bow foremost beneath the sea. Accounts of the casualties on the two ships differ, and are uncertain; it would be safe to estimate those on the *Richard* as within one hundred and fifty killed and wounded and those on the *Serapis* as within two hundred. There never was a more bloody and frightful battle fought on any sea. Its happy result for the Americans was unquestionably due to the exertions of Jones and Dale. There is no battle on record where the individual personality of one man so contributed to the result obtained as much as this.

The little squadron now made its way to the Texel. Jones was compelled by the Dutch at the instigation of the English either to accept a French commission and set the French flag over the *Serapis* and the *Scarborough*, or else give up his prizes. To his eternal honour he chose the latter alternative, and shifted his colours to the *Alliance*, deposing Landais who was afterward dismissed the service. In spite of thirteen Dutch ships of the line in the harbour urging him to get to sea at once, and the presence of a large fleet of English ships in the offing intent upon his capture when he did come out, Jones calmly refitted the ship, and choosing his own time, in the midst of a howling gale on the night of the twenty-seventh of December, put to sea in full view of the blockaders, boldly made his way through the narrow English

Channel crowded with ships on the lookout for him, passed two fleets of the enemy, and finally reached Corunna, in Spain, and shortly after Groix, in France. From the moment he entered the Texel he had not ceased to fly the American flag, even in the face of the overwhelming enemy from whom he was desperately trying to escape. A most unusual incident this, but one which well illustrates the character of the man.

Commodore Jones died in Paris in the year 1792. He was alone in his chamber at the time, and when his friends found him, he was lying face downward upon his bed. The hand of the conqueror whom no human power can resist had been laid upon him, and for the first time in his life the face of Paul Jones was turned away from the enemy.

Since writing the above I have learned that John Paul assumed the name of Jones out of regard for the family of the celebrated Willie Jones of North Carolina, who, with his charming wife, greatly befriended the young Scotsman in his days of adversity. The subject is treated at length in my life of John Paul Jones.

The Saratoga Campaign: The Defeat of the Detachments

1. TICONDEROGA, HUBBARDTON.

Of all British officers who fought in the American Revolution the name of the one who is regarded with the most consideration by the Americans is that of John Burgoyne. The esteem in which he is still held takes its rise from two circumstances; he was the finest gentleman of the lot, and the most terribly unfortunate of them all. His personality, from all accounts, must have been charming, and his kindness of heart and loftiness of spirit is shown by many little anecdotes. As, for instance, when he was charged by Gates with licensing rapine and outrage on the part of the Indians he was forced to employ by the orders of the home government, and whom he endeavoured vainly to restrain, he replied indignantly, "I would not be conscious of the acts which you presume to impute to me for the whole continent of America, though the wealth of worlds was in its bowels, and a paradise upon its surface." He was a pleasure loving, cultivated, easy going gentleman, and in a small way a man of letters beside. As a commander he was a conspicuous failure. Carlyle speaks somewhere of certain English armies being led by wooden poles wearing cocked hats. Burgoyne was certainly a brilliant illustration of the epigram.

The best of all the haphazard plans, and the only one showing any real military insight, which were devised by the English during the American Revolution, was that which resulted in Burgoyne's expediton. There are some spots upon this earth's surface which are naturally marked out for battle grounds, like the plains of Beth-Horon or the pass of Thermopylae; such a place was the valley of the Hudson. It had been the scene of numberless encounters, and had been fought over by Indians, French, Provincials and British again and again. The

51

English government saw that the only way of separating the revolted colonies into manageable units would be by possessing themselves of the line of the Hudson. If that could be obtained and held they could deal with the colonies to the south and west at their leisure, or even with the New England colonies, as they wished.

The idea was certainly a good one; the details of its execution as they were marked out by the ministry, as we shall see, were radically bad, and the expedition was doomed to disaster from the beginning. Of all military manoeuvres, that which necessitates the converging on a given point, at a given time, of a number of entirely independent units with no means of communication between them, is the most difficult to carry out. The difficulty increases when every unit is compelled to fight its way to the junction point through determined resistance. In such cases a single defeat or check may overthrow the whole plan. That was why Washington failed at Germantown. The plan was for General Howe in New York to come up the Hudson with his force, while General Burgoyne came down. Albany was the place of meeting of the two main forces and of several auxiliary expeditions. To begin with, the English minister, Lord George Germaine, pigeon-holed the order for Howe to cooperate and forgot about it, while he was visiting at a country house, until it was too late.

In the spring of 1777 the British made their supreme attempt to cut the confederated colonies in two. Burgoyne, who had distinguished himself in a subordinate capacity in Portugal, was appointed to succeed Sir Guy Carleton, whose previous attempt in the same direction the year before had been checked by Arnold's heroic naval battle off Valcour Island on Lake Champlain. Carleton was, with the exception of Cornwallis, the best soldier the English sent over; but Burgoyne was a man of great influence and he displaced the older and better soldier. The government allowed Burgoyne everything he wanted. They gave him an absolutely free hand in fitting out the expedition; if he failed, it would be no one's fault but his own.

The force that he took with him consisted of nearly ten thousand men; four thousand English regulars, three thousand Germans, five hundred artillerists, a large body of Canadians, and an indefinite number of Indians. The troops were selected with especial care and included one of the best regiments in the British army, Ackland's Grenadiers. The second in command was Major-General Fraser, a distinguished and able soldier with a long and brilliant record; Phillips, the chief of the artillery, was among the first in his profession;

Lord Balcarras, a dashing soldier, commanded the light infantry; Baron Riedesel, an experienced and capable veteran, led by the German contingent, with Colonels Baum and Breyman among his subordinate commanders. The wives of many of the officers accompanied the expedition—perhaps they thought it was going to be a picnic on a large scale. On the first day of July Burgoyne and his army reached the famous fort at Ticonderoga. Meanwhile Howe, who, when left to his own discretion—which is a figure of speech, for he had none—was the most stupid and wooden of all the cocked-hatted poles in command, had gone off on a little expedition of his own to capture Philadelphia, which was of no earthly use to him whatsoever. That he was urged thereto by General Charles Lee, as great a traitor as Arnold subsequently became, does not excuse his blundering. He succeeded in effecting the capture after great delays, and two desperate battles with Washington at the Brandywine and Germantown, in the latter of which he just barely escaped a disastrous defeat; alter which he went into winter quarters in Philadelphia and left Burgoyne to his own devices. Truly an able and energetic commander.

General St. Clair was in command of the extensive works at Ticonderoga, with an insufficient garrison of about three thousand men. He had proposed to defend the place to the very last, but the American engineers, though previously warned, had neglected to fortify Mt. Defiance, a precipitous and rugged height, towering some six hundred feet above the water of the lake about a mile away from, and entirely commanding, the works. They had laughed at the possibility of mounting a battery there and were greatly surprised on the morning of July fifth to find the place swarming with the red-coats who were busily mounting a heavy battery.

Phillips and his engineers, with incredible difficulty, had effected the apparent impossibility; that General remarking sapiently, "Where a goat can go, a man may go; and where a man can go, he can haul up a gun." The battery, which would be in position the next day, absolutely commanded the fort and rendered it untenable, so there was nothing to do but to abandon the position without loss of time, or to surrender the army.

It was a terrible blow, not only on account of the munitions of war and the supplies which could not be destroyed, and which would naturally fall into the hands of the enemy, but the holding of the position, on account of the romantic manner in which it had been captured by Ethan Allen, was looked upon as a point of honour. However, there was nothing for it but to leave. When St. Clair was afterward reproached for abandoning the position, he replied pithily and wisely, "Yes, I lost a post, but saved a province." He was subsequently tried and acquitted for his action. On the following night of the fifth, therefore, the women and the children and invalids were embarked in two hundred boats and sent down the lake under strong guard toward Fort Edward; and St. Clair, committing the charge of the rear-guard to Colonels Seth Warner (Ethan Allen's whilom associate), Francis and Hale, retreated toward Castleton in all haste, quietly spiking the guns and destroying the stores as much as possible before leaving, without giving the alarm.

Unfortunately, however, and by the orders of General de Fermoy, it is said, a house was set on fire by the retreating soldiers and its brilliant illumination gave away the whole affair. The British immediately occupied the fort and Fraser with nine hundred men started in hot pursuit. They came up with the rear-guard the next morning at Hubbardton where a desperate encounter took place. The Americans, numbering about one thousand men, fought with the greatest spirit, beating off the British several times, and, in fact, charging fiercely in return, drove back Fraser in confusion, until the British were reinforced by Riedesel and his Hessians, when the Americans were forced to withdraw, leaving on the field about three hundred killed or wounded, including many officers. The brave Colonel Francis was killed while leading a charge upon the enemy, Colonel Hale was captured and Colonel Warner, with the remnant of his regiment, retreated eastward through Vermont. Though somewhat delayed by this sharp action, the British pursued the Americans so closely that the fugitives burnt and abandoned Fort Ann, and retreated with all speed south to Fort Edward, where St. Clair's men joined General Schuyler's little force on the twelfth of July.

General Schuyler, who was in chief command of the surrounding American department at that time, worked in the most heroic and wise way to check the British advance, summoning the wilderness to his aid. The inhabitants withdrew from the country entirely, all of the provisions and stock they could not take with them they destroyed; bridges were broken down, the rivers and creeks choked up, and stalwart woodsmen felled the mighty trees in the forest paths and otherwise blocked the roads, so that the British progress was slow in the extreme. It took Burgoyne thirty days to advance his army nearly twenty-four miles through the wilderness, though up to that time he states that he had built some forty bridges—as a bridge builder he was an unrivalled success! Every step of the road had to be made anew, the Americans retiring in good order before the slow British advance. The army, of course, carried its provisions and supplies and the men were in heavy marching order which made progress through the thick woods extremely difficult. Burgoyne had hoped to have lived off the country, but found it impossible. The inhabitants did not rally to his standard to any great extent, as he had been led to believe they would, and his position was rapidly becoming a difficult one. Finally he reached Skenesborough, where he rested; he and his were tired, and it was time they did so.

2. FORT STANWIX. ORISKANY.

Meanwhile another expedition had been organized, which had started out at the same time as his own by way of Lake Ontario, to make an attack upon Fort Stanwix, situated at the headwaters of the Mohawk River where navigation ceased. It comprised about seventeen hundred British regulars. Provincials, Sir John Johnson's Tory contingent, and numbers of Indians, and was under command of Lieutenant-Colonel St. Leger. After they had captured the fort, they were to swoop down the Mohawk Valley and, gathering stores therefrom, were to join Howe and Burgoyne at Albany. They landed at Oswego about the middle of July and made their way to the fort without opposition, and immediately invested it on the third of August. It was defended by Colonel Peter Gansevoort with about six hundred men. The stout old colonel refused to surrender and, as the fort had been recently strengthened, St. Leger feared to assault and saw no way to effect its capture except by a regular siege.

Schuyler had called out the militia of Tryon County, under the command of General Nicholas Herkimer, a veteran soldier in his sixtieth year, who resolved to relieve the fort. His little army of some eight hundred men pursued their way up the Mohawk Valley unmolested until, very early in the morning of the fifth of August, while it was yet dark, they came near to the Oriskany Creek, about eight miles from Fort Stanwix. At that point the advance was halted and three messengers were despatched to the fort with a request from Herkimer that Gansevoort would fire three guns immediately upon their arrival and make a sortie to engage the enemy, when Herkimer would advance and endeavour to break through the besieging lines and gain the fort, and thus it was hoped the siege would be raised. The men found it difficult to reach the fort; the long hours dragged away and no sound came to announce their arrival; the impatient militia under Herkimer chafed bitterly at the delay, finally going so far as to reproach the general for not permitting them to go on. He was suspected, most unjustly, of Tory leanings, and his principal officers. Colonels Cox and Paris, did not refrain, in the stress of their excitement, from apprising him of their suspicions and charging him with cowardice. The wise old man resisted their importunities and disregarded their taunts until they became unbearable, when he reluctantly ordered an advance.

The road, or way, led across a causeway of logs carried over a marsh in a narrow defile thickly wooded, in which an ambush had been carefully prepared. St. Leger, to intercept them, had despatched a large body of "Johnson's Greens" under Major Watts, many of them neighbours and acquaintances of Herkimer's men. Between these antagonistic bodies, on account of their differing political views, a most acrid and bitter feeling had developed, so that they literally longed to get at each other. This Tory regiment was accompanied by a large body of Mohawks under the famous Brant, and under his direction the ambush was arranged. The Americans marched carelessly into the defile about nine o'clock in the morning and would have undoubtedly been massacred to a man, had it not been that the impetuosity of the Indians, who fired precipitately, apprised them of their danger. They were met after a shot or two by a smashing volley. Herkimer's rear-guard immediately retreated incontinently, but the rest stood their ground stoutly and returned the fire; old hands at this sort of a game, the men at once sought cover behind trees and commenced in that narrow valley a woodmen's battle, which for sanguinary ferocity and determined persistence was hardly paralleled on the continent.

To their political differences they added personal antagonisms of the bitterest kind, and as the conflict grew fiercer, the opposing bodies of sometime friends and neighbours, and the ferocious Iroquois, drew nearer to each other, until they fought during the long hot morning through the woods and marshes hand to hand. A furious thunderstorm accompanied by vivid lightning now broke over the horrid scene, and the rain which began to fall in torrents rendered the firearms useless, but conflict was actually carried on with knives. Colonels Cox and Paris were both killed. The Americans presently gained a more advantageous position on higher ground, and the Indians began to give way. Watts with the Tories now made a desperate charge with the bayonet. The struggle became a confused bloody conflict between men mad and raving with the lust of battle, from which, after more than five hundred had been killed or wounded, the Indians finally fled and the Tories and the Americans alike sullenly and bitterly withdrew from the field in complete exhaustion.

Herkimer was early disabled by a bullet which shattered his knee and killed his horse. The noble old man refused to withdraw from the conflict and directed his aides to place him on his saddle with his back against a great tree. There, while smoking his pipe, he calmly directed the conflict. The passions of men had turned the pretty little valley into a hellish slaughter-pen, and about half of those engaged on both sides had been killed or wounded—a terrible proportion, indeed! So bitter had been the strife that even the agonies of death itself had not separated the fighters; men were found locked in each other's arms, a knife in each heart, in a grasp, the tenacity of which bespoke their infernal passion. Herkimer's advance was, of course, checked; he did not succeed in reaching the fort, but the dreadful slaughter he had inflicted greatly discouraged St. Leger's men and correspondingly encouraged the garrison.

In the heat of the conflict Herkimer's messengers reached Gansevoort, who had been wondering what the distant firing meant, and he immediately sent out Colonel Marinus Willett with two hundred and fifty picked men, who fell upon St. Leger's camp and stampeded a portion of his force with great slaughter; they captured five standards, and twenty wagon loads of plunder, and returned to the fort in safety without losing a man! The five captured flags were immediately hoisted below an improvised American banner, the only one they possessed in the fort, which had been made out of a white sheet, a blanket and a woman's petticoat—this was the first time that an English flag had been hoisted beneath the Stars and Stripes! Fiske says, in fact, this was the first American flag with its stars and stripes that was ever hoisted. St. Leger, however, still pressed the siege vigorously and Colonel Willett finally volunteered to carry the news of their condition to Schuyler. He succeeded in escaping through the lines, after some thrilling adventures, and Schuyler immediately despatched Arnold, the only one of his brigadiers who would volunteer, with twelve hundred men to the rescue.

Arnold had but a small force, but he was himself a host. In strategy he proved himself as wise as he was in battle brave; so he caused reports to be spread greatly exaggerating the number of his forces and their nearness to St. Leger. He actually succeeded in creating a panic among the troops of that disgusted soldier, which caused the Indians to withdraw after first filling themselves with whisky and raiding his camp, so that finally the English were forced to raise the siege and fly precipitately from their camp, leaving tents, artillery, provisions, and everything for the Americans. This was August the twenty-second. During his rapid retreat St. Leger's army disintegrated and nothing more was to be feared from them. They never appeared on the scene again. Fort Stanwix was saved, and the Mohawk Valley, from which the British had expected to gain large supplies, remained in possession of the Americans. The heroic Herkimer died at his own home a few days after the battle, mainly from the effects of unskilful surgery; his end was that of a philosopher and a Christian. Fully conscious of it, he smoked his pipe and read his Bible to his assembled family at the thirty-eighth Psalm until he expired.

May his name be held ever in grateful remembrance. This defeat was blow number two to the hapless Burgoyne.

3. BENNINGTON.

Blow number one was delivered on the sixteenth of August. Burgoyne, in great straits for provisions, forage and horses, had learned that there was a large depot of supplies at Bennington, in Vermont. On the thirteenth of August he despatched a force of five hundred men, most of whom were dismounted Hessian dragoons, under the command of Colonel Baum, to seize the supplies; one hundred Indians followed Baum's force. Major Skene, a royalist of the neighbourhood, also accompanied the expedition. A skeleton organization for a regiment of royalists, which it was hoped might be raised among the people, was also sent along—that regiment never amounted to more than that skeleton, and even that was soon lost!

On the news of Burgoyne's descent, the New Hampshire militia had rallied under the command of that famous veteran of the old French and Indian war, John Stark. It was he who had held the rail fence stuffed with straw at Bunker Hill. He had fought in all the battles around Boston and New York. It was he who led the advance of Sullivan's column on the famous Christmas night at Trenton. He had been unjustly treated by Congress in the matter of rank and had retired from the service, with the pithy remark that, "an officer who could not protect his own rights could not be entrusted safely with those of his country!" He had accepted the command of the militia with great reluctance and expressly stipulated that he should be amenable only to the authorities of New Hampshire.

By his orders the men assembled at Bennington, where there was a large supply depot. They were a rude and motley array; there was not a uniform among them; many came in their hunting frocks, or in home-spun shirts, but every man carried a bright, well-kept rifle, which he knew how to use, and, in their way, they made up a very effective force. No loyalists joined Baum, and appearances were so threaten-ing that he stopped near Bennington on the fifteenth of August and entrenched on a little hillock near a creek during a long rainy day, and sent back a message for reinforcements. Before the battle the next day, August sixteenth, in the early afternoon, Stark in his plain and homely way made a brief speech to his men, concluding with these significant words, "Now, my men, there are the red-coats! Before night they must be ours, or Molly Stark will be a widow!" The morning had been consumed in preparing for the battle. Stark had sent parties of men through the woods in every direction, past the unconscious Germans, who, never having seen an army out of uniform, paid but little atten-tion to them, until he had assembled a force of two hundred men on one side, three hundred on another and two hundred on a third side of Baum's little redoubt. It has been said that Baum had surmised that these detached parties were the expected rank and file of that skeleton regiment. He was soon bitterly undeceived.

The Americans were three times as great in numbers as their an-tagonists, but every advantage was with the Germans. They were well-trained, disciplined soldiery, in a commanding position of their own choosing, strongly entrenched and provided with cannon. But in spite of this "the men who fought at Minden," under the famous Ferdinand of Brunswick, were no match for the Americans under Stark! The Indians who had accompanied Baum were wiser than he. They knew what deadly foes these men in their hunting frocks could be, and they fled incontinently. Finally about two o'clock in the afternoon, all his dispositions having been made satisfactorily, Stark moved across the shallow stream and gave the signal to begin the battle.

The enemy was entirely surrounded. The Germans had two field pieces which, at first well-served, did great execution, but the experi-enced American riflemen from their various points of vantage picked off the men at the guns, sometimes creeping to within eight or ten paces of the redoubt in order to do it effectually, until the space about the artillery became a regular death-trap. Stark was everywhere around the fort inspiring his men. Finally, after several hours of conflict, the ammunition of the Hessians began to diminish, and the Americans actually stormed the position! Stark led one of the columns in person and fought with his sword, hand to hand, with the rest. The Hessians met the charge with the bayonet and with the swords of the dragoons, but nothing could stem the splendid advance of the Americans. Baum was killed, many of his men fell with him, and the rest threw down their arms and were captured. A militia army without bayonets had captured a fortified position defended by artillery and garrisoned by veteran soldiers!

At this juncture Colonel Breyman, with six hundred German and English troops whom Burgoyne had despatched to succour Baum's men, made his appearance on the scene, and immediately charged the disorganized Americans, who began to give ground before the onslaught of these fresh soldiers. At this critical moment, Warner's men, whom we have seen gallantly fighting at Hubbardton, led by the colonel in person, came running on the scene, not yet having been engaged. By Stark's order they immediately charged Breyman's troops. The other Americans rallied and returned to the conflict and in a short time Breyman was forced to retreat, which he did expeditiously and disastrously. He lost heavily in killed, wounded and captured. Attended by only sixty or seventy soldiers, he finally succeeded in reaching the force which Burgoyne in person had led out to succour him. In this action over two hundred were killed or wounded; some seven hundred prisoners and one thousand stand of arms, nearly as many dragoon swords, and four guns, together with many other equipments, fell into the possession of the victorious Americans, who lost only about sixty killed and wounded! This was blow number one, and the two strokes almost completed the undoing of Burgoyne's hapless expedition.

The Saratoga Campaign: The End of the Main Army

1. Freeman's Farm

The position of Burgoyne was now become desperate. The American militia came pouring in upon him from all sides. The murder, by the Indians, of a beautiful young girl, Jane MacCrea, betrothed to a lieutenant in the British camp, had aroused the most intense feeling among the American farmers; and animated by a burning desire to revenge and punish this and other atrocities, they flocked to the American standards in great and ever increasing numbers. Burgoyne was horrified at the outrages perpetrated by his savage allies and did what he could to prevent them, finally dismissing the Indians altogether; but it was then too late, the mischief had been done.

Congress on the first of August had removed the brave and able Philip Schuyler and replaced him with the weak and inefficient Horatio Gates! It was a most unjust change, and the subsequent victories of the Americans were due not to Gates, but to Schuyler's wise measures and unflagging energy—it was too bad that he should have been robbed of the glory after having sustained the hardships, met the difficulties, and laid the plans, which brought success, for Burgoyne was practically beaten before Gates appeared. If Burgoyne was a hoop-pole in a cocked hat. Gates was scarcely more than a toothpick similarly clad! Schuyler behaved like the hero, the patriot, the gentleman, that he was; remaining with Gates and assisting and advising with him to the end of the campaign, though treated with scorn and contumely by the latter.

The defeats of Baum and St. Leger had terribly crippled the British. Nothing whatever had been heard from the expected movement of Sir William Howe up the river. As we have seen, that gentleman had gone on a wild-goose chase toward Philadelphia. Later on Sir Henry Clinton had moved up from New York, outgeneraling old Putnam in a rather clever campaign, and captured Forts Washington and Lee on the Hudson. After this brilliant exploit, his action not having effected the final issue in the slightest degree, he had retired to New York again. Prudence would have dictated that Burgoyne should retreat at once to Canada if it were yet possible, but he was a chivalrous gentleman and could not bear the idea of withdrawal, for the reason that it would permit the large American army in front of him to attack Howe, then, as he supposed, coming up the river, and crush him! Besides, his main army had not yet done any serious fighting, and in common with all the British officers he despised the Americans and probably counted on an easy victory when he attacked, which might materially alter the situation. His experience at Bunker Hill ought to have taught him differently. He therefore determined, against the advice of some of his best officers, upon giving battle. On the thirteenth of September he crossed the Hudson on a bridge of rafts to the west side of the river, where he strongly fortified a camp. On the nineteenth of the same month he moved his army out to make the long expected attack, from which so much was hoped.

The American position had been established on Bemis Heights. It was well-fortified, and the lines had been laid out by the distinguished Polish volunteer, Thaddeus Kosciusko. Gates' force amounted to about fifteen thousand men, mostly militia and volunteers. His second in command was the famous Benedict Arnold. Washington had sent him from the southern army and with him the famous corps of riflemen under Daniel Morgan, as well as some other veterans of the Continental line, whom he could ill spare, by the way, as he was having his hands full at the Brandywine and Germantown. Putnam also despatched some veterans to Gates.

Burgoyne's plan of attack seems to have been to turn the left flank of the American position at the same time that he made a direct attack on the centre and right: General Fraser had command of the right wing, Riedesel and Phillips of the left, and he, himself, led the centre. The movement commenced in the early morning. The American scouts and pickets, posted in the thick woods, caught the gleam of the rising sun reflected from hundreds of bayonets of the silently advancing army; here and there through vistas in the forest might be seen little groups of red-coated men. By noon Burgoyne's plan had been entirely discovered. Arnold, who commanded the left wing, was not inclined like Gates to play a waiting game, and when he found that the latter was disposed to remain inside his strong entrenchments to await the attack, he protested with all the force of his impetuous nature. His representations were so far successful that finally Gates gave him leave to take Morgan's and Dearborn's brigades of Continentals, and move out to the attack.

It was about three o'clock when he fell upon the advance of the British centre under Burgoyne himself at Freeman's Farm. The conflict at once became sanguinary and desperate. Arnold had slightly the greater force at the point of contact, and the British centre was driven back, fighting stoutly and contesting every foot of the way. General Fraser on the right made all haste to join the centre, but Arnold, flushed with success, daringly thrust his men forward and interposed between Fraser's left and the British centre, and Fraser had a desperate time to maintain his division intact. The battle was now general; Arnold was attacking and driving the British centre straight back; charge and countercharge were delivered, guns were taken and retaken, and the battle became a fierce hand to hand struggle in the woods. Arnold was everywhere, in the thick of the fray, fighting like the commonest soldier, and animating his men to more desperate exertions. Burgoyne, Fraser and the English did not spare themselves in the fight either, and soldiers and officers fought side by side. Part of Arnold's men were moving on the right flank of the British centre, and another part on the left flank of Fraser's right division, and the enemy's lines were fairly broken. The situation of the British army was precarious in the extreme. The bold tactics of Arnold had completely disorganized and nullified Burgoyne's plan of attack.

Meanwhile, during the long afternoon up on Bemis Heights, Gates held eleven thousand impatient men in reserve who did nothing at all. Arnold repeatedly sent to him for reinforcements and declared that with two thousand more men he could have utterly routed the whole British army, which was probably true. Gates paid no attention whatever to Arnold's requests, and as the shades of night drew on, Phillips and Riedesel, in command of the left wing of the British, who had intended to make the direct attack on the entrenchments, gave over their purpose, and summoned to his aid by urgent messengers from Burgoyne, hastily turned away to the river, and by hard marching struck the right flank of Arnold's division. The preponderance of force was now the other way. The American advance was checked, the British line re-formed, and the advantage previously gained was lost.

The battle still raged, however, until nightfall, when Arnold sullenly withdrew his men in good order, leaving the British in possession of the field whereon they had fought. They, therefore, claimed a victory; but inasmuch as their attack on the American line had been foiled and their advance checked, the victory—if it may be so called—was a barren one, and the honours rested entirely with Arnold. He had in action about three thousand men as opposed, at the close of the fight, to four thousand five hundred of the British. About one-fourth of the combatants were killed or wounded—a tremendously large proportion—the British suffering the greater loss. The combat was known as the Battle of Freeman's Farm.

There was a wild scene of recrimination and reproach at headquarters that night between Gates and Arnold, and the former finally relieved the latter of his command and sent him his passports to Philadelphia. Arnold refused to go. In the despatches which Gates sent to Congress announcing the victory, he basely made no mention of Arnold's name. The two armies remained in camp until the seventh of October, keeping up a constant skirmishing and picket firing, although the net was drawn more and more closely about Burgoyne with every succeeding day. During this period he received word that Lincoln's men had recaptured the outworks of Ticonderoga, and the fort was besieged. His boats on Lake George were taken and destroyed, his lines of communication cut, his base of supplies menaced. Henceforward no supplies of any kind were received, and provisions became very scarce; the whole army was put on short allowance and the hardships were very great.

2. STILLWATER

On the seventh of October, in utter desperation, Burgoyne resolved upon a final attempt to break through the ever-tightening circles drawn about him by the enemy. He selected from his depleted force a picked column of about fifteen hundred men, the very best in the army. He led it in person, and Fraser, Riedesel, Phillips, Balcarras and Ackland accompanied him. A strong battery of artillery went with them. General Fraser, with five hundred chosen men, led the advance. The rest of the army remained under arms in camp, ready for any success or emergency. As he advanced toward the American line, his movement was discovered, and Morgan, with three thousand riflemen, attacked him furiously on the right, while the New England militia moved out upon his front.

The heroism of that little party of English soldiers was nothing less than marvellous; such stubborn fighting as they made had not been witnessed on the continent and was not seen again for a long time; they and their leaders fully sustained the national reputation for valour. Fraser, on a big gray horse, was everywhere in the conflict, animating his men, and contesting every point with the most determined courage and skill. The British were slowly forced back by the overwhelming Americans. Ackland's Grenadiers, one of the finest regiments in the British army, began to give ground under the furious attacks of the riflemen. Ackland himself was desperately wounded and taken prisoner. Fraser succeeded, however, in re-forming his shattered lines on the hills of Freeman's Farm, the scene of the previous battle; he was ably seconded by the other commanders who exposed themselves with the highest degree of personal gallantry.

The story goes that Morgan, seeing the value of Fraser's services, called two of his most expert riflemen and pointed to the unfortunate soldier, with the words, "That is General Fraser. He is a brave man, I honour him, but for the success of our cause it is necessary he should die." The bullets began to fall thickly about the brave Englishman, and some of his staff officers begged him to retire. "My duty forbids me to retire from danger, my place is here," he replied, and immediately after a rifle bullet struck him in the breast mortally wounding him. No loss, not even that of Burgoyne himself, could have been more serious. He was carried back to camp in a wheelbarrow, suffering dreadfully.

Arnold, who had been chafing bitterly at his enforced idleness on the Heights, watching the battle in which he had no right to interfere, as he was without command, and even had no status at all in the army, at this moment perceived that if the attack were pressed home, the most brilliant results might be expected. Without asking anyone's permission, mounting his horse he galloped away to the scene of the conflict. Gates, fearful that his impetuosity might lead him to undue lengths, sent a staff officer to call him back. The staff officer was not born who could catch Arnold that day. As he swept down along the American lines the men recognized him as their fighting leader, and with wild cheers followed him in a succession of desperate charges upon the shattered British column, which began a precipitate retreat to the camp, hard-pressed by the Americans.

As Arnold was the senior in rank on the field, his orders were obeyed everywhere without question. He despatched Morgan to attack the extreme right flank of the British camp, and with those immediately about him, fell like a storm upon the lines where were stationed the light infantry under Balcarras. The men of that famous regiment stood up like a rock. Seeing the attempt to break through was hopeless there, Arnold moved on to his left, falling upon the Canadian contingent, routed them, crashed into Breyman's Hessians, who were assailed at the same moment by Morgan's riflemen on the other flank, and who gave way at once. Arnold raged up and down the line in a fury of battle, a perfect incarnation of war. Well had it been for him if he had died at that moment on that bloody field!

The slaughter among the British was dreadful. Breyman himself was killed, and the right flank of the enemy's camp was in possession of the Americans. At this moment a ball from a rifle fired by a wounded German, lying on the ground, struck Arnold in the leg, breaking both bones and killing his horse—one likes to think that Arnold saved the life of the man who shot him. Reinforcements from the other flank and the centre of the British camp were now brought up, and the Americans finally retired, taking with them their disabled leader, who at this moment was overtaken by the staff officer carrying Gates' orders to return!

The gathering twilight stopped the progress of the conflict, called the Battle of Stillwater. Had Gates been a little more enterprising, he could have absolutely beaten the British to pieces on this day. It was the second opportunity he had lost. Nothing was now left for Burgoyne but to retreat. He gathered up his army skilfully enough, leaving his sick and wounded in camp, and precipitately moved back to Saratoga. The American army followed closely upon his heels. When Burgoyne reached Saratoga he found a force of three thousand men drawn up on the opposite side of the river, which would prevent his crossing.

Fraser had died the morning after the battle. The journal of the Baroness Riedesel who, with her three little children endured the hardships of the campaign, tells of the fortitude with which the gallant soldier bore his sufferings. He was buried, by his own request, on a high hill in the centre of the camp, at six o'clock on the evening of the day in which he died, Burgoyne delaying his retreat to carry out the last wishes of his friend. He was carried to his grave by the grenadiers of Ackland's regiment in his division. Burgoyne and his principal officers stood about the grave while the chaplain of the grenadiers, the Rev. Mr. Brudenell, calmly read the burial service. The cannon of the American batteries, not realizing the nature of the movement, played upon the little group. Bullets struck so near as to actually scatter the earth over the chaplain, who continued to read the Church service in his usual calm and even way. Before the service was finished the Americans discovered what the British were about and, in honour of the dead, minutes guns were fired until the burial was over, when the business of war was resumed again.

Lady Harriet Ackland, the wife of the commander of the grena-diers, who had devotedly followed the army from Quebec and nursed her husband through an attack of illness, and a wound received at Ticonderoga, now applied to General Burgoyne for a pass to the American lines to go to her husband who had been captured, after being desperately wounded in the battle of the day before. Accompa-nied by the plucky chaplain, Mr. Brudenell, in the dark, rainy night, they rowed down the river to the American camp. Gates received her with every courtesy and permitted her to have access to her gallant husband.

3. SARATOGA AND THE SURRENDER

The situation in the British camp was absolutely hopeless; their provisions were gone and there was no water. The American riflemen killed every man who attempted to go to the river to get water, and it was not until a woman, the wife of a British soldier, volunteered and made the attempt, that they got even a scanty supply—the American army would not fire upon a woman! The American batteries raked the camp with their shot, and the long rifles of Morgan's men searched out every point—there was no safety any place. The situation was now plainly unbearable. On the eighth of October Burgoyne sent a flag of truce to Gates, asking what terms would be accorded him. Burgoyne indignantly refused the first demand that he surrender uncondition-ally, and after further argument, on the seventeenth of October the articles were signed which were called *The Convention of Saratoga*.

In them Gates, on behalf of the United States, bound himself to the effect, that after the British army had marched out with the hon-ours of war, they should pile their arms at an appointed place and then be marched to Boston, whence they would be sent back to England. The arrangements which were made by Gates, to give him his due, were marked with the most distinguished consideration. When Bur-goyne, a tall, imposing man, brilliantly attired in the gorgeous scarlet and gold uniform of the British army, approached the small, unpre-possessing American soldier, in his plain blue frock-coat, he handed

Arnold wounded in the attack on the Hessian Redoubt at Seratoga

him his sword and said: "The fortune of war. General Gates, has made me your prisoner." Gates immediately returned the sword with a profound bow and the gracious remark, "I will be ready to testify that it was through no fault of your Excellency." Gates had been a major in the British army in earlier days, where he had served with some credit. Notwithstanding the fact that he received the surrender and did it well enough, as a commander he was thoroughly incompetent. The credit of the victory belongs first to the enterprising and devoted patriotism of Schuyler, and secondly to the bold work of Arnold.

One or two statements regarding matters under consideration may be of interest. In the first place, the American Congress deliberately and wilfully, and without cause, broke faith with the English, and the articles of the convention were never carried out. The captured army was taken from Boston to Virginia, where they were held as prisoners of war. Some of the officers were exchanged from time to time, but the army disintegrated and, as a body, never got back to England. The Baroness Riedesel and her three children, and the other women also, were treated with the most delightful hospitality and courtesy by the Americans, whom they ever after held in grateful remembrance.

Major Ackland, under the careful nursing of his devoted wife, recovered, was exchanged and went back to England. Sometime later, while at a dinner party, he undertook to resent some remarks which were made in disparagement of the courage of the Americans. A duel followed in which Ackland was killed. Lady Harriet lost her reason when she heard the news and continued insane for the space of two years. Would that the romantic chronicle might end here. Alas! When she recovered she married again, this time the Rev. Mr. Brudenell, the intrepid chaplain! Thus does romance veil its head before stern fact. Some have ventured to suggest, however, that Lady Harriet had not fully recovered her reason when she spoiled her charming story by that other marriage.

Talking with General Lew Wallace one day, he related the following anecdote. While minister of the United States to Turkey, he was seated with some English friends looking over the Golden Horn. A little boat flying the English flag crossed their field of vision.

"There," said his friend, reflectively, "is a flag which has never been surrendered by a general at the head of an army on a field of battle to a foreign foe,"

"You are mistaken," said Wallace, quietly, "I recall two instances."

"What are they?"

"Saratoga and Yorktown!"

"Oh," said the Englishman, quickly, "you are our people. They do not count."

But they did count, nevertheless, very highly; for Sir Edward Creasy, the distinguished historian, includes Saratoga, with Marathon, Arbela, Tours, Blenheim, Waterloo, and the others, among the fifteen decisive battles of the world! Frederick the Great, trailed, experienced soldier and statesman that he was, had seen the importance and value of Trenton and Princeton. The most ignorant and the sceptical could read the lesson of Saratoga. It wrote in large letters the prophecy of the ultimate success of the American cause, brought about the open alliance with France, and paved the way for Yorktown.

Greene's Campaign in the Carolinas

1. THE BEGINNING, THE COWPENS AND GUILFORD COURT HOUSE

A campaign which for brilliancy in conception and success in working out, may fairly challenge comparison with Washington's Trenton and Princeton campaign, was that of General Nathaniel Greene in the Carolinas. In some respects I would even award it the palm over Washington's more famous New Jersey manoeuvres. While the general conditions were not so desperate and the issues were not so great, in that failure would not have terminated the Revolution, yet locally nothing could have been more difficult, nay, impossible, than the problem which Greene was set to solve; and in the solving of which he demonstrated his right to be considered after Washington— and not far after him either—the ablest tactician, the most brilliant strategist, and the greatest fighter of the Revolution.

Indeed, we have come down to the Civil War to find his equal, and even then the search must be made with some care. General Scott, for instance, who gained a much greater reputation in the War of 1812 and in the Mexican War, is not to be mentioned in the same breath with this Rhode Island blacksmith, either for ability or achievement; he does not compare with this plain man who so highly educated himself by his own unaided efforts, that, for relaxation in the midst of desperate campaigns, he read the Latin poets in the original by the light of the camp fire, and annotated, for the use of the army, Vattel's famous treatise called "*Droit des Gens!*"

He began his service at the breaking out of the war and was never out of the harness until the end. He and Washington were the only general officers present at the siege of Boston who remained in the army until the British withdrew from the United States in 1783. He fought in every battle in which Washington commanded, except one, until he went South, with ever increasing success and skill; and although he had no previous military experience whatsoever, he developed himself, by observation, study and reflection, not only into the strategist which he naturally was, but into a brilliant tactician as well—strategists are born, tacticians largely made. His tactics on the field of battle were as great as was his strategy in his campaigns. He was a man of impetuous, dashing nature, yet he schooled himself and so checked his natural impulses that he became the incarnation of caution. It is difficult to find anything to blame in his military work from the beginning, and impossible in those years in which he exercised independent command. His plans and his methods were moulded largely after those of Washington himself. No man could be more wary, more prompt, or more bold than he, when the exigency demanded the one course or the other.

When the British under Sir Henry Clinton invaded South Carolina in 1780 and finally succeeded in capturing Charleston on the twelfth of May, thus eliminating the army—containing over two thousand Continentals, by the way, which Lincoln had foolishly permitted to be cooped up in Charleston—from the campaign, in the absence of any other organized forces, they easily overran Georgia and particularly South Carolina. In order to make secure their possession, they established a number of well-fortified posts on every hand, the more important being located at Camden and Ninety-six, in North Carolina, and Augusta, in Georgia. Lord Cornwallis, a very able man, was left in command by Sir Henry Clinton, who went back to New York under the impression that the provinces south of Virginia had been absolutely and finally won back to the crown. Quite an unwarranted conclusion, as we shall see.

After the capture of Charleston, Washington, though he could ill spare them himself, had detached a splendid division of Continental troops under the Baron de Kalb, a most capable officer, to stem, if possible, the tide of the British success in the South, and form a nucleus upon which the militia of the invaded sections might rally. In opposition to his wish, Congress had designated the incompetent Gates for the command of these forces, his friends expecting him to repeat what they were pleased to call the "Burgoynade" of his Saratoga campaign, in the South. In the words of Charles Lee, "His Northern laurels changed to Southern willows," and in the disastrous Battle of Camden he was utterly and entirely defeated; said defeat being due to his own stupidity, carelessness and gross inefficiency as a commander.

The Baron de Kalb heroically fought with his veterans, whose courage and devotion somewhat redeemed the day, until he fell covered with sixteen wounds and died a prisoner a short time after the battle was over. The larger part of his veteran division was absolutely annihilated, a smaller part cut its way out of the British lines at the point of the bayonet and effected a retreat. The generalship of Cornwallis had been excellent and the conduct of his troops beyond question. It seemed as if nothing whatever could redeem the South from the British and that they had at last established themselves securely in one not unimportant portion of the revolted colonies.

At this desperate juncture, Nathaniel Greene, Washington's right arm, who had been originally chosen by that commander for the purpose, was sent to take command of the department, *i.e.*, all south of and including the State of Delaware. Except territory he had but little to command. Washington, however, generously detached the famous legion of "Light Horse Harry Lee," composed of light infantry and cavalry from his army, and sent them with Greene. He also sent another small squadron of horse—a very efficient body—commanded by Lieutenant-Colonel William A. Washington, a kinsman of the great general and a man of the same school. The famous Daniel Morgan, who had withdrawn from the army on account of his ill-treatment in the matter of rank, by the blundering and incompetent Congress, rejoined the army after the defeat at Camden, nobly saying that an occasion of such public disaster was not the time in which to indulge private griefs.

Lieutenant-Colonel Otho Williams, another distinguished soldier and cavalry leader, was also attached to Greene's skeleton army, the nucleus of which was the famous brigade of the old Maryland line, which had escaped after Camden; two regiments of troops, about six hundred in number, which I think did more and better service than any other in the Revolution; there was also a remnant of the Delaware regiment, another good lot of men. In addition to this nucleus of veterans, a very efficient auxiliary existed in the Carolinas in the shape of partisan bands of rangers, who were led by such men as Pinckney, Sumter and Marion, than whom no more efficient leaders in the sort of warfare in which they excelled ever bestrode a horse, laid an ambush, or headed a charge. Gates had been inattentive to their services and had not recognized the possible value of these men. Greene utilized them to the greatest possible extent, and their brilliant and daring manoeuvres, under his direction, contributed as much as anything

THE DEATH OF BARON DE KALB AT CAMDEN

else to the success of his campaign.

Von Steuben, with a few Continentals and the Virginia militia, was left in charge of the operations in the State of Virginia by Greene as he went South. Before he arrived in the South to supersede Gates, a body of one thousand men, mostly Tories, led by Colonel Patrick Ferguson, a very distinguished officer, had been utterly defeated in a hand to hand conflict in a strong position of their own choosing on King's Mountain, North Carolina, by an irregular assemblage of backwoodsmen, who had assembled for the purpose of wiping them out, and who dispersed as soon as they had done so. Ferguson was killed, with three hundred of his men, and the remainder were made prisoners; their arms and equipments being of great value to the Americans—indeed, during this campaign, the Americans lived off the country and armed off the enemy!

Inasmuch as this was the force which Cornwallis had intended to use as a flying column to keep himself in touch with the chain of posts he had established on the borders of the State, its loss was felt by him rather severely, though, of course, it was neither vital nor irreparable, especially as he was soon reinforced by a large body of troops despatched from New York by Sir Henry Clinton. When Greene arrived at Hillsboro, North Carolina, in December, 1780, he found about two thousand men had assembled. Cornwallis, with the main body of the British, numbering about three thousand men, was at Camden. Large detachments garrisoned the posts at Ninety-six and Augusta, and smaller ones were scattered about at various forts in different parts of the State, such as Granby, Motte, Watson and others.

The British had carried things with a high hand in their conquests and had actually attempted to force the inhabitants either to enter the British service or to be declared rebels. The policy was disastrous, as it raised up for the British a host of enemies, for many of the otherwise peaceable inhabitants, if they had to fight, naturally preferred to fight for, rather than against, their own. Colonel Banastre Tarleton, a very capable and enterprising young man, who commanded Cornwallis' cavalry, had made himself particularly obnoxious by his method of carrying out his harsh orders and, as the inhabitants of the country had divided themselves between the British and the Americans, they added the usual neighbourhood animosities to the political differences which separated them; and hanging, plundering and outraging in every way were evidences of the hatreds engendered, as always, in the internecine conflict which was waged.

Since two complete American armies had been captured or destroyed by the British, Greene had the greatest difficulty in collecting more than two thousand men. The American force was not only smaller in number but it was not to be compared in quality to that of Cornwallis', whose troops included some of the finest of the British army—as was shown by their fighting on every field on which they were engaged—the chief of which were two battalions of the famous "Household Guards." Cornwallis had no illusions whatever regarding Greene. "He is as dangerous as Washington," he wrote to a friend. He knew his quality; he had felt his attack and witnessed his tactics on many a hard fought field in the Revolution. He remembered him at Trenton; he recalled how he had brought up his division on the run for four miles, charging "toward the sound of the cannon" at Brandywine.

He knew that Greene and his officers had been trained in the school of the great Washington—for whom the earl had conceived the most profound respect—and he resolved to employ all the skill and address of which he was capable to defeat this new enemy, leaving nothing undone to accomplish his purpose; so the two armies faced each other, neither, for the moment, daring to take the initiative. For Greene knew that Cornwallis was the ablest of the British commanders also, and he could not afford to take even ordinary chances. They were like two wary fencers who have just crossed swords and are gently moving the blades up and down, looking for the necessary opening, neither being willing to disengage for fear of the other.

But the pause could not be allowed to last long; every day strengthened the British hold on the South and made his own task harder, so it was incumbent upon Greene to do something. He could not attack with any possibility of success, and he had before him one supreme necessity, which was, that at whatever hazard and under whatever circumstances, he must preserve his army intact. So long as he had an army, even a little one, the British were not safe in their positions; but that last army once destroyed and dispersed, there was no further resource. After careful thought he came to a determination; first despatching Marion and Sumter to harry the flanks and communications of the British and cut off the scattered detachments and bodies of loyalist reinforcements in the rear of the enemy—which they did with thoroughness and precision—and throwing Williams to skirmish in Cornwallis' face, he decided to divide his little army into two great partisan bands.

To do this was contrary to the usual laws of strategy, but the conditions were peculiar and anomalous, and subsequent events showed the wisdom of his action. He gave Daniel Morgan about nine hundred men, including the Maryland Continentals, Washington's cavalry and some North Carolina militia, and sent him off toward the British left, where he threatened in force Cornwallis' rear. Greene, with the main body of eleven hundred men, hurried down to the South and began that series of perplexing and annoying marchings and countermarchings in which he became such a master; playing a game of hide-and-seek with the English on a large scale and never getting caught.

Cornwallis hesitated to move forward to attack Greene lest he should have Morgan down upon his rear. He also hesitated to turn and crush Morgan lest he should have Greene upon his rear; also he could not leave Camden unprotected on account of the large quantity of stores and supplies there. His position was, therefore, a difficult one. He finally determined to follow Greene's example and divide his force, so he despatched Tarleton with eleven hundred men to take care of Morgan, left a strong body under Leslie at Camden, and moved out to attack Greene, when, or if, he could catch him. But the wary American had no intention of being attacked, and manoeuvring his light force—which was without baggage or tents, or even shoes for that matter, such was their destitution—with great skill, he never permitted Cornwallis to force an action. He was here today and there tomorrow, never remaining more than a night in one spot; it was humiliating and exasperating to be always on the run, but it succeeded admirably. Cornwallis and his men were kept fearfully busy, and accomplished nothing except to weary themselves in body and spirit.

Meanwhile Tarleton had impetuously dashed away after Morgan. Morgan, a man of humble extraction, the son of a day-labourer, but of great native ability, was one of the striking figures of the Revolution. He had been a wagoner in Braddock's unfortunate expedition, had felt the British lash upon his back for striking a comrade—he never forgot the feel of it, either, and paid back every stroke a thousandfold—had been given a commission for distinguished gallantry in that battle, and so made his way upward. When the Revolution broke out he led a splendid corps of backwoods riflemen "from the right bank of the Potomac" to Washington's army. He had participated in many desperate actions from Quebec to Saratoga and had served always with the greatest distinction and success.

Morgan had emulated Greene's tactics—he was an old backwoodsman, and could do it to perfection—until he was ready to give battle; and he led Tarleton a long, perverse chase until he was almost worn out; then he resolved to hazard an action at the Cowpens. It was a small affair in point of the numbers engaged—all the battles of the campaign were that—but tactically it was an unusually brilliant combat. Morgan selected as a place to light a slight acclivity behind which an unfordable river, the Broad, bent in a wide circle. The ground was open or but thinly wooded. There was no possibility of retreat. He said that he wanted his militia to feel that there was no method of getting away, they would have to fight or die. If he had possessed any boats, no doubt, like Cortez, he would have burned them. There were no marshes about into which the possible retreaters could plunge, there was no open country through which they could break in wild panic as they had done at Camden and elsewhere. The night before the probable battle Morgan clearly explained his plan to his officers, and then walked up and down among the men, stopping at the various camp fires, and in plain, homely phrase talked over the matter with them, animating them with his own heroic purpose, and promising them, with their assistance, that the old "wagoner would crack his whip over Tarleton," etc.

Word had been brought to Tarleton, through Morgan's connivance, that the Americans proposed to wait for him, and at three o'clock in the morning of January 17, 1781, he put his men in motion to take them by surprise. He was not early enough to catch the old hunter napping, however, for when he appeared upon the scene Morgan had his force under arms and was ready for the attack. He had the militia drawn up in line about three hundred yards in front of the hill. Above them on the hill he had drawn up the Continental line; on the bank of the river and screened by the brow of the hill from the observation of the enemy, was the cavalry under Washington in reserve. Morgan had ridden up and down the line commanding and exhorting the militia to fire at least two well-aimed volleys, when he would permit them to retreat, if the British advanced, around the left flank of the Continentals, and re-form in safety back of the hill; imploring them for the sake of their country and their homes to heed his words, deliver the two volleys and retire slowly in good order, preserving their ranks. They promised to do so. He also cautioned the Continentals that the militia would retire and bade them withhold their fire until the order was given, and he further admonished Washington to be on the alert with his cavalry all the time, but to make no move until directed.

Tarleton's men, who had been marching half the night over the muddy roads, were tired out, but their restless leader gave them no opportunity for rest. Just as the sun rose he came in sight of the American camp and immediately sounded the charge. The British rushed through the woods and fell on the militia under Pickens, who, remarkable to state, stood up manfully and delivered not only one or two, but several well aimed volleys before they retired in good order around the left flank. The British had become somewhat disorganized in the attack, but they were led forward by the dashing Tarleton himself, with the utmost bravery, and their superior numbers permitted them to overlap the right flank of the Continental line. Morgan, to prevent this flank, refused his line, and to do that it became necessary for the Continentals there to withdraw a little. The British mistaking the movement, which was successfully carried out under fire by the Marylanders under John Eager Howard, for a retreat, rushed forward shouting victory. When Howard had reached his proper position, he immediately turned about and delivered a volley at close range, and rushed forward with the bayonet.

At this juncture, by Morgan's orders, Washington's cavalry dashed around the hill and fell upon the British right, the Continentals opposite the British centre advancing at the same time. Meanwhile the militia, elated by their successful resistance, had been re-formed at the back of the hill by the heroic Pickens, and came on the field on the dead run, circling around the left flank of the British just where they were being severely pressed by Howard. Old Morgan at once ordered a general advance and the British forces were surrounded. The Continentals broke their ranks with a deadly fire at thirty yards and rushed upon them in a stern bayonet charge. The greater part of the British army threw down its arms and surrendered at once. Six hundred prisoners were taken, and only about two hundred and fifty escaped from the conflict, Tarleton being among them. He only got away after a furious hand to hand conflict with Washington in which he was wounded.

The British lost about three hundred in killed and wounded, two field pieces and one thousand stand of arms, two colours, thirty-four wagons, one hundred horses and a large number of tents, all very useful indeed as the Americans were mainly without them. The victory was complete and decisive. The Americans had absolutely captured or killed more than their entire force engaged. The tactics of Morgan had been crowned with the most brilliant success. He had so manoeuvred that with an inferior force he had literally surrounded and captured a larger force opposing him, and he had actually made his militia fight! His loss in killed and wounded only amounted to seventy-three.

The tidings reached Green and Cornwallis about the same time. Cornwallis immediately made for the fords of the Catawba to intercept Morgan and his men. During this period, however, and it was the only occasion during the campaign that he did not move with his accustomed celerity, he hesitated and appeared undecided. Greene at once put the main body of his army in motion under the command of General Huger, and told him to move north at all speed, collecting all the boats as he went, while he himself, attended by a single officer and an orderly, rode at full speed one hundred and fifty miles to join Morgan. By desperate marching Morgan, though he had the greater distance to cover, succeeded in reaching the fords of the Catawba, where Greene found him, and crossed with all his prisoners and booty before Cornwallis arrived there. Then the British commander at last waked up. Summoning all his detachments to his aid, he started on a furious pursuit of the Americans, led by Greene and Morgan. There never was such desperate marching. Greene gathered up the boats as he went, destroying those he could not use, and actually mounting the rest on wheels like wagons!

Cornwallis was close on the heels of his enemy all the time and, in spite of the disadvantages under which he laboured, he almost caught him on several occasions. To accelerate his movements, the British commander burned all but the absolutely necessary baggage and followed hard the retreating Americans. Leaving Morgan to push ahead. Greene essayed to rouse the militia, but with little success, as Cornwallis was too quick for him and too close on his heels to give them time to assemble. We get a fine picture of the desperate straits to which the Americans were reduced in effecting their escape and the fierce energy of the pursuit, when we see Greene riding up late at night in a drenching rain to the tavern at Salisbury on the night of February first, after receiving the news that one detachment of militia, upon which he had counted to dispute the passage of the Catawba, had been cut to pieces and its commander killed, and that Cornwallis had almost reached Morgan. The tavern keeper expressed surprise at seeing him alone.

"Yes," he said sadly, "tired, hungry, alone and penniless!"

But it takes such conditions to develop some men best, and Greene, like Washington, was never so dangerous as when he was pushed to the wall; the British were to learn that presently. Cornwallis was unable to prevent the junction of the two armies near Guilford Court House, but in spite of the fact that he was outnumbered, he still persisted in the pursuit. Greene's forethought and his travelling boats enabled him to make his escape, and Cornwallis was foiled at the Catawba, the Yadkin and the Dan in quick succession. Finally, when he had driven Greene into Virginia, as he was far away from his base of supplies, and as he was in great need of that baggage which he had burned some time since, he gave over the pursuit, saying that he had successfully forced the enemy out of the State, which was perfectly true. This was the first act of the drama. Things looked dark for the Americans then. They did not intend to stay forced out, however, and the second act began when the indefatigable Greene recrossed the Dan and moved out on the heels of, though at a safe distance from, Cornwallis, who began to move slowly to the southward to reach his base of supplies again.

By detachments of militia and a brigade of Virginia Continentals, who were mostly raw troops, Greene's force was increased to something like four thousand men, and with it he resolved to give battle at Guilford Court House. Cornwallis was nothing loath to engage, indeed, he was desperately anxious for a fight, by which he trusted to retrieve his somewhat precarious situation. On the morning of March fifteenth, Greene drew up his men in three lines; the North Carolina militia in the first, the Virginia militia in the second, the famous Marylanders in the third, which was placed on the top of a hill, and the Virginia Continentals in reserve. Lee's legion was on one flank of the first line, Washington's cavalry and some Delaware riflemen on the other, and Singleton's two guns in the centre. Cornwallis had about twenty-two hundred men, the best in the service. Their fighting that day was simply magnificent. He boldly attacked the first line early in the morning. Most of the battalions comprising it fled without firing a shot, as usual. Singleton withdrew with his guns on the run.

The legion and cavalry and the riflemen retreated on the second line, which stood firm and actually checked the British advance for a time, but the heroic Englishmen pressed forward with the bayonet and finally succeeded in breaking the line. Detached parties engaged the riflemen, the cavalry and the legion, and gradually drove them down the field, separating them in the centre. Meanwhile the main body of the British rushed for that part of the hill held by the Second Maryland; this regiment, not so good a one as the First, was broken by the furious British attack and the two guns belonging to it were captured.

Greene immediately threw the First Maryland into the breach and they recaptured the guns by a dashing bayonet charge which pierced the British centre. At the same time Lee and Washington, who had succeeded in getting clear of their antagonists, fell simultaneously on the British flanks. The British line was broken in the centre and began to give ground slightly, in the face of the furious American attack. To stay their retreat, Cornwallis brought his artillery into action and, in spite of the remonstrances of his officers, fired at the approaching Americans through the lines of his own troops, some of whom were killed by shot from their own guns. It was a desperate measure, but the exigency of the situation warranted it. Cornwallis now put in his reserves and Tarleton's cavalry and the advance of the Americans was first checked and then they retreated back to the hill in disorder.

By great exertions Cornwallis re-formed his lines and, concentrating them, advanced his artillery, which continued to play upon the broken Americans with great effect. The Virginia Continentals had not yet been actively engaged. It is possible that if Greene had thrown them in at this moment, he might have crushed Cornwallis and won the day. Whether or no it could have been done is a grave problem. The Virginians were green hands and the British were veterans already flushed with success. If the Virginians failed in their attack, Greene's army would be ruined. His personal preference would have been to put in every last man and try out the issue to the bitter end, but the loss of the army would mean the loss of everything, and, bitterly against his inclination, as the British advanced, he gave the order to retreat. It was a sad moment for the young commander, but stern and inexorable necessity dictated his course. That retreat at the crisis of that still undecided battle was much more heroic and evidenced more courage and generalship than anything else he could have done. The British were too badly shattered to pursue, and Greene withdrew to the northward in good order, taking his guns with him—they had done well, but they had been defeated.

We have to look along the pages of history for a hundred years to find such fighting as the whole British army did on one side, and as the famous First Maryland did on the other, on that day, and we do not find it until we come to old Thomas at Chickamauga. It was a glorious and splendid victory for Cornwallis and his outnumbered army, but the winning of it cost him dear. He had lost in killed and wounded over six hundred men, more than one-fourth of his total force! "A few more victories like that and we are undone," said Fox, when he heard the news. The situation of Cornwallis was now more precarious than ever, in spite of his triumph. He had almost expended his supply of ammunition, he was over two hundred miles away from his base of supplies, Marion and Sumter were pressing heavily upon his flanks, Williams was skirmishing boldly in front, and he found himself actually compelled to retreat. But where should he go? To return to Charleston was intolerable. He finally determined upon making his way to the seaboard, whence he could communicate with headquarters and look for assistance from the fleet.

So on the third day after the battle, leaving his sick and wounded, he put his army in motion for Wilmington, North Carolina, leaving the command of the troops in South Carolina to Lord Rawdon. The decision was really forced upon him; he did not dare to attempt the long march back to South Carolina in his condition, and there is where Greene displayed another touch of his splendid strategy. He surmised that Cornwallis could only go one of two ways when he reached the seaboard, *i. e.,* back to Charleston, where he wanted him to be, or up to Virginia, where he could be brought in contact with the terrible Washington. Therefore, instead of following Cornwallis, Greene at once gathered up his army and thrust himself boldly between the two British commanders; leaving Cornwallis to pursue his way unhindered and unpursued, he at once turned south to fall upon Rawdon. The American commander had actually forced Cornwallis out of the field and eliminated him and his army from future operations! When the astonished earl found out that he was not being followed, it was too late for him to retrace his steps, and with, I imagine, a heavy heart, he made his way into Virginia. We shall see what became of him there later on.

2. Hobkirk's Hill, Eutaw Springs and the End

After carefully considering the situation, Greene determined upon his course of action. Pickens was directed, with his partisan band, to threaten the left flank of the British lines at Ninety-six, Marion and Lee were to move upon the small posts on the right flank between Camden and Charleston, Sumter was to operate in the rear, while he, himself, with the four Continental regiments—two Maryland and two Virginia—and Washington's cavalry moved down to attack the centre. The campaign was planned with the greatest skill and care, and though the forces were inconsiderable—Greene's whole command scarcely amounting to fifteen hundred men—the game was played as brilliantly and the results are as instructive to the student of military matters as if the armies had been as great as that of Xerxes.

On the sixth of April the march began. Marion and Lee at once struck for Fort Watson, an irregular stockade which had been erected on an old Indian mound which dominated the plain for several miles around. It was defended by one hundred and twenty soldiers, under Lieutenant McKay. Neither Marion nor McKay had any artillery, and rifle fire was of course ineffective against the stockade. Marion cut off the water supply, but McKay dug a well. The fort had been amply provisioned, and the Americans were in a dilemma. Finally it occurred to one of the officers, a certain Colonel Maham, to build a wooden tower high enough to command the fort—it was an undertaking as old as Caesar. The country was heavily wooded and the stalwart men quickly acted upon the idea.

When day broke on April twenty-third the astonished garrison saw that their position was commanded by a high wooden tower which had been erected during the night. Its top was covered with men who were protected by heavy planking from their fire, and who picked them off at leisure. At its foot was a breastwork lined with riflemen; a sortie to destroy the tower was out of the question. There was nothing to do but surrender, and they accordingly hauled down their flag. The success at Fort Watson was repeated by Marion at Forts Motte and Granby. On the other side, Sumter took Orangeburg and various small posts, and cleared the country. Pickens and his militia raided the country, destroying parties of royalists in every direction, and constantly hovered about Ninety-six. To anticipate a little, on the fifth of June, the post at Augusta, after a most obstinate and desperate defence, was captured by Lee and his partisans.

The British had now nothing left except Camden and Ninety-six. Since the defeat of the previous year the post at Camden had been carefully fortified and strengthened, and when Greene moved down to it on the twenty-fifth of April, he found it too strong for attack by his little force of about eleven hundred men, so he withdrew and took up a strong position on an elevation called Hobkirk's Hill, a few miles north of the town. Rawdon, who was in command of all the British forces, at once determined to attack him. Early in the morning of April twenty-fifth he moved out with his whole force, numbering a few more than nine hundred men. Greene had drawn up his four regiments in line upon the hill, the two Virginia regiments on the right and the two Maryland on the left. The North Carolina militia, small in numbers and poor in quality in this instance, were placed in the rear of the hill, Washington's squadron of cavalry was stationed in reserve. What remained of the Delaware regiment was thrown out on the picket line.

The British came on gallantly, led by Rawdon in person. As they struggled up the road and through the narrow clearing before the American position, Greene determined, since he had the most men, to flank them. He therefore swung the Virginia and Maryland regiments on each end of his line in toward the British column, at the same time ordering a general advance. Washington meanwhile was directed to sweep around the British left and attack their rear. He did this with brilliant success, capturing over two hundred men of Rawdon's little army, including all the surgeons. The North Carolina militia were also ordered to advance, which they did reluctantly.

The little battle on the side of the hill was joined with the utmost fury. The outnumbered British displayed their usual resolution and bravely advanced in the face of a furious discharge of grape from Greene's two guns. The attack of the Americans, however, was proving too much for the British and they commenced to give ground, though still preserving good order and battling furiously. At this juncture, Captain Beatty, leading the charge of the famous First Maryland, was killed. His company of Continentals halted and under a bitter return charge led by the intrepid Rawdon, they gave ground a little. The veteran commander of the regiment seems to have lost his head at this moment, for he gave the order to fall back, intending, as he said, to form a new line on the company which had given ground; but it is a bad thing to order a regiment to fall back during a battle, and these famous veterans, who had shown their mettle on nearly every field in the Revolution, and may be considered the very flower of the famous Continental line, hastily broke and ran.

Rawdon was quick to see his advantage and the attack was pressed more vigorously than ever. The defection of the Marylanders, who had been to Greene what the Tenth Legion had been to Caesar, was simply heartbreaking, and it occurred at the very moment when victory was within their grasp. The panic unsettled the other regiments, which had done so well, and there was a moment of indecision all along the line—another moment or two and the army would have been routed.

The Americans were wavering and retiring and the fight had reached their guns. Greene was in the very thick of it, as was Rawdon, and both narrowly escaped being killed. The efforts the two men made were prodigious—Greene to stand his ground and Rawdon to continue his advance. The First Marylanders were rallied by their officers and came on again, though, of course, not with their usual spirit and success. Rawdon's attack, however, would have been successful, had it not been for the arrival of Washington, who had learned of the disaster and had acted with the promptness of Greene himself; releasing his prisoners, he brought up his cavalry on the gallop. His quick eye detected the critical nature of the situation, and he boldly charged through the scattered ranks of his own army and fell like a thunderbolt upon the British about the guns.

By the mad impetuosity of his charge, Rawdon's men were borne back and driven down the hill. But a moment's respite was afforded by this rugged little band of heroic cavalrymen, and as soon as the force of their dash was spent Rawdon re-formed the men. But that moment had been enough for Greene. He had instantly taken advantage of that diversion to withdraw his guns in good order and effect a retreat! Rawdon hovered in his rear, which was covered by the remnants of Washington's intrepid cavalry, for a little while, but finally returned to Camden.

The loss on the American side was nineteen killed, one hundred and fifteen wounded and one hundred and thirty-six missing, most of the latter being militia, making a total of two hundred and seventy. The British loss was thirty-eight killed and two hundred and twenty wounded and missing. The total number engaged on both sides was about two thousand, making the total percentage of loss about twenty-five! As usual, Greene had lost a battle but had won a campaign. Rawdon, finding his communications cut off in every direction, was forced to abandon Camden and retreat upon Charleston. Greene was very much chagrined over his lost battle, which he would have won but for an unaccountable accident, but he philosophically made the best of the situation and resolutely girded up his loins for another fight.

To the "French minister he wrote at this time: "We fight, we get beat, rise and fight again," and the state of his mind is indicated by his orders for the day after the battle. The parole he gave was "Perseverance," and the countersign, "Fortitude." There was something very fine in the grim tenacity and persistence of this devoted soldier.

Greene at once moved forward and. laid siege to the last British post in the interior at Ninety-six. It was the strongest of the British fortifications and the most heavily garrisoned. The commanding officer was Colonel Cruger, of the famous New York regiment of loyalists. He skilfully and bravely defended his post. On the twenty-second of May, Greene and Kosciusko, the Polish engineer, made a careful reconnoissance of the position. The works were so strong that the American despaired of effecting their capture with his small force, yet he determined to attempt it. The operations carried on were those of a regular siege, approaches being made by parallels, and the first parallel was broken at about seventy yards from the fort on a dark, rainy night. It was too near the works and, by a brilliant sally, which was a complete success, Cruger broke up the intrenching party, captured their tools, destroyed the parallel, and returned without loss to his entrenchments.

The next parallel was opened at four hundred yards—a proper distance—and the work was thenceforward carried on vigorously and successfully, though interrupted by frequent bold sorties from the fort. A mine was begun at the end of the first parallel, guns were mounted on the second, and the cannonading began. Cruger was summoned to surrender on the third of June, and indignantly refused, whereupon the third parallel was opened close to the works. To facilitate their operations, the besiegers made use of the Maham tower, which they found so effective at Fort Watson and elsewhere.

Meanwhile reinforcements had arrived at Charleston for Rawdon, and he at once advanced to relieve Ninety-six. Lee had come in from the successful siege of Augusta, which had raised the number of Greene's force somewhat, though the other reinforcements, which were to be sent to him from Virginia, had been retained to defend that state against Cornwallis's incursion. On the twelfth of June a man from Rawdon succeeded in reaching Cruger with the advice that the British commander had passed Orangeburg and was marching hard to raise the siege. But little time was left for the Americans, and as Greene could not bear to abandon the siege without making a final effort to capture the post, he decided to attempt to storm the works.

The assault was delivered with the greatest gallantry and was partially successful, as the attacking forces succeeded in establishing themselves in one of the bastions. It was quite possible, if Greene had put in every man he possessed, to have made good his footing and captured the fort. It was equally possible that he might do so and still get no further than he had. It was the old question that presented itself to him at Guilford Court House, and he wisely chose to give up a possible success in the face of a possible lost army, so he reluctantly abandoned the siege. The defence of Cruger had been magnificent. The American loss had been one hundred and forty-seven; that of the British, eighty-eight.

Rawdon arrived on the twenty-first of June with about twenty-five hundred men. He immediately left in pursuit of Greene, but the wily American was not to be caught by him anymore than by Cornwallis. The two armies never came in contact, though Rawdon's advance did some heavy skirmishing with Lee and Washington. Greene established himself on Rawdon's flanks, changing his camp daily, until the enemy gave up the futile pursuit in disgust. Abandoning Ninety-six, his last stronghold in the interior, which was untenable now that the other British posts had been captured. Rawdon retreated once more to Charleston. Again Greene had been defeated, but had won a campaign!

As soon as Rawdon faced toward the sea, Greene was on his heels again with the partisan cavalry hovering about his flanks. No man was ever better served by his scouts than Greene, and did Rawdon stop his march and face about, the wary American at once withdrew from his vicinity. It was impossible to bring him to battle or to force him at bay, so the superior and victorious army continued its dogged march to the seaboard, pursued and aggravated and goaded on by the inferior and defeated force. They might defeat Greene, but they could not disarrange his plans or break his spirit; and his men seem to have entered into the feelings and aspirations of their leader.

It has not been mentioned before, but in this whole campaign, from beginning to end, Greene never had anything that was necessary to make an efficient army. His men were deficient in everything. He had no money, no tents, no provisions, no supply-train, but little ammunition, and arms which were mainly captured from their enemy; the men were barefoot, ragged, hungry, tired, sick and wounded—but they were men! And they showed it in the whole campaign. On the tenth of July Sumter and Marion joined Greene with about one thousand state troops and militia, bringing up his total force to about two thousand men. He at once determined to give battle again, and moved closer to the retreating Rawdon, who had by this time reached Orangeburg.

Greene occupied a strong position in front of Rawdon, expecting that the British commander would come out and attack him. Rawdon, however, declined to do so, his experience at Hobkirk's Hill had been sufficient to discourage him; and finding the British position too strong to be carried, Greene withdrew to the high hills of the Santee to give his tatterdemalion heroes an opportunity to recuperate during" the hot months of the summer, while the partisan bands continued their adventurous raids with much success in the vicinity of Charleston.

Rawdon, sick and worn out with his arduous campaigning, started to New York on leave of absence, turning over the command to Colonel Stewart. The vessel in which Rawdon sailed had the ill-luck to be captured by De Grasse, and the unfortunate commander had the privilege of sharing the fate which soon after befell his old leader and chief, Cornwallis. On the twenty-third of August the indomitable American commander broke camp and moved for Stewart's right flank in the hope of interposing himself between that commander and Charleston. On account of the lack of river transportation, a circuitous march was necessitated which led him through Camden. As soon as Stewart heard that Greene was on the move, he began a retreat toward Charleston, and finally established himself in a strong position at a place called Eutaw Springs. Greene, sending all his heavy baggage to the rear, at once moved forward in pursuit. On the eighth of September the two armies were almost in touch.

Greene formed his little force of about twenty-three hundred men, one half of whom were Continentals and the rest militia, in two columns, the North and South Carolina militia in one column, the Continentals from North Carolina, Virginia and Maryland in the other, and advanced early in the morning as usual, to make the attack; this time he determined to begin the battle instead of waiting the British attack as heretofore. Lee was stationed on the right flank, Henderson, with some South Carolina cavalry, on the left, Washington and the remnants of the Delaware battalion in the rear. Two three-pound guns went with the first column and two six-pound guns with the second. Stewart's force amounted to about twenty-five hundred men—or about the same number as Greene had—and comprised the Sixty-Third and Sixty-Fifth regiments, a battalion of grenadiers, Cruger's loyal New Yorkers, and the third regiment from Ireland, known as the "Buffs." They were encamped in a little clearing in the midst of thick woods.

Greene stole up to them without being observed. Two deserters apprised Stewart of Greene's proximity, but he did not credit their story. Nevertheless, early in the morning a small detachment of cavalry was sent out to cover the "rooting parties," who were accustomed to dig for sweet potatoes for the various regiments every morning. This cavalry picket, under Captain Coffin, met the advance guard of the Americans at eight o'clock in the morning about four miles from Eutaw Springs. Thinking that he had to do with militia as usual. Coffin charged, but retreated immediately, leaving forty prisoners in the hands of the Americans and a large number of dead and wounded on the field.

The unarmed potato pickers, hearing the fire, came out on the road and were all captured—it was an auspicious opening of the day. The rattle of the small arms in the woods at once apprised Stewart that something serious was about to happen, and he drew up his force under the trees across the road leading through the forest, his three pieces of artillery commanding the road. A battalion of light infantry protected the right flank, the British reserve being stationed on the left. Greene deployed his two columns into line as quickly as the thickly wooded ground would permit, and sent the artillery on ahead to open the battle. He moved his forces forward slowly until he came upon the enemy's lines.

The militia, who formed the first line, under Pickens and Marion fought with the greatest determination, holding their ground for a long time, but they were finally forced back in the centre. The North Carolina Continentals were then ordered forward to reinforce the first line, which again renewed the battle and gained some ground, though it was afterward slowly driven back again. Greene then despatched Washington and his cavalry against the British right, under Major Marjoribanks, and Lee, with the light infantry and the cavalry of the legion, against the British left. At the same time, Colonels Williams and Campbell, with the Virginia and Maryland Continentals, were sent forward to the first line and were instructed not to fire but to make free use of the bayonet, Greene himself leading the charge. Their determined assault was bravely met all along the line.

Meanwhile Washington was unsuccessful on the left; Marjoribanks put up a desperate defence, and the thick woods did not allow the cavalry to be used to advantage. Washington's horse was shot under him, he was thrust through with a bayonet, and would have been killed had it not been for a British officer who took him prisoner. All his officers but two were killed or wounded, and he lost over one half of his men.

The remnant of his force was driven back and their retreat was covered by Colonel Wade Hampton and some South Carolina partisans. In the centre, however, things had gone better. The men came to close quarters and crossed bayonets. Colonel Campbell was killed, Colonels Henderson and Howard likewise, and many others wounded. The struggle was maintained with the utmost fury and without advantage on either side, the lines swaying back and forth like gigantic wrestlers, until Lee, who had succeeded in breaking the British left, turned and took the British line in reverse. As the light horse came sweeping down on the flank, the British gave way in every direction. Two of the three guns were captured, three hundred prisoners were taken, and finally the whole line broke and fled for life, hotly pursued by the triumphant Continentals on the dead run.

The British forces rushed pell-mell through the woods until they reached the clearing, where Stewart finally succeeded in rallying them some distance in the rear of the camp. Cruger and Sheridan and the New Yorkers threw themselves in a stout brick house on the edge of a garden surrounded by a high fence. Marjoribanks and his men took possession of the fence and poured in a heavy fire. The British and Lee's men had reached the house at the same time; there was a furious struggle for its possession, but the British finally secured it, and by the most heroic exertions, Stewart got his line re-formed. From the upper windows of the house the New Yorkers poured a hot fire on the Continentals. Unfortunately, the American advance had led straight through the British camp, which was filled with good things to eat, as breakfast was being prepared when the fight began. The men would have resisted the temptation which lay in ordinary plunder, but they were actually hungry. They fell into great disorder in the presence of the first substantial breakfast they had seen for perhaps six months!

The British seeing the state of affairs made a determined advance. It was met with varying success; in some parts of the line they took prisoners and drove the Americans back, in other parts they were repulsed. The balance of the advantage, however, was with them, and in the confusion, in which the Americans had been led by their appetites, Greene determined to withdraw—another bitter resolution but, as usual, a wise one. It was now nearly noon, the battle having lasted about four hours. Greene fell back to his camp of the morning and Stewart, of course, attempted no pursuit. On the next day the Englishman destroyed his baggage and supplies and leaving his sick and wounded and one thousand stand of arms, he began a hasty retreat

The Battle at Eutaw Springs

toward Charleston.

This may be counted, fairly enough, a victory for Greene, though the British have always claimed it as a drawn battle. Greene reported to Washington that it was the most bloody battle and obstinate fight he ever saw. The American loss was five hundred and twenty-two, one fourth of their entire strength, the loss of the officers being unusually severe. The British loss, according to their own figures, was seven hundred, but the number of prisoners which Greene carried off the field of battle brought the British loss up to at least nine hundred, which made it almost forty *per cent*, of the number engaged! Thereafter the British withdrew within the walls of Charleston and there they stayed, and there was no more war in the Carolinas.

For about eight months Greene had been in the field. His force had fought four pitched battles, one of which, the Cowpens, had been an overwhelming victory, two others, Guilford Court House and Hobkirk's Hill, defeats, and the last one, Eutaw Springs, a substantial victory. He had won from an enemy, who always overmatched him in their total numbers, three provinces. He had carried on one determined siege—Ninety-six—himself, and through his lieutenants had captured every other fortified post in his department. He had so manoeuvred as to always have the greater force—with the exception of the action at the Cowpens—at the point of attack, although the total number of his command was always greatly inferior to the total of the British. He had forced Cornwallis and his troops out of the field, had out-manoeuvred Rawdon, had beaten Stewart, and had captured every position for which he had made an attempt.

He had been pursued with the most determined persistence by all the British commanders in turn, and had outwitted them all, marching over a thousand miles at the head of his men. He had done this with an army which at no time consisted of more than one thousand regular soldiers; he had made the best possible use of the irregulars, the militia, and the partisan bands of Marion and Sumter, and had preserved peace and harmony between those dashing soldiers, unaccustomed to brook restraint from any one. He had done this without a military treasure chest, without supplies—almost without assistance from any one—single-handed and alone. All this constitutes a military achievement almost unparalleled.

There was no more fighting, for six weeks after the battle of Eutaw Springs Cornwallis surrendered, and one year afterward Charleston was evacuated. At the head of his ragged veterans, on December 14,

1782, the gallant Rhode Islander entered the city. The grateful people, crowding the streets in the sunshine of that winter morning, rained flowers and blessings upon the great soldier, who had so brilliantly fought their battles. The legislatures of the various States gave him large grants of land and some gifts of money, most of which went to redeem the personal pledges he had made from time to time, of his personal credit, to get bread and powder for his devoted men. Four years after the war he died of sunstroke in that South land for which he had warred and in which he had chosen to make his home. These are the words regarding him, written by one of his friends, his comrade "Mad Anthony Wayne."

> My dear friend. General Greene, is no more. He was great as a soldier, greater as a citizen, immaculate as a friend. Pardon this scrawl, my feelings are too much affected, because I have seen a great and good man die.

In the long roll of men who made possible that glorious liberty which we now enjoy, by their sacrifices and struggles and their heroic devotion in the hard days of the Revolution, no name, save Washington, should stand higher than that of the great and heroic soldier to whom the South owes her independence.

Storm and Surprise

1. TICONDEROGA

Up to the date of the Civil War there was more fighting around the point which Lotbinière fortified at the head of Lake George than in any other spot on the continent; from the days of the advent of the romantic Champlain, who fought a severe battle with the Iroquois where the fort was subsequently located, to and including the War of 1812, it was the scene of innumerable conflicts. In the year 1775 the fort, which had cost the English so much blood and treasure to capture from the French, was negligently garrisoned by forty-three men under the command of Captain Delaplace. It was an immense depot of supplies, there being not less than two hundred cannon, besides large quantities of other military stores of great value, kept there and at the adjoining post of Crown Point.

Fired by the news of Lexington and Concord, Benedict Arnold had suggested the possibility of the capture of the fort at Ticonderoga. His proposed enterprise had been sanctioned and he was granted a colonel's command by the State of Massachusetts, with permission to enlist a regiment wherever he could, to carry out his project. A similar idea, however, had occurred to one Ethan Allen who, in command of a small party of hardy men known as the "Green Mountain Boys," had been maintaining, à la Robin Hood, a bold freedom in the hills of Vermont and New Hampshire, in open rebellion to the authority of the Province of New York, which claimed jurisdiction over the disputed country. Before Arnold had time to enlist any men, he heard of Allen's design and at once joined him, claiming the command of the assembled force by virtue of his commission.

The Green Mountain Boys, however, would have none of him. Choosing Allen for their leader, and being joined by some fifty Massachusetts men and a number of others from the adjoining country,

under the redoubtable Seth Warner and Jonathan Easton, they determined upon the capture of the fort at Ticonderoga. The unrecognized
Arnold was fain to go along with them as a volunteer.

On the night of May 6, 1775, the little band, amounting to about
two hundred and fifty men, reached the lake opposite the fort. They
found that but few boats could be collected and, even by using the
greatest diligence, they were unable to get more than eighty-three
men across the river before morning. What was to be done? If they
waited for the rest to come over they would of course be discovered
and all hope of a surprise would be lost. To many they seemed too
few in numbers to do anything but retrace their steps and try it over
some other time. It was a critical moment, but Allen was equal to it,
he knew that other time would probably never come, it was then or
never. He drew his men up in line and addressed them in the bombas-
tic but effective style of which he was a master.

He announced his intention of attacking the fort without waiting
for the rest to join and concluded with these words:

> It is a desperate attempt and I ask no man to go against his will.
> I will take the lead and be the first to advance. You who are
> willing to follow, poise your firelocks.

Inspired by his words and example the men fairly threw their pieces in the air in their eagerness to be off. Guided by a country boy of
the vicinity, they made their way through the woods, and in the gray
of the morning climbed the hill silently and without noise. As they
came creeping softly around the wall of the fort, they observed that
the main gate was closed, but the wicket was open. Before the sleepy
sentry at the sally-port had more than time to snap his musket, which
missed fire, Allen and Arnold, who were in the lead, were upon him.
He was knocked down, his piece was wrenched from him, and with
loud cheers the Americans poured into the fort through the covered
way.

Another sentry inside made something of a fight, discharging his
piece ineffectively and gallantly rushing forward to use the bayonet,
when he was wounded and overpowered. By Allen's direction, his
men drew themselves up in a hollow square in front of the barracks
and the officers' quarters, facing out, and when the surprised British
rushed out on the parade, they found themselves looking down a row
of polished gun-barrels. Under threat of instant death, the captured
sentry pointed out the commandant's house, and Allen ran over and

thundered against the door with the hilt of his sabre. "Come forth instantly," he shouted, "or I will sacrifice the whole garrison." Delaplace, who had been awakened by the confusion, at once opened the door. He was still in his night clothes and carried his trousers in his hand. Behind him appeared the white-capped face of his frightened wife. "Deliver me up the fort instantly," cried Allen.

"By what authority do you ask?" asked the surprised and startled commander, who had not even heard that there was a revolution in the land. Allen's famous answer has rung through the years from that day to this and is enough to have gained him immortality.

"*In the name of the Great Jehovah and the Continental Congress!*" he replied. Either of these adjurations was sufficient. Delaplace began to remonstrate, but was sternly silenced, and with Allen's sword at his throat he reluctantly gave up the post and ordered his men to be paraded without arms.

Thus the fort, which had been so brilliantly defended by Montcalm, which had cost England eight million pounds sterling, a succession of desperate campaigns and many lives before she took it from the French, was captured in ten minutes by less than one hundred provincials and undisciplined volunteers, without the loss of a man! At the same time, Seth Warner, another Green Mountain Boy, captured the fort at Crown Point while Arnold, with some other men, sailed down Lake Champlain and captured St. Johns, and a third detachment took possession of Skenesborough, at the foot of Lake George. Thus the whole country came into possession of the Americans. They secured over two hundred cannon and vast quantities of military stores, which were immediately forwarded to Washington's army, and without which, at that time, it would have been almost impossible to carry on the Revolution.

2. STONY POINT

While Washington and Clinton were warily watching each other about New York in 1779, the British commander amused himself by sending predatory forces in various directions to raid the country. The British some time before had captured Stony Point, a rocky peninsula commanding the Hudson, which extended into the water and was surrounded by it on three sides, connection with the mainland being only practicable at low tide by a causeway which led through a morass. The Americans had begun the erection of a fort on the point when it was captured by Clinton, and which he had completed. It was strongly garrisoned, provided with cannon, rifle-pits and two rows of abattis. Washington determined to take the position; first to let Clinton know that he was still to be reckoned with, and second, to effect the recall of some of the marauding excursions. He selected to command the attack Brigadier-General Anthony Wayne, one of his distinguished subordinates.

Wayne was a Pennsylvanian, a wealthy, cultivated gentleman, of fine military ability and the highest courage. He had various nicknames in the army and among the Indians, with whom he afterward fought, among which were "Black Snake," "Tornado," and "Dandy Wayne,"—the last from his love of military finery. But the best known epithet and the one which has clung to him is that of "Mad Anthony," from his reckless and daredevil courage; the name gives a false impression of his character, however, as none could be more cool and wary or provident and determined than he, especially in his later years when he fought the Indians with such signal success.

When Washington asked him if he would accept the duty and storm Stony Point, he said tersely, "I'll storm Hell, General, if you will lay the plan !" The great commander-in-chief did lay the plan with the utmost care, even going so far as to have all the dogs for three miles in the vicinity of the fort privately killed to prevent them giving the alarm.

"As most of the affairs of this kind are attempted in the early morning before daybreak," he remarked, "at which hour a good commander is most alert, we will deliver this attack about midnight."

Orders were sent to put in another co-operating force from West Point in case the attack succeeded. The light infantry, who were to make the attack, marched to within a mile of the fort without discovery on the night of the fifteenth of July. None of the muskets of the men were charged and orders were given to rely entirely upon the bayonet—this is the first time it was to be formally tried as a main dependence in the Continental army. The assaulting force, numbering about twelve hundred men, was divided into three columns, and a reserve of three hundred under General Muhlenberg, with Lee's light cavalry, were left on the shore. Wayne and his principal officers had carefully reconnoitred the fort to enable them to proceed understandingly. About half after eleven at night the men were paraded and told the object of their expedition which, until then, had been kept profoundly secret. They were eager to make the attempt.

Guided by a negro of the neighbourhood, who had frequently sold fruit and vegetables to the garrison and who knew the countersign, they advanced quietly through the darkness in two main columns to attack right and left, with a smaller column in front. One hundred and fifty volunteers, commanded by Lieutenant Colonel Fleury and Major Posey, formed the van of the right column under Wayne himself, one hundred volunteers under Major Stewart, the van of the left column under Colonel Febiger; in advance of each of these assaulting columns was a forlorn hope of twenty men each, led by Lieutenants Knox and Gibbons, whose duty it was to remove the abattis. The negro guide was accompanied by two stout soldiers disguised as farmers. He gave the countersign to the first two sentinels they reached in succession, and while he held them in conversation, they were seized and gagged by the pseudo-farmers, without having been able to fire a gun. They found the causeway overflowed when they reached it and were forced to wait until half after twelve until the water subsided, there- upon the charge was ordered. The British were at once called to arms.

The Americans silently rushed upon the pickets in spite of their fire. The forlorn hopes threw aside the abattis, losing, in one instance, eighteen men out of the twenty, and the two columns dashed through the openings, brushing aside the inner guards, and under a heavy fire of grape from the cannon of the bastions, most of which overshot their mark, and a brisk musketry discharge, they sprang upon the walls of the fort shouting the countersign, "The fort is our own!" Colonel Fleury was the first man to leap over the ramparts, where he lowered the English flag with his own hands. At the inner row of abattis, Wayne was struck down by a musket shot which grazed his head. Thinking, in the confusion, that he had received his death wound, he cried feebly, "Carry me into the fort, and let me die at the head of the column."

His *aides* picked him up and rushed forward with him until he recovered himself. The two columns scaled the ramparts at nearly the same time and met in the middle of the fort, before the garrison had entirely awakened or fully recovered from their surprise, whereupon the place was at once surrendered. The loss of the Americans was eighty-three killed and wounded; that of the British ninety-two, and about five hundred prisoners. No inhumanity marked the capture and no surrendered man was put to the sword—there was no massacre and murder—according to the British practice on similar occasions.

At daybreak the guns of the fort were turned upon Fort Lafayette and the ships-of-war, and the latter at once cut their cables and dropped down the river. Through some blunder the supporting detachment, which was to come down from West Point, did not arrive in time and, when they did come, brought no ammunition for their siege guns. Fort Lafayette therefore held out.

Clinton at once moved up the Hudson in force, hoping to tempt Washington from his strong defensive position, and get him to hazard a battle to hold Stony Point. Washington inspected the fort carefully, and finding that it would take at least fifteen hundred men to hold it properly, which he could ill spare, and as he had no wish to risk a battle on unfavourable terms, he determined to abandon the post, which he did on the eighteenth of July, after removing the cannon and stores and destroying the works; taking away property to the value of one hundred and sixty thousand dollars, which had fallen into the hands of the victors.

The storming of Stony Point was the most brilliant achievement of the war. The Americans captured the position without firing a gun, relying entirely upon the use of the bayonet. Wayne gained the greatest credit for the courage and daring with which he carried out the plan of the commander-in-chief. When he heard the news of their evacuation, Clinton occupied the position after the American withdrawal, but he soon abandoned it as untenable; he had previously recalled his marauding parties and thereafter kept his army together in New York, well in hand, uncertain where he would be attacked again.

3. Paulus Hook

He was not left long in doubt, however, for the daring exploit of Wayne had kindled the imagination of another young soldier, equally hardy and bold. Richard Henry Lee, commanding the famous Virginia cavalry and known as "Light Horse Harry Lee," in one of his scouting expeditions, discovered that the British fort at Paulus Hook was negligently garrisoned by an over-confident enemy. Paulus Hook is a long, low point on the Jersey shore just opposite New York, stretching out into the Hudson and connected with the mainland by a sandy isthmus. It is almost an island in fact; for a creek, fordable in but two places, rendered the Hook difficult of access.

Between the fort and the creek a deep trench had been cut across the isthmus, over which access to the post was to be had by a drawbridge and barred gate on the land side of the fort; there was also a double row of abattis around the walls. The garrison amounted to about four hundred men. To take it was a smaller but much more desperate undertaking than the attempt on Stony Point, on account of the difficulties the attacking party would have, even if successful, in getting away, owing to the nearness of the enemy's main army in New York and vicinity.

On the eighteenth of August, 1779, the expedition started. Lee divided his forces, sending a portion of them in a different direction, under Captain Allan McLane, who was to join him before the fort, while he himself commanded the main attacking column. In the darkness of the night and through some misunderstanding, when Lee reached the Hook at midnight the others did not come up. The contingent of loyal Americans, who ordinarily garrisoned the position, had been withdrawn, and some of the best of the Hessian mercenaries had supplanted them. Lee did not know this, but if he had it would have made no difference. The failure of McLane to arrive had seriously weakened his force, of course; but, as he said, he had come to attack, and if he could not take the fort with his party, they had at least enough men to get in it and die there.

That is the kind of man Lee was. The watchword he gave was "Be firm." It was after three o'clock in the morning, on account of their very long wait for McLane, when he gave the word to advance. Although the tide was rising, the men plunged in boldly and struggled across the morass without a sound. They waded through the ditch and as they climbed up the bank they were discovered. The startled garrison sprang to arms and opened a hasty fire at once, but the "foot cavalry," the dismounted light horse, were too quick for them. They rushed into the works, clearing their way with the point of the bayonet.

Twelve of the British were killed and wounded, and but five of the Americans. Sutherland, the commander of the post, with sixty of the Hessians threw himself into a small blockhouse on the left of the fort and opened a scattering fire which did no damage. The rest of the garrison, to the number of one hundred and fifty-nine, including three officers, were tumbled out of their quarters and captured before they had time to thoroughly awaken, and Lee, in accordance with the strict orders which he had received from Washington, abandoned the fort at once, without disturbing the men in the blockhouse or attempting to spike the guns.

After some desperate adventures he reached Washington's camp in safety with all his prisoners. As a brilliant *coup de main*, it would be hard to surpass this enterprise; it was like pulling the nose of the king on his throne in the very presence of his assembled court and getting away safely; and it gave the British a very healthy regard indeed, in conjunction with the affair at Stony Point, for the American troops thereafter.

Some Minor Sea-Fights
of the Revolution

1. BIDDLE AND THE *RANDOLPH*

After John Paul Jones, the most daring naval officer of the Revolution was Captain Nicholas Biddle, a notable scion of the distinguished American family of that name. From his early youth he had followed the sea, experiencing in full measure the hardships and dangers, including several shipwrecks, of that arduous calling. On the occasion of a threatened outbreak between England and Spain over the Falkland Islands, at his own request he had been appointed a midshipman in the British navy. When it was seen that there would be no war, moved by a spirit of adventure, he applied for and received a leave of absence, during which he shipped before the mast—as the orders were to take no midshipman or boys—in Captain Phipps' expedition to the North Pole. Another lad who had been actuated by the same spirit had done the same thing—his name was Horatio Nelson! The two boys, who became great friends, were both promoted to the rank of coxswain before their return and both gave promise of their subsequent ability.

Of course Biddle was commissioned in the Continental navy at the outbreak of the Revolution, and in the early part of the war, while in command of the *Andria Doria*, a small vessel armed with four six-pound guns, he made a brilliantly successful cruise, capturing ten prizes in a short time, including two armed transports carrying over four hundred soldiers! When the *Andria Doria* reached port after this cruise she had but five of her original crew on board, the rest being distributed on her various prizes. After this, in February, 1777, he was given the command of the new thirty-two-gun frigate *Randolph*, just built by the Government, and at that time the best ship in the navy.

He made two successful cruises in her off Charleston, taking many prizes, one of them a twenty-gun war vessel with a convoy of three valuable merchant ships, all of which he captured. He was a great favourite with the gallant South Carolinians while he was blockaded in Charleston Harbor for nearly a year, and they fitted out a State fleet of five small vessels which, under his command, set forth to seek the erstwhile blockading squadron of the enemy which had disappeared before they sailed. They were not successful in finding this squadron, however, although they captured several prizes while cruising to the southward.

On March 7, 1778, a large sail was sighted off Martinique, some accounts say at five in the morning, some at the same hour in the afternoon; the difference is not material however, for it was the action not the time that counted. The squadron made for the approaching vessel, but as the hours wore away she was discovered to be a large ship-of-the-line—the *Yarmouth*, 64. Biddle now signalled to his squadron of small and lightly armed merchant vessels and prizes to make sail to escape. He then stood boldly down toward the enemy, to cover their retreat. It was an act of the greatest hardihood and resolution for a small thirty-two-gun frigate to engage a heavily built ship-of-the-line with her massive scantling and frames. The difference in the number of guns on the two ships, two to one, does not by any means indicate the difference in effective force between them, which could be better expressed by the ratio of four or five to one, especially considering the greater size and weight of the liner's guns. It was like matching a bull terrier against a mastiff in a finish fight to pit these two ships against each other.

Biddle was game for anything—no braver man ever trod a ship's deck than this young captain, just twenty-seven years of age—but although he was heroic, he was not foolish, as it would seem at first glance, for he knew what he intended to do and what was necessary. He intended to sacrifice his own ship in order to protect the State cruisers and the prizes under his command! The odds against him were fearful, but the American navy has ever laughed at odds. So Biddle took his life in his hands and, supported by as stout-hearted and reckless a crew as ever hauled a sheet or passed an ear-ring, sailed boldly down on his huge antagonist. Heroes one and all! At eight o'clock the two ships had drawn within gunshot of each other when the *Yarmouth* hailed and asked the name of the smaller vessel, and then demanded that she strike.

"This is the American Continental ship *Randolph*," replied Biddle, gallantly, at the same time pouring in a broadside, which was at once returned with fearful effect by the two-decker, as the ships were within pistol-shot distance. It has been surmised that Biddle desperately hoped to capture the *Yarmouth* by boarding, though what he could have done with three hundred men, if he had gained her decks, against six hundred of the English is difficult to see. However, during the whole of the action he endeavoured to close—to get nearer the enemy was his instinctive desire, that is the kind of man he was! For forty minutes the action was kept up with the greatest spirit, the ships edging nearer together with every passing moment, until at last they came in contact. At the end of that time with a tremendous roar the *Randolph* blew up, probably a shot had reached her magazine, though we are certain of nothing except the fact of the explosion which tore her to pieces.

The *Yarmouth* was hurled over on her beam ends and covered with burning timber, sails, spars, and other debris and wreckage from the *Randolph*, including a small, tightly rolled up American flag. She had great difficulty in successfully fighting the flames and repairing her rigging and spars, which were much cut up by the fire of her puny and desperate antagonist, and her other casualties amounted to four killed and twelve wounded. When she was in condition to chase, the American ships were too far away to be overhauled by the weakened battleship, and they all escaped. Thus Biddle's heroic resolution had effected his purpose. Five days after the battle, the *Yarmouth* again cruising in the same vicinity, four men, starving and exhausted, were picked up from a spar to which they had been clinging.

They stated that they belonged to the ill-fated *Randolph*, and they were the only survivors of three hundred and fifteen officers and men who had gallantly fought her until she was destroyed. From them it was learned that Biddle had been severely wounded in the leg in the early part of the action, but that he had refused to go below and had remained sitting in a chair on the deck encouraging his men and directing the fighting, while the surgeon dressed his wounds—a gallant picture of an heroic seaman. Before he had sailed away on this cruise he wrote to his brother as follows:

I know not what may be our fate; be it, however, what it may, you may rest assured it will never cause a blush in the cheeks of my friends or countrymen.

And so Biddle was not only a sailor, but a prophet as well; for no

American fighter, in so short a career, ever gained more honour on the sea than he.

2. NICHOLSON AND THE *TRUMBULL*

Another American naval officer who had a distinguished career was Captain John Nicholson. After the dismissal of Esek Hopkins he became the senior officer of the navy. On June 2, 1780, this officer, in command of the small twenty-eight-gun frigate *Trumbull*, discovered a strange sail about four hundred miles east of Cape May. Captain Nicholson ran in his guns, closed his ports, set his sails carelessly, to give the impression that his ship was a clumsy merchantman, and throwing out drags to check his speed, succeeded in luring the stranger under his guns. When the character of the *Trumbull* was ascertained on closer approach, the stranger, a large armed ship, much greater in force than the *Trumbull*, made sail to escape, but was speedily overhauled by the more rapid American frigate which had meanwhile assumed her true character. Nicholson then immediately cleared for action.

When within one hundred yards of each other, the two ships began a murderous and obstinate fight which lasted for three long hours. There appears to have been no manoeuvring to speak of on either side; and the two vessels, pouring into each other a rapid fire the while, sailed side by side, sometimes drifting so close together that the yard-arms interlocked for the moment. Each ship in succession was set on fire by burning gun-wads, so near were they to each other. At the end of the fight, when the fire of the enemy had almost ceased, and Nicholson already considered the other ship his prize, the mainmast of the *Trumbull*, which had been badly wounded, carried away, bringing with it spar after spar until only the foremast of the frigate was left standing. While the Americans were in this helpless condition, the enemy, who had received more than enough of it, made his escape; though, had he been in condition to continue the fight, he should easily have been able to compel the *Trumbull* to strike. It was afterward learned that he was the British privateer *Watt* of thirty-eight guns, mostly twelve-pounders, which had been especially fitted out to take an American frigate.

The loss of the *Trumbull* was thirty-nine killed and wounded, that of the *Watt*, ninety-two! As she sailed away it was seen that she was terribly cut up and her main top-mast carried away; this loss was followed later by that of most of her other spars. Some days after the action, when his completely disabled ship was towed into the harbour of New York, the captain of the *Watt* was asked the name of his antagonist's commander; his answer was, "It must have been Paul Jones or the devil. There never was a ship fought before with such frantic desperation." There was no question but that the *Watt* was a heavy overmatch for the *Trumbull*, and in thus beating the English ship to a standstill, and virtually winning the fight, Captain Nicholson had done a very gallant thing. Many of the American crew were green hands who had never been to sea before and suffered from the debilitating illness incident thereto during the fight. With the exception of Jones' greatest battle, this is considered to have been the severest seafight of the Revolution.

In the summer of 1781, the *Trumbull*, still under the command of stout old Nicholson, was convoying a fleet of merchantmen off the Capes of Delaware. She had a worse crew on than before. She was actually short nearly two hundred of her quota, the total number of souls she carried being one hundred and twenty, when her proper complement should have been over three hundred. Of those she had, a large number were British seamen who had conceived the plan of mutinying and capturing her, influenced by the heavy rewards offered by the British Admiralty for such actions. Captain Nicholson had as his lieutenants, however, three men who were worth a ship's company; they were Alexander Murray, afterward highly distinguished, Richard Dale, who had fought on the *Bonhomme Richard* with such conspicuous devotion and courage, and Christopher Raymond Perry, the father of the subsequently famous Oliver Hazard Perry.

The little squadron had been chased by three British cruisers and the merchantmen had put back and escaped, though the *Trumbull* continued at sea, desirous of getting a fight out of the pursuers, could they be separated. During the chase they all ran into a heavy gale which scattered the British ships and in which the *Trumbull* unluckily lost her foretopmast and main topgallant-mast late in the evening. About ten o'clock on the night of the eighth of August, two of the ships which had formerly chased her again overhauled the American.

The British thirty-two-gun frigate *Iris* came down on the starboard side, another vessel ranged alongside on the port quarter, and they both opened fire. The weather was rainy and squally with the sea running high; the *Trumbull* was still encumbered with wreckage, which had not been entirely cleared away on account of her being undermanned. Almost any officer would have struck at once, but Nicholson was not made that way. At the first fire of the enemy, the

Englishmen on the *Trumbull*, having no interest in the fight, ran below, where their withdrawal so affected a large number of the green crew that they also deserted their stations and fled below in great terror. Nicholson had less than fifty officers and men left to work the crippled ship, clear away the wreck, and fight the enemy—but those left, like Gideon's three hundred, were of the very best. He did not think of surrendering even then, and for more than an hour they actually kept up a desperate and hopeless battle, the captain and officers serving the guns with their own hands. Finally when nearly forty *per cent*, of the little band had been killed or wounded, a third English ship came up and took position across the stern of the helpless *Trumbull* and prepared to rake.

The *Trumbull* had only one mast left standing, her gun-ports had been beaten in, many guns dismounted, and Lieutenant Murray was badly wounded; to fight longer was to be murdered at their stations or to sink alongside; there was nothing more to gain, and Nicholson reluctantly struck the flag he had so gallantly defended. With less than fifty men, on a wrecked ship, he had fought nearly a thousand men in three ships, two of which were larger than his own. This was certainly as honourable and singular an action as was ever fought upon the seas, it reminds one of Sir Richard Grenville's heroic defence of the *Revenge*. The *Iris* was much cut up and reported seven killed and wounded, the loss on the other ships was never ascertained.

3. Barney and the *Hyder Ally*

The only naval officer of the Revolution who survived to bear a successful part in the War of 1812 was Joshua Barney. He had served with credit on a number of small cruisers and private armed vessels, and had been commissioned a lieutenant in the navy when in the year 1782 he was placed in command of the *Hyder Ally*, a converted merchantman owned by the State of Pennsylvania, and armed with sixteen six-pounders. She was to be used to convoy merchant ships between Philadelphia and the Capes of the Delaware. On the eighth of April, in the same year, in company with a large fleet of some forty merchantmen she dropped down to Cape May Roads. While they were waiting for a favourable slant of wind to get to sea, three English cruisers were seen coming in past the Capes, which at once made for the merchant vessels. In obedience to Barney's signals to fly, all but one of the convoy made sail up the bay. That disobedient one attempted to get to sea on her own account, struck on a shoal and was captured. Barney leisurely followed the fleeing merchantmen, hugging the shore the while, which his lighter draft permitted, in order to cover their retreat.

The first of the English chasing ships edged in toward the *Hyder Ally* and exchanged broadsides with her. Finding her rather heavier than she thought, she made off, continuing in her efforts to overhaul the fleeing convoy. She was a smaller ship than Barney's, so he made no effort to chase and coolly waited for larger game. The third English ship, the frigate *Quebec*, had been forced to make a wide detour and could not come within gunshot of the American on account of the shoal water; but the second, a twenty-gun sloop-of-war, called the *General Monk*, dashed boldly at her, expecting an easy prey. Barney had instructed his quartermaster at the wheel to do the very opposite thing that he commanded, thus if he ordered the helm to starboard, it was to be put to larboard, and so on.

As the English ship drew near, Barney loudly gave a number of orders which, if they had been carried out, would have resulted in laying his ship parallel to that of the enemy. As the Englishman made his preparations for the expected manoeuvre, he was astonished to see the *Hyder Ally*, after exchanging a fierce broadside with him, swing in toward him and cross his bow, before he could prevent it. He was raked at once and as the two ships came together, his jib-boom was thrust across the American's deck, when it was at once securely lashed to the main-shrouds by Barney's own hands.

As the English ship swung partially around on the quarter of the *Hyder Ally*, some of her guns bore so that she was not completely helpless. The Americans now delivered the fire of their battery with unexampled rapidity, discharging not less than twenty broad- sides in twenty-six minutes, the English reply growing more feeble after each broadside. The *General Monk* was terribly smashed up fore and aft, losing fifty-three out of her crew of one hundred and thirty-six, or forty *per cent.*, and in thirty minutes she struck her flag! The English ship carried twenty nine-pounders throwing ninety pounds to the broadside, as against Barney's sixteen six-pounders throwing forty-eight! Throwing a prize-crew on board, not even taking time to ascertain the name of the ship he had captured, the *Hyder Ally* and the prize at once made sail up the bay, and though hotly pursued by the British frigate when they reached deep water, the other armed vessel keeping considerately out of way, they succeeded in effecting their escape.

The comment of J. Fenimore Cooper on this tidy little fight is as follows:

> This action has been justly deemed one of the most brilliant
> that ever occurred under the American flag. It was fought in the
> presence of a vastly superior force that was not engaged; and
> the ship taken was, in every essential respect, superior to her
> conqueror. The disproportion in metal between a six-pounder
> and a nine-pounder, is one half; and the *Monk*, besides being a
> heavier and larger ship, had the most men.

The *General Monk* had been originally an American armed ship called the *General Washington*. She was restored to the service under her old name and Barney made several successful cruises in her. In the War of 1812, after making some brilliant and successful privateering cruises. Commodore Barney commanded the gunboat flotilla in the Chesapeake and on the Potomac, in which he fought several courageous actions against superior force. At the disastrous land battle of Bladensburg, which preceded the capture of Washington, when the American militia were routed by the British regulars, Barney and five hundred of his seamen, who manned a battery posted on a little hill in the American lines, almost redeemed the disgrace to our arms by the desperate courage with which they fought their guns and repulsed the enemy, until the commodore himself was seriously wounded, many of his men killed, and the little force surrounded by overwhelming numbers, when they reluctantly surrendered. Barney died in 1818, after nearly forty years of conspicuous and daring naval service.

4. BARRY AND THE ALLIANCE

After Jones and Biddle the most eminent of the American naval commanders in the Revolution was John Barry, a native of Ireland, who came to America in early youth and followed the sea for a livelihood. He was the first regularly commissioned officer of the navy to get to sea as a lieutenant in command of the small armed brig *Lexington*, sixteen guns and seventy-five men. On April 16, 1775, he fell in with the armed tender *Edward*, eight guns and thirty-five men. After a spirited action of an hour in which the *Edward* was cut to pieces and lost a large portion of her crew she was captured. For this service Barry was made a captain and given command of the *Effingham*, 28. In the summer of 1777 she was blockaded in the Delaware by the British expedition under Howe, but the gallant Barry, pining under his enforced inaction, planned a cutting out expedition, and with four boats captured a ten-gun schooner-of-war without the loss of a man. In the face of superior force he burned the schooner and retreated safely.

He was next given command of the frigate *Raleigh*, 32. In this vessel he was chased off the New England coast for several days, in 1778, by two ships, the *Unicorn*, 28, and the *Experiment*, 50. Barry manoeuvred his vessel brilliantly but was unable to escape. The *Unicorn* succeeded in closing with him and a spirited action ensued. The *Raleigh* was much cut up, but the *Unicorn* was beaten and would have been captured by boarding, had it not been for the advent of the *Experiment*. Under a heavy fire from both ships, which he returned with spirit, Barry ran the *Raleigh* ashore, intending to burn her. While he was on shore, however, superintending the erection of a battery and making preparations to land the crew, the *Raleigh* was surrendered by one of her officers. She lost twenty-five in killed and wounded, while the *Unicorn* had lost ten killed and many wounded. Barry gained much credit for his determined and gallant resistance to vastly superior force.

In 1781 he was given the command of the *Alliance*, 32, the best frigate in the American navy. After taking Laurens to France, he sailed on a cruise in English waters in company with the *Lafayette*, a French letter-of-marque. On April third, the two ships made prizes of the twenty-six-gun privateer *Mars*, and the ten-gun privateer *Minerva*. Leaving the prizes to the care of the Frenchman, the *Alliance* continued her cruise alone with much success, taking many merchant ships. On May twenty-eighth, two sail were discovered. The wind, which had been very light, entirely died away and left the *Alliance* becalmed. A little breeze still remained with the strangers, however, and aided by large sweeps, they succeeded in taking up positions on both quarters of the frigate, where they commenced action. For over an hour they poured their broadsides into the American ship, which only had three nine-pounders she could bring to bear to return the attack of an eighteen-gun brig and a fourteen-gun brig.

The unfortunate *Alliance* lay like a log in the still water and was an easy mark for her antagonists, who were calmly pounding her to pieces at their leisure. After an hour's combat, just as Barry, who had been severely wounded by grape shot, was being carried below and the American flag had been shot away, a little breeze sprang up which filled the sails of the frigate. The British thinking the *Alliance* had surrendered had left their guns and were cheering gaily—they were soon undeceived. As the American swung around, her heavy batteries came into play. Sailing down between the two ships, delivering her fire right and left, she soon forced them to strike. They proved to be the brigs-of-war *Atalanta* and *Trepassy*. The English loss was twenty-one killed and thirty wounded; the American, eleven killed and two wounded.

Still in command of the Alliance, in 1782, Barry fought the last action of the war. Coming out of Havana carrying specie, he was chased by three British frigates. As the day wore away, a French fifty-gun ship appeared on the horizon, whereupon, supposing he would be supported by her, the brave Barry immediately went about and stood for the nearest English frigate. The other two frigates manoeuvred about the Frenchman without coming into action with her. Meanwhile the *Alliance* was hotly engaged with her enemy, which proved to be the *Sibylle*, 38, a slightly superior ship to the *Alliance*.

After an hour's conflict the two English ships, in obedience to a signal of distress from the *Sibylle*, abandoned their projected attack upon the French fifty-gun ship and made for Barry, who was forced to haul off without taking possession of his beaten enemy. The *Sibylle* was a wreck. She had lost eighty-seven killed and wounded, while the loss of the *Alliance* was only three killed and eleven wounded. Barry had spurned several attempts which the British made to bribe him to renounce his allegiance. One offer is said to have amounted to fifteen thousand pounds and the command of the best frigate in the British navy. He lived to become the head of the American navy and performed good service in the war with France. He died full of honours in 1803.

Yorktown

The drums were beating a parley. An alert officer in an American battery heard a faint *tap-tap-tapping* above the roar of the cannonade; at his word the battery he commanded ceased its discharge; the drum taps were heard more plainly, rolling, rattling with ever increasing volume. Presently other ears caught the welcome sound and gun after gun became curiously silent. The tremendous roar which for the past week had filled the air gradually diminished in volume until a stillness like death supervened. As the smoke blew away from the muzzles of the silent guns the soldiers came running from their tents on the hills back of the batteries; the long roll of the drums was plainly audible now; *rap-a-tap-tap-tap, rap-a-tap-tap-tap*—what was it?

With hopes high they listened. There were trained ears there and they recognized the cadence; yes, they were beating a parley, and there, above the battered embrasures, rose a white flag in the clear morning. It was a surrender then! The great fleet of De Grasse down in Lynn Haven Bay actually heard the wild cheering which rose from the throats of the excited men. The war was over! They were free!

When the noise had partially died away, two scarlet-coated horsemen could be seen under a flag of truce, advancing from the British works:—the cheering rose in volume until it might have drowned the cannonade! Instantly all was commotion in the staff of the great general, who calmly sat his white horse keenly overlooking the scene and apparently unmoved by the wild tumult of joy about him—only apparently, however, for his heart beat as madly as that of the youngest blade in the army; it meant so much to him and so much more to his country, these beating drums with their message of submission.

By his orders, two young officers, one a Frenchman, the other an American, separated themselves from the cortege surrounding Washington and Rochambeau, and galloped rapidly forward to meet the newcomers. There was a sweet interchange of courtesy between the lines, a little colloquy, and then with military salutes each group returned to its entrenchments; on one side "the robings of glory" on the other, "the gloom of defeat!" As the Americans rode through their line, though they spoke no word until they reached their general, they wore that in their faces which gave the dullest soldier official confirmation of what had not been doubted. Cornwallis wished—or rather he did not wish, but was forced—to surrender!

We left him, after his disastrous victory at Guilford, slowly making his way to the seaboard, having been shouldered out of North Carolina by Greene's strategy and determination. When he reached Wilmington he found no transports nor vessels of war and, in great perplexity, he decided to march into Virginia. To go back to Charleston would involve a tremendous journey through the country swarming with Greene's partisans, and besides it would be tantamount to a confession of defeat, for that had been his point of departure. There was a large British force already in Virginia, which was distant only a few hundred miles, under the command of Phillips, whom we saw at Saratoga, and the traitor Arnold. He might get there easily enough and combine his little force, now less than two thousand men, with the troops of Phillips and, in a whirlwind campaign, overthrow the great State of Virginia. A brilliant stroke or two would also serve to redeem his reputation as a strategist, which was somewhat dimmed in the light of Greene's superb campaigning, though no man ever could or did question his character as a skilful fighter and a man of courage.

Arnold and Phillips were opposed by a few Continentals detached by Washington and some militia under Lafayette and Steuben. Cornwallis despised the Frenchman; "The boy cannot escape me," he exclaimed, when he took command. The famous marquis was only twenty-three years old at the time, yet neither of the veteran British generals had ever succeeded in bringing him to an engagement, and Cornwallis found it equally impossible. He hovered on their flanks, cutting off light parties, and rendering foraging unprofitable and kept his little army together which was about all anyone could expect of him. When Cornwallis effected a junction with the English troops in Virginia, to the great joy of all the subordinate English officers, he displaced Arnold, who had succeeded to the command on the death of Phillips from illness; and "allowed" him to return to New York on the plea of urgent business—for the gallant soldier and nobleman never could stomach a traitor. It was a lucky thing for Arnold in the end that he received this permission, and a lucky thing, perhaps, in the end for the Americans, for had they captured him they would certainly have hanged him, and perhaps it was better to let him live out his life and die as he did, than to offer him even the poor expiation of the gallows for his ineffable treachery.

The indefatigable Tarleton had recovered somewhat from his defeat at the Cowpens, and in command of a new legion of cavalry, mounted on the swift horses for which Virginia was famous, ravaged the country far and wide; at one time capturing the Legislature and being within twenty minutes of taking the coveted person of Thomas Jefferson himself. The marauders did much damage and destroyed great quantities of private property, but in the end effected little—to maraud is not to wage war, it makes mad people madder, that is all! Washington now sent Wayne to reinforce Lafayette with the veteran Pennsylvania Continental line. Cornwallis then moved back toward the coast; not retreating, for he was under no necessity whatever of doing so, but because he was desirous of establishing a strong base on the Chesapeake, and opening communications with his commander-in-chief, Sir Henry Clinton, at New York.

Lafayette followed closely and actually attacked the British rear at Williamsburg. Wayne, in command of the advance, was partially ambushed and found himself with about nine hundred light infantry in the presence of the British rear-guard of about two thousand men, having a further advantage in their position. To retreat was to be destroyed. The situation was one in which Wayne gloried. He immediately attacked with such spirit that the British imagined he was supported by the whole army and, though they drove him off after a stubborn combat, in which each side lost about one hundred and fifty men, they made no attempt to pursue—which was lucky for Wayne! Cornwallis finally reached Yorktown on the Chesapeake, at which point he had ordered the garrison at Portsmouth to assemble and where he threw up strong fortifications, unwittingly digging in the place the grave of his hopes.

Lafayette moved down with his little army to Malvern Hill, a good position to retreat from if attacked, or to attack from if the enemy attempted to cross the James. The Frenchman had displayed great tact and ability in his conduct of this campaign; he was too feeble in force, he wrote to Washington, even to be beaten, and more afraid of his own impetuosity than of the enemy! Secure in his forts, Cornwallis was actually so little aware of the thunderbolt which was about to be launched upon him and of the imminent peril of his situation, that he offered to send some of his force to Clinton whom he imagined to be hard pressed by Washington at New York.

But in the mind of that prescient commander a great campaign had been evolved. By the strenuous efforts of the French Minister of Marine, a splendid fleet of twenty-eight sail-of-the-line and six frigates had sailed from France to the West Indies under the command of the Comte de Grasse, their most efficient admiral—supposed—and the command of the sea passed from the British on account of this French preponderance of force; only for a time, however, but long enough for Washington. The great American realized that if he could make a combination between the sea forces of De Grasse and the land forces under his command, the result would be finally disastrous for the British.

His mind at first had determined upon New York as the point for the combined attack, but he easily accepted the turn of the situation given by the assemblage of the large army under Cornwallis in Virginia. As soon as he learned of the earl's arrival, he had outlined his plan to Rochambeau, and they had jointly written a letter which he despatched to De Grasse by a fast ship, imploring him to meet them in the Chesapeake as soon as possible; which he at once promised to do. On August 14, 1781, Washington received his reply, stating that he had started with his whole fleet for the bay.

The Continentals were cantoned on the Hudson, the Frenchmen in Rhode Island and Connecticut; at Newport there was a squadron under De Barras, who was the senior in rank to De Grasse but generously agreed to serve under him in the campaign, at the solicitation of Washington and Rochambeau, and he at once made ready to sail for the Chesapeake to join the French fleet; while Washington prepared to hurl his army a distance of four hundred miles, presenting his flank en route to an enemy strongly posted at New York, in an effort to capture Cornwallis and his army. It was a strategic conception of surpassing boldness and, if there were nothing else, would stamp Washington as a strategist of the first order; the only other similar military achievement which compares with it was the famous manoeuvre of Napoleon, when he threw his army from the channel seaboard into Bavaria in the Ulm campaign.

Washington communicated his plan absolutely to no one but Rochambeau; not an officer in the army, not even those of the highest rank, had the slightest idea of what he intended to do. It was one of the best kept secrets of military history. It was a maxim with Washington that it was impossible to deceive an enemy by manoeuvres unless his own force was deceived at the same time. He therefore caused entrenchments to be laid out in the Jerseys below New York; bake-ovens and quarters to be built as if for an extended stay; and gave out everywhere that he intended to move his army to the southward and from that point effect the dislodgement of Sir Henry Clinton *via* Staten Island.

On the nineteenth of August the troops began to cross the Hudson River. Washington left a large force strongly fortified on the Hudson under General Heath and took with him two thousand of his best Continentals and about four thousand Frenchmen. The army marched in extended order with the greatest rapidity. Everybody, including the English themselves, felt certain that Washington was about to be- gin a campaign against New York, and Sir Henry Clinton, watching the long dusty ranks defiling before his works on the other side of the river, made every preparation for a determined resistance, concentrating his troops and strengthening his works and recalling all his detachments, which left him more in the dark than ever. It was not until the advance reached New Brunswick and the men found they were still headed for the south, that an idea where they were going began to dawn in the minds of the soldiers and officers. When they reached Philadelphia on the second of September, it was a secret no longer. "Long live Washington," was the toast of the day. "He is gone to catch Cornwallis in his mouse-trap!"

The Americans led the march and passed through the capital to the music of fife and drum at quick time. In their ragged uniforms and covered with the dust of the march, those old Continentals made a strange sight, but the spectators looked from the great general riding at the head of his staff to the army following rapidly after, and noted the long, swinging step, the disciplined easy carriage, the polished gun-barrels and gleaming bayonets, and felt that the rags could not hide the quality of the soldiery. The patriotic women of the city, matrons and maids, showered flowers and cheers upon their countrymen and under the influence of their bright smiles with hearts growing lighter as each step brought them nearer their goal, they marched away.

They were followed the next day by the French contingent. The latter had lost time and distance, caused by a halt outside of the town to brush the dust from their uniforms and equipments and put on their bravest attire. A very different showing they made as they marched down Chestnut Street past the State House where they were reviewed by Congress; regiments with old world names which spoke of the glory and power of France, Rochambeau and his brilliant staff in the lead, their uniforms of gold and white sparkling in the sun; but they were men, too; they had shown it in the past, they were to show it then; aye, and in the future as well. Among the aides of the French commander was one Berthier, whom history saw later as a Marshal of France under the great Napoleon!

When the eager Washington—ever in the lead—reached Chester, he received the news that the combination was a success, and that De Grasse had entered the Chesapeake on the thirty-first of August! A cloud, like the famous man's hand, had arisen above Cornwallis' horizon with the entrance of those ships in the bay, but as he never dreamed but that the British would brush them away presently, he remained reasonably confident still—and there was no Elijah in his camp to read the future for him. Washington was so delighted with the news that he rode back to Philadelphia and informed Congress and Rochambeau. Cornwallis might have broken through the thin ranks of Lafayette, but where would he have gone afterward? North into the hands of Washington; or south, into the arms of Greene? He had had enough of both of these generals, so he concluded to await the arrival of the British fleet, still unconscious of the storm cloud looming up very black now on every side of the horizon.

When the armies reached the head of the Chesapeake Bay on the fifth of September, they found transports had assembled, upon which they were embarked and taken down the bay. Meanwhile De Grasse had landed three thousand troops under St. Simon and on the eighth of September, while Eutaw Springs was being fought in the Carolinas, by Lafayette's command the allied armies moved down and took a position squarely across the peninsula in front of Yorktown. Cornwallis was "corked," like another later commander, "in a bottle;" and the cork was pressed down, driven in.

Washington stopped for two days at his beloved Mount Vernon, which he had not seen for six years, entertaining Rochambeau and the French officers with old time Virginia hospitality, while his army swept down the Chesapeake. On the fourteenth of September he arrived at the camp and took command; by the twenty- sixth of September the whole of his army had joined forces with Lafayette and St. Simon, and on the sixth of October Cornwallis withdrew into his fortifications and the investment began. There were about seven thousand Frenchmen, five thousand five hundred Continentals, and three thousand five hundred militia under Governor Nelson in Washington's army. The first parallel was opened within six hundred yards of the British works on the same night by General Lincoln; it was completed in three days, batteries were mounted and, with his own hand, Washington fired the first gun.

Before all this had happened, however, Admiral Graves, who commanded the British fleet at New York, having been reinforced by a squadron sent him by Sir Samuel Hood, had sailed down the coast with twenty ships-of-the-line to dispute the control of the sea with De Grasse. Although a large number of French seamen were absent with the vessels transporting the American army down the bay, and De Barras had not yet joined them with his squadron, De Grasse immediately put to sea on the fifth of September with twenty-four ships, leaving the rest to continue the blockade. The two fleets manoeuvred for four days, the French skilfully keeping the weather-gage, and an indecisive action was fought on the seventh of September in which the British, fewer in numbers, sustained considerably more damage than the French, losing one ship-of-the-line and many killed.

The two admirals learned at the same time that De Barras had entered the Chesapeake and Graves, now greatly inferior in force and disheartened by his repulses, went back to New York and De Grasse returned to the Chesapeake. It was substantially a victory for the French, but it was a good thing for De Grasse, and it was a good thing for the Ameriican Revolution, too, that Rodney was sick in England and not in Graves' place. Sir Henry Clinton found means to communicate with Cornwallis on the return of Graves, and informed him that the British sea power would soon be augmented by the arrival of another squadron and that he would sail for his relief as soon as possible. Cornwallis replied that he was entirely confident of holding out as long as necessary. That was before Washington's arrival.

To return to the siege, the cannonading was kept up from an ever increasing number of guns with the utmost fury. At first there had been much skirmishing between Tarleton's Legion and the French Hussars, under the Duc de Lauzun, without decisive results; though there were individual encounters on both sides in which great personal gallantry was displayed. On the night of the eleventh of October the second parallel was opened within three hundred yards of the British works. Unfortunately for this parallel, however, the British had two redoubts on the river side which enfiladed the works and rendered them unten-

SIEGE OF YORKTOWN

able. Washington determined to carry them by storm. The one nearest the river was allotted to the Americans and the one further inland, larger and more formidable, was claimed by the French. Two storming parties, the Americans under the command of Alexander Hamilton, and the French under the leadership of the Baron de Viomenil, were detailed to make the attempt. At eight o'clock on the evening of the fourteenth, when it was quite dark, the attacks were delivered.

The Americans, without waiting for the pioneers to clear the way, rushed impetuously up to the abattis and tore it apart with their hands, the little Hamilton, using a soldier's back as a stepping-stone, sprang into the fort sword in hand, followed by his men. There was a sharp conflict in the redoubt and the British, surrounded and outnumbered, threw down their arms and surrendered. The guns of the redoubt were at once swung to the inside and added their death-dealing missives to the American cannonade which was going on furiously at the time. Hamilton immediately despatched an *aide* to the Baron de Viomenil to inform him of his success. The French had waited to deliver their attack while their pioneers cut down the abattis, according to rule. Hamilton's *aide* found the French chafing in impatience under a hot fire from the fort, which was inflicting considerable loss. When the Baron de Viomenil was informed that the Americans had captured their fort, he sent the officer back to tell Hamilton that he was not yet in his, but would be, in five minutes.

The Gatinois grenadiers had the honour of leading the French advance. They had formerly belonged to the old Auvergne regiment which had been once commanded by Rochambeau himself, and which, for its heroic gallantry on many fields, had been known as *Auvergne sans tache*. When Rochambeau had addressed them before the attack they had promised everything if he would get their old name restored to them. By their heroic conduct in this action they obtained their desire, and were henceforward known as the Royal Auvergne. As soon as the abattis was broken down, the Frenchmen with resistless valour rushed into the fort, effecting its capture in short order. Washington had ridden into the parallel nearest the British batteries and a member of his staff, in great anxiety lest his commander-in-chief's life should be sacrificed thus uselessly, ventured to suggest that it would be safer to retire as the place was much exposed.

"If you think so, sir," said Washington, with unusual sharpness, "you are at liberty to step back."

The next moment the cannon by which Washington was standing

was struck. As his officers sprang to his side, fearful lest he had been wounded, General Knox grasped his arm exclaiming, "My dear general, we can't spare you yet."

"It is a spent bullet and no harm is done," he replied. I have no doubt that he would have given his rank itself for the mere soldier's privilege of leading the advance of either of these storming parties, for that was the kind of soldier Washington was. He was, above all things, a fighter from beginning to end. Presently his practised eye saw that both assaults had been delivered successfully and the works were in possession of his troops. "The work is done and well done!" he remarked triumphantly, turning away.

The cannonade was now resumed from the new parallel with renewed vigour. Governor Nelson, who had lived in Yorktown, on being asked what were the best points at which to direct a fire, pointed out his own house which, as it was the largest in the place, was most likely to be the headquarters of Cornwallis, which was afterward ascertained to be a fact. One pleasing little incident which places Cornwallis in an agreeable light is this. Governor Nelson had a brother living in Yorktown, a very old man, who had been secretary of the colony under the crown for over thirty years and was habitually called "Mr. Secretary Nelson." The secretary had two sons who served in Washington's army and they besought him, if possible, to secure the enlargement of their father. Washington wrote a personal letter to Cornwallis requesting that "Mr. Secretary Nelson" be allowed to leave the city. The generous Englishman granted permission at once, and the boys had the satisfaction of not being compelled to fire upon the abiding place of their father.

The night after the capture of the redoubts, Cornwallis, whose men were being cut up by the heavy bombardment, whose headquarters were made untenable from the same cause, whose provisions were giving out, and whose ammunition was almost exhausted, determined upon a sortie. A heavy column under Lieutenant-Colonel Abercrombie made a gallant attack upon the American works. It was partially successful, though they had not time more than hastily to spike one or two of the guns, when they were dislodged by the return attack of the Americans and forced to retreat with considerable loss in killed, wounded and prisoners. The spikes were easily drawn from the guns and they recommenced their useful service.

The situation of the earl was now desperate; although he received word that Sir Henry Clinton was about to sail with seven thousand men and a large fleet of twenty-five ships-of-the-line, and two fifty-gun frigates, he could hold out no longer. Word was brought to De Grasse of this at the same time and he immediately determined to abandon the siege and get to sea, in order to be prepared to run away or fight as circumstances would permit. It was only by the strongest pleas and representations from Washington, Rochambeau and Lafayette that he was induced to reconsider his purpose and remain for a few days longer; so his ships moved down to Lynn Haven Bay and were kept in readiness for constant action. Yorktown had been almost destroyed by the cannonading, many of the British ships and boats in the harbour were set on fire and burned, including the *Charon*, a forty-four-gun frigate.

Cornwallis, in his desperation, determined to pass over to Gloucester point, opposite Yorktown, across the river, where he had a fortified post, assemble his forces there and break through the small American force opposing and get away. It was a foolhardy plan at best, but any hope he might have entertained of carrying it out was frustrated after he had succeeded in getting one brigade across, by a violent storm which arose during the night, wrecking and scattering his boats so that it was with the greatest difficulty he managed to get that brigade back to his army in the morning.

On the seventeenth of October he determined to surrender. There was nothing left for him to do with his defeated and exhausted troops; he could not escape by withdrawing in the face of the French fleet and he could not sustain the siege longer. So, as I have said, on that bright, sunny morning, the drums began beating a parley. And this was the end of all the hard marching, the mad chasing, the desperate fighting, in which he had indulged since he landed at Charleston two years before. Nay, more, this was the end of a greater thing than Cornwallis and his army; though they knew it not, it was the end of the British empire in America with all its "stamp acts," and non-representations and oppressions; its scorn and contempt of things colonial. "It is over, it is over," seemed the message of the drums on that October morning.

The rest was soon arranged. In order to protect his loyalists from the rancour of their countrymen, Cornwallis was allowed to send a ship back to New York in which they escaped. The terms insisted upon were the same which had been forced upon the Americans when the British had captured Charleston—the officers retaining their side-arms and everybody his private property. As the Americans had been compelled to play an American march when they surrendered, it was insisted that the British should do the same by playing a British air in this instance. At noon then, on October 19, 1781, the allied armies were drawn up in two lines, the Americans on the right, and the French on the left. The British marched out between them, sullen, dejected, bitterly indignant, their bands playing, significantly enough, a quaint old English tune called, "The World Turned Upside Down!" The red standard of England was lowered before the banners of her oldest antagonist and her newest enemy.

The white flags of France with their golden lilies, which had gone down in the dust at Crecy, at Agincourt and at Poictiers, now beheld the banners of their ancient foe drooping in submission before them and before the Stars and Stripes; the flag that Paul Jones' hand had hoisted at the masthead of his ship; the flag which had fluttered above the bastion at Fort Stanwix; which Cornwallis himself had seen at Mon- mouth and at Guilford Court House—the flag of the child who had broken away from the cruel mother. General O'Hara, who led the British troops in the indisposition of Cornwallis, surrendered his sword to General Lincoln, who had capitulated at Charleston. The British soldiers grounded arms and marched back, and that was the end.

It was a great day for Washington and for that Revolution which had been conceived when the minute men of Lexington and of Concord rallied to the midnight summons of Paul Revere, riding hotly through the night; that Revolution which had quickened on the blood-stained slopes of Bunker Hill, which had travailed at Trenton and Princeton and had been born on the plains of Saratoga, which had starved and frozen at Valley Forge. It was now an accomplished fact. The fighting was over. The dullest could see that a new nation had arisen—a country that could not be conquered—that freedom had been achieved. The great patient man who sat his horse and watched the sullen soldiers pass before him, must have felt this with a thankful, grateful heart; for with the deep piety which was part of his nature, the first general order after the surrender was accomplished bade the troops to a service of thanksgiving and prayer!

It was two o'clock in the morning when the news of the surrender reached the quiet city of Philadelphia. "Past three o'clock," cried the watchman in the still night, "and Cornwallis is taken!" There was no more sleep in the staid old town that night. "Past three o'clock and Cornwallis is taken!" The citizens rushed from their houses glad-hearted in the dawning of a new day.

It was later still when the news reached England. Lord George Germaine was awakened early in the morning by the arrival of a courier who had brought the despatches telling the disastrous story. Sir Henry Clinton with his great "*armada*" had arrived too late. The surrender was accomplished when he got there; De Grasse had gone to the West Indies, and like the King of France who marched up the hill and then marched down again. Sir Henry had returned to New York. Lord George jumped into a carriage and, picking up the chancellor by the way, drove to the house of the prime minister with his dreadful news. "How did he take it?" he was asked by a friend.

"Like a bullet in the breast," was the reply. "He threw up his hands in great agony crying, 'O God, it is all over, it is all over!'" and the words were even so. The king blustered awhile, and vowed that he would do this, or that, or the other, but in the end peace was declared, independence was acknowledged and the United States of America began to be.

St. Clair's Defeat

Late in the evening of December 19, 1791, a tired officer in a weather-stained uniform, on a played out horse, rode up to the door of the house of President Washington, in Philadelphia, and demanded admittance on the plea of carrying urgent despatches for the President. Upon the refusal of the officer to deliver them to Mr. Lear, his private secretary, Washington was sent for. He excused himself to his dinner guests and came into the hall and read the despatches. After dismissing the officer, he resumed his seat at the table without disclosing the purport of the communication he had received, although one of the company states that he heard him mutter under his breath, "I knew it would be so." Washington, with his usual calm serenity, appeared in the drawing-room, where his wife was holding a reception after supper, and it was not until after ten o'clock that he was left alone with his secretary. Then his iron self-control was broken, and he gave way to the agitation which the despatch had induced.

After pacing up and down the room a few minutes, he sat down and motioning Mr. Lear to a seat, he exclaimed passionately, "It's all over!—St. Clair's defeated!—routed; the officers nearly all killed, the men by the wholesale; the rout complete; too shocking to think of, and a surprise in the bargain!" His secretary watched him in dead silence, appalled, perhaps as much by the furious passion of the general as by the news of the overwhelming disaster. Washington presently sprang to his feet and walked up and down the room again in great agitation, endeavouring to control himself anew. He finally stopped near the door and broke out again.

"Yes," he exclaimed, "here, on this very spot, I took leave of him; I wished him success and honour. 'You have had your instructions from the Secretary of War,' said I, 'I had a strict eye to them, and will add but one word, BEWARE OF A SURPRISE. You know how the

Indians fight us. I repeat it, BEWARE OF A SURPRISE.' He went off with that, my last warning, thrown in his ears. And yet! To suffer that army to be cut to pieces, hacked, butchered, tomahawked, by a surprise—the very thing I guarded him against. O God! O God!" he exclaimed throwing up his hands, while his very frame shook with emotion, "He's worse than a murderer! How can he answer it to his country! The blood of the slain is upon him—the curse of the widows and orphans—the curse of heaven!"

After this outbreak, to which Mr. Lear dared venture no reply, Washington struggled with himself until his strong will once more regained its habitual mastery over his feelings. After some minutes, as if ashamed of and regretting his passion, he broke the silence again by saying in a subdued and altered tone, "This must not go beyond this room." After another and a longer pause, he added, in a tone quite low and distinct and with great deliberation, "General St. Clair shall have justice; I looked hastily over the despatches, saw the whole disaster, but not all the particulars. I will receive him without displeasure; I will hear him without prejudice; he shall have full justice."

The cause of this extraordinary fit of passion, the like of which only occurred a few times in the life of the great Washington, was one of the most frightful disasters that ever befell the American arms. There had been trouble with the Indians for years in the Northwest, in what is now the States of Ohio, Indiana and Illinois. The British at the close of the Revolution had not yielded their control of the lake possessions in their desire to preserve their monopoly of the lucrative fur trade, and they cannot be held guiltless of inciting and encouraging the border warfare on the part of the Indian and the frontiersmen, which was in any event a natural and legitimate outcome of the situation. The great west bound tide of men which, since the Garden of Eden, has ever flooded on in the path of the sun, had swept across the Alleghanies in rolling waves; and it speedily became necessary to secure an outlet for the ever increasing, onrushing deluge of humanity in the great waste of untilled fields, dense forests, and fertile valleys of the West.

The Indian, who had roamed the country freely, looked upon the advance guard of civilization with jealousy and suspicion, and wherever the wave of progress came in contact with the men of the Stone Age, it broke into the wild spray of irrepressible conflict. The Government of the United States did not appreciate the situation, and desired nothing but peace on its frontiers, never dreaming of the immense power latent in the straining nation, striving to break the tightening circles in which the rapid increase of population constricted the people. It was the old story of the Anglo-Saxon going up to possess the earth. The Stone Age had enjoyed its period, it was old and left behind in the race; a new day was dawning, a new people desired the place, and were not to be denied. The weakest must go to the wall again. But every foot of the advance was to be marked with blood and met with desperate resistance. Of such always is the path of civilization.

The history of the eight years following the Revolution is one of merciless outrage and bloody reprisal, of ruthless, cruel and terrible warfare in which cupidity and guile played leading parts. From a moral standpoint the American was the more blameable for he knew more; from a physical standpoint, the savage, for he knew less, and his methods of warfare were in accordance with his lack of knowledge. It was his land, too, but on the other hand he could not use it. The question of right is a deep one, here we are only concerned with the facts. The innocent and guilty suffered alike on both sides from the play of passion, and outrage after outrage occurred on the part of the thoroughly aroused savages, until the Government was at last compelled to take notice. Expeditions under Harmer and others had been rather severely handled, and public opinion had been so aroused by several unusually atrocious depredations, that an army for the chastisement of the savages was authorized by Congress, and Major-General Arthur St. Clair was placed in command.

His force, which had assembled at Fort Washington on the Ohio, now Cincinnati, comprised two small regiments of regulars, newly organized, two regiments of six month levies, and a large body of militia, to which were added two small batteries of light guns and several squadrons of inferior cavalry. Headquarters were eventually established at Fort Hamilton, twenty-five miles north of Fort Washington, where months of inactive waiting for the arrival of nearly every sort of necessity for campaigning passed away. The pay allowed by the Government was so miserable that the better class of men absolutely refused to enlist. The bulk of the army came from the purlieus of the seaboard cities, *the prison, the wheelbarrow and the brothel,* for two dollars per month a head! The six month levies were no better, and the militia, much worse.

The officers were mainly men of spirit and courage but of limited military experience. The experienced frontiersmen like Brady looked askance and would have nothing to do with such an army for such an expedition, and the whole assemblage was as ignorant of Indian warfare as if they had been babies in arms. Braddock's famous army, though made up of much better men, was not more confident nor more stupid. The second in command was General Richard Butler, who was an old Revolutionary soldier, as was the Adjutant-General, Colonel Winthrop Sargent, who was the only really capable man among the leaders of the party. St. Clair was nearly sixty years old. He had served with credit in the Revolution and was a man of undoubted honour, probity and courage, but he was seriously ill with the gout and other ailments, and was frequently unable to ride a horse and had to be carried on a litter. Butler was in much the same condition.

The arms, equipments and other supplies were as bad as possible. Much of the powder was spoiled or was of inferior quality. There was no food for the men, no fodder for the horses, which were broken down old hacks. The commissary and quartermaster departments were woefully inefficient. It was the old story so often repeated of an absolute unpreparedness for action, and the Republic never seems to learn the lesson of it. The two regular regiments had been assiduously drilled during the long days of weary waiting, and in ordinary warfare might have proved fairly efficient, but nothing on earth could ever make woods- men of them or fit them for their present purpose. The six month levies and the militia, if anything, deteriorated rather than improved during the delay. It is only justice to St. Clair to state that he protested vigorously against this state of affairs, but without result. Still he never seems to have entertained a doubt of ultimate success, even considering the wretched quality of the army.

On October 4, 1791, the miserable army began its forward movement. Its rate of progress was about six miles a day! For nine days it cut its way through damp, dense woods, or dragged itself wearily over the sodden prairies, wet with the heavy autumnal rains. Then it stopped and built a fort which was called Fort Jefferson, where the large numbers of sick and some scanty supplies were left. On the twenty-fourth of October the march was resumed. The straggling was awful, desertions frequent, and although St. Clair, in the endeavour to preserve discipline, hung three of the deserters summarily, the measure did not seem effective. On the thirty-first of October they had made about twenty miles, without seeing any great force of Indians, though there was some little skirmishing from time to time, and the advance was greatly galled and disheartened by stray warriors who took pot shots at the hapless Americans from the underbrush, and disappeared before they could be apprehended or even seen. There were no organized parties of flankers or scouts, and what few men were detailed for that vital duty were left mainly to their own devices.

On the night of the same day sixty of the militia deserted in a body, after proclaiming their intention to live off the supply trains, which were lagging unaccountably in the rear. To capture and to bring them back and to protect this supply train as well St. Clair very foolishly detached one of his two regular regiments, the second, under Major Hamtranck, on the first of November. This most seriously weakened his army.

On the third of November the army camped in the evening on the east fork of the Wabash, at this point a little stream scarcely twenty yards wide and fordable anywhere. It was St. Clair's design, as he was near the principal Miami villages, to throw up another fortification, leave the sick and all except absolutely necessary baggage in it, and push on to destroy the towns, and then, after leaving strong garrisons in the various forts, return to the Ohio for the winter. He did not have a chance to put his plan in operation. The army, now reduced to about fourteen hundred men, including camp followers and about thirty wretched women, was camped in a clearing on a narrow rise of ground about three hundred and fifty feet long. The place was surrounded by dense virgin woods, through which they had been compelled to cut a narrow road. The main body, consisting of the regulars and the levies, was drawn up in two lines facing out, with the batteries in the centre and the cavalry on either flank, making a sort of elongated hollow square. On the other side of the creek the militia and a small scouting party were thrown forward.

The officer in charge of the scouts came back to headquarters in the night and told St. Clair that he had discovered signs of large bodies of Indians. He was thanked for his information and told to return to his post, the matter would be looked into in the morning; the tired soldiers were plunged in slumber and could not be disturbed for rumours of this kind—for most of them there was to be a dreadful awakening in that coming day. The men were paraded as usual at sunrise, and had just been dismissed to prepare their breakfast, when rifle shots rang out in the cold, raw morning. It was the thing they had been warned against, a surprise! There was a slight snow on the ground, which was very wet and muddy, and the little pools were covered with a thin coating of ice, which soon melted away as the day advanced. The firing in the front at once became general.

After the briefest possible stand and a volley or two, the advance party of the militia were routed by the charging Indians, and came running back pell-mell across the stream and plunged into the regiments in camp, which were hastily reassembling to the long roll of the drums, causing much disorder and confusion.

Such was the impetuosity of the Indians' pursuit, as they rushed forward through the creek, and so close were they on the heels of the craven militia that they almost broke through the startled lines of the camp, and a stampede was with difficulty averted by the officers. One or two hasty volleys from the first line of the regulars, however, drove the savages out of the open to seek shelter in the thick and almost impenetrable woods. At the same moment the army found itself surrounded and assailed from every side. Every tree trunk, every fallen log, every clump of bushes hid a crouching foe, and the bullets fairly rained in among the exposed men in the clearing, who sent volley after volley in every direction without doing any perceptible damage. The artillery was unlimbered and the guns were served with furious energy; so that the army was soon covered with clouds of its own smoke through which the men fired aimlessly in the greatest bewilderment.

The officers strove with the greatest courage to re-form the lines which had been broken and disorganized by the fleeing militia. St. Clair in person took command of one line, Butler the other. One likes to think of the old general walking calmly up and down the line, his gray hairs floating in the wind, striving to encourage the men; it somewhat redeems the man after all, so splendid a virtue is courage. For a time they stood their ground manfully under a hail of bullets from their concealed foe—pushed to the wall, even the most craven and ignoble will fight in the last extremity. But the situation was more than they could stand; the poor frightened outcast from the towns firing blindly into the smoke suddenly would be appalled by the sight of a feather-crowned head, a pair of burning eyes gleaming fiercely upon him from out a painted face; and before his terror-dried throat could frame a shriek, with a wild cry screamed in his ears, the tomahawk would be buried in his brain, the scalping knife circling his head. The groaning wounded were given sudden relief from their agonies by the thrust of a gleaming knife in the hand of some crawling, stealthy prowler who had made his way unnoticed into the camp in the awful confusion.

But the Indians had grown bolder from their own immunity, and noting the numbers of those who fell, from time to time they advanced from the underbrush and under cover of the smoke rushed recklessly upon the Americans, a thing most unusual for them. Whenever they could be seen in force, they were met with the most determined courage and repelled time and again by furious bayonet charges. Again and again the officers led their men forward. The Indians, however, would never remain to face the advancing detachments, but would melt away on every side and when the charging party had gone a little way from the camp it would be necessary to execute a return charge to get back through the interposing bodies of the foe, and in these little retreats more would be lost than had been gained in the charge. Particular attention was paid by the Indians to the artillery. Every officer and most of the men connected with it were soon killed or wounded. Every officer in the only regular regiment remaining met a like fate.

Several times the Indians succeeded, under cover of the smoke, in breaking through the lines in force, killing and scalping the wounded wherever they were, and were only prevented by heroic efforts from capturing the camp. General Butler, who was shot in the arm in the early part of the action, walked up and down cheering on his men until another bullet brought him down. As he lay on the ground he was tomahawked by one of the Indian attacking parties.

St. Clair had eight bullets through his clothing, a shot grazed his head, cutting off a lock of his hair, but he was otherwise unharmed. In spite of his age and his infirmities he several times personally led charges, sword in hand, upon the Indians, but his experienced eye saw that the battle was going seriously against him; the spirit of his men was giving out, their resistance was becoming feebler, ammunition was getting low, most of the officers were gone—the game was up. The numbers of the slain and the wounded were increasing at a fearful rate, the ground was covered with bodies, the Indians were coming in closer and closer and the violence of their fire did not slacken in the least degree. Something would have to be done and promptly, else they would all be massacred where they stood.

Under the orders of St. Clair, Colonel Darke, the commander of the second regiment, although badly wounded, assembled what men he could and led a charge upon the encircling line of the Indians as if to get in their rear; while St. Clair, with some of the bolder soldiers, taking advantage of the diversion thus caused, broke through in another direction and circling round upon the rear, succeeded in opening a way of escape by gaining possession of the road which they

MAJOR-GENERAL ARTHUR ST. CLAIR

had made through the trees in prosecuting their advance. With the desperate courage of despair the little band held the way open while the terror-stricken men tore through the pathway thus made without a moment's hesitation. They lost all semblance of organization and discipline and the retreat at once became a frightful rout. The hapless wounded were left behind or thrust aside; arms and equipments and everything which would impede flight were cast away, and in one long, maddened mob they ran frantically down the open road in wild panic.

Darke and a few remaining officers and men laboured heroically with a skeleton rear-guard to prevent pursuit; St. Clair, mounted on a wounded pack horse, endeavoured to get to the front to stop the rout and restore some kind of order, but the wretched animal could not be pricked out of a walk. Meanwhile the ruthless Indians, like silent shadows, flitted through the heavy woods on either side of the road and picked off the frightened, helpless, unresisting men at their pleasure. But their desire for the booty of the camp and their utter lack of military organization caused them to withdraw from the pursuit about four miles from the camp, and the fugitives were left to pursue their mad flight unhindered.

The temporary withdrawal of their savage pursuers made no difference to them, they ran on through the long day until they dropped from exhaustion; many of them, especially those who were wounded, crawled into the woods and were lost in its fastnesses, where they perished miserably from fevers, starvation, or under the tomahawks of the triumphant war parties which scoured the country for days after the battle. The wounded remaining in the camp were butchered and tortured in the most ferocious manner, until death gave them welcome relief. The unfortunate women of the camp, who were all captured, were staked out upon the ground and their fate can hardly be imagined; they were all finally put to death, a welcome relief. Some of the ruder tribes indulged in a wild cannibalistic orgy!

It was six o'clock in the evening when the army reached Fort Jefferson, having met on the way Hamtranck's regiment which with pusillanimous hesitation had failed to advance to cover the retreat, and could not now be driven forward. It had taken the army seven days to advance twenty-nine miles—the distance in retreat was covered in as many hours.

The number of the killed was six hundred and thirty, seriously wounded, two hundred and eighty. Only about five hundred escaped, most of whom were slightly wounded or in some way bore marks of the awful disaster. The Indian loss was rather less than a hundred and the total number of Indians engaged was probably not as much as a thousand. The Indian leader was, according to some accounts, Little Turtle, the noted war chief of the Miamis; according to others, Thayendanegea, otherwise known as Joseph Brant, the chief of the Six Nations, the illegitimate son, according to some records, of the famous Sir William Johnson, and the inveterate foe of the Americans. He is remembered for his participation in the Wyoming and the Minnisink massacres; and he was, with the possible exception of Pontiac, and it may be, Tecumseh, the ablest Indian who ever lived.

The Indians who fought were Algonquins and belonged to the Wyandottes, Shawnees, Ottawas, Miamis, and Delawares. Brant was an Iroquois and, as the head chief of their great confederacy, was probably attended by a small body of these ruthless and famous warriors. The Delawares had been hitherto designated by the haughty Iroquois as women; in this action they wiped out the stigma and proved themselves men.

Resting for a day or two at Fort Jefferson, the defeated Americans retreated to Fort Washington, and the wretched St. Clair despatched a staff officer with the news of the disaster to the President. How that news was received we have seen. The unfortunate St. Clair resigned his commission soon after, and Washington appointed Mad Anthony Wayne to succeed him. Wayne was a soldier of a different stamp and after some vigorous campaigning, culminating in the Battle of the Falling Timbers, August 20, 1794, he completely broke the savage power, and there was peace in the Northwest thereafter. General St. Clair was explicitly exculpated from blame by a committee of Congress after a rigid examination, partly, it is supposed, on account of his long and honourable career, and the great personal sacrifices he had made during the Revolution. Although severely reprehended by the general public, he continued to enjoy the confidence and friendship of his old commander. Such was the "justice" of Washington toward his old comrade-in arms!

Truxtun and the "Constellation"

To know we're resolved, let them think on the hour,
When Truxtun, brave Truxtun off Nevis's shore.
His ship manned for battle, the standard unfurled.
And at the Insurgente defiance he hurled.

Then raise high the strain, pay the tribute that's due
To the fair Constellation, and all her brave Crewr;
Be Truxtun revered, and his name be enrolled,
'Mongst the chiefs of the ocean, the heroes of old.

Old Song.

This is a story of a forgotten ship and a forgotten captain in a forgotten war. The names of Paul Jones, Hull, Decatur, Bainbridge, Stewart, Perry; the ships or squadrons they commanded, and the battles they fought, are as familiar in our mouths as household words; but who today thinks of Truxtun and the *Constellation?* Yet he was quite on a level with any one of the others in the matter of personal gallantry, professional skill and unvarying success. In the frigate Constellation he fought two most brilliant single ship duels; in one instance with *L'Insurgente*, a frigate of slightly less force than his own, and in the other with *La Vengeance*, a very much larger and heavier ship; the latter action was the more notable when it is recalled that in the War of 1812, in which the United States Navy gained such everlasting re nown, in almost every instance our ships were larger and carried heavier guns and more men than those of the enemy; certainly this is true of all the more important actions. This detracts nothing from the glory of these combats, but it certainly enhances Truxtun's reputation to have thoroughly beaten a ship which, in every particular, save in the quality of the man on the quarter-deck and the men behind the guns, entirely outclassed his own.

The man himself is a most romantic and picturesque figure; he was, with one possible exception, the only one of the sea officers of the Revolution who subsequently rose to any degree of eminence in the naval service. Born on Long Island, on February. 17, 1755 (and his natal was also his lucky month, as we shall see), he was the son of an eminent English lawyer settled in the then royal colony of New York. Through the influence of a relative who cared for him after the death of his father early in his own life, he went to sea in the merchant service when only twelve years old. His opportunities for education were limited therefore, but he had diligently improved them and by application in later life more than made up what he might more easily have acquired had he remained on shore. One or two books, technical in character, of which he was the author, a treatise on navigation, and letters and despatches still extant, bear out this statement. The educational standard of the day was certainly not high and he easily surpassed it.

He made many voyages in distant seas, and at one time was pressed in His Britannic Majesty's ship *Prudent*, 64, where his ability attracting attention, he was offered a midshipman's warrant, but he declined it and was shortly after released from the English service. In 1775, at the age of twenty, he actually commanded a ship—the *Andrew Caldwell*—in which, by his daring and address, he succeeded in bringing large quantities of much needed gunpowder into the rebellious colonies. In the same year, his ship, in which he had acquired a half ownership (good for a boy of that day), was captured, condemned and sold, and he was made a prisoner. Nothing daunted by this reverse of fortune, he finally escaped from surveillance at St. Eustatius and made his way to Philadelphia. Early in 1776 he shipped as a lieutenant in the *Congress*, the first to get to sea of a long line of bold privateers which swept the waters for British ships, and in the next war with that country, in 1812, nearly drove the merchant vessels of the English from the Atlantic Ocean.

In 1777 he fitted out the privateer ship *Independence*, boldly dashed through the British guard ships in Long Island Sound, out around Lord Howe's tremendous fleet, and made a brilliantly successful cruise, capturing several ships, one larger and with more guns and men aboard of her than his own.

On this cruise the young privateersman had a rather unpleasant encounter with Captain John Paul Jones with regard to his flying a pennant in the presence of the latter's regularly commissioned ship-of-war. The offending pennant was most properly hauled down after a sharp correspondence at the demand of Captain Jones, always a fighter for his prerogatives and for everything else as well, but not until the peremptory request was backed by one Richard Dale with two heavy boat crews fully armed. While the incident speaks little for Truxton's discretion, it says much for the pluck and courage of a boy in daring to withstand even for a moment so great a captain as Paul Jones, who taught him in the end a needed lesson.

The next year, in command of the *Mars*, a larger and better ship, still gaily privateering, he emulated the example of Wickes and Connyngham and ravaged the English Channel, sending so many prizes into Quiberon Bay that an international question was vigorously raised by Lord Stormont. Later, in the *St. James*, a ship of twenty guns and one hundred and twenty men, while carrying Mr. Thomas Barclay, just appointed Consul-General to France, he beat off, after a desperate action, an English frigate of thirty-two guns! A bold, dashing, hard fighting, thorough-going sailor was Master Thomas Truxtun, Revolutionary Privateersman.

In person he was short and stout, red-faced and gray-eyed, but handsome and strong looking. To the day of his death he always wore a quaint, old-fashioned naval wig. He was quick tempered with men, especially when he had the gout, which, as he was a high liver, was not infrequently; at such times he was wont to make it somewhat unpleasant for his body servant, an old seaman who had sailed with him for many years. With women he was always courteous and charming, and seeing that he had thirteen daughters and only one son, it may be conceded that he had no lack of experience with the ruling sex. In short, he was of that quaint, old-fashioned, forgotten type of sea officers which vanished when the romantic and beautiful sailing ship of the past was supplanted by the prosaic, but intensely business-like iron pot of the day. He was a good Churchman too, and sleeps after his tempestuous life in Christ Church burying ground in Philadelphia— well, he earned his rest.

After the war he again engaged in the merchant service, visiting at different times in his own ships all quarters of the globe and becoming in time wealthy, substantial and respected. When the United States Navy was organized, in 1794, under the stimulus of the Algerine piratical depredations, he was made the last of the six captains for the six new ships authorized by Congress. In his case, the last certainly became the first. He was appointed to the new ship *Constellation*, 38, then building at Baltimore, and superintended her building and equipment. She was launched on September 7, 1797, and is at present the oldest ship on the United States Navy list, the frigate *United States*, 44, which was launched two months prior, having long since been destroyed.

The Algerine difficulty having been temporarily adjusted. Congress, smarting under the arrogant aggressions of the French upon our ships and flag abrogated all treaties and, in July, 1798, began a little naval warfare on its own account; which is chiefly remembered for the exploits of the *Constellation* and for having given rise, a little time before the beginning of hostilities, to Pinckney's famous saying, "*Millions for defence, not one cent for tribute;*" or, as a modern, iconoclastic, and more probable version writes his answer to the French demands, "*Nary a penny!*"

About noon on Saturday, February 9, 1799, while the *Constellation* under easy canvas was cruising off the Island of St. Kitts, a sail was sighted to the southward, whereupon she squared away and headed for the stranger. The wind was blowing fresh from the northeast, and all sail was at once crowded on the frigate in chase, reefs were shaken out of the topsails by the eager topmen, the royals and topgallant sails set, the light studding sails on their slender booms were rapidly extended far out beyond the broad yard-arms, and the gallant ship, "*taking a bone in her teeth,*" as the sailors say, tore through the waves and bore down upon the stranger at a tremendous pace, the water boiling and foaming about her cutwater, the spray flying over her lee cathead, the waves rushing madly along the smooth sides of the great ship, and coming together again under her counter, making a swirling wake in the deep blue of the tossing sea.

The stranger bore up at once, hauling aboard his port tacks, and showed no disposition to avoid the expected attack of the *Constellation*. The two ships were both very speedy and weatherly; the *Constellation* was certainly the fastest vessel in the American navy then and for many years after, and the French ship had the reputation of being one of the fastest ships in the navies of the world. They neared each other rapidly therefore, but the fresh breeze blew up into a sudden squall. The watchful Truxtun, who had noticed its approach, however, was ready for it, though he held on under all sail till the very last breathless minute. Just before the blow fell, the order was "In stun's'ls, royals and topgallants'ls, all hands reef tops'ls."

The nimble crew executed the orders with such dashing precision that, when the squall broke a few moments after, everything was snug alow and aloft, and the ship bore the fury of the wind's attack unharmed, having lost not a foot of distance through shortening sail before the emergency demanded it. As soon as the squall cleared away and the rain, which had hidden the ships from each other, had abated, the *Constellation's* people found that the chase had not fared so well as they; less smartly handled, with a less capable crew, she had lost her main topmast. The wreck had been cleared on her, her course changed and, with the wind now on the quarter, she was heading in, hoping to make a harbour and escape the conflict.

Truxtun and the *Constellation* would not be denied however, the yard-arms were covered with canvas again, the men sent to quarters, and all preparations made for the action. The other ship, after hoisting various different flags, finding escape impossible, finally set the French colours, ran oft' to the southeast, and gallantly fired a lee gun as a signal of readiness to engage. At 3 p.m. the *Constellation* having taken in her light sails, and stripped herself to fighting canvas, drew up on the Frenchman's weather quarter. This was the first great action in which the United States Navy had ever borne a part. It was, in fact, the first great action in which Captain Truxtun had ever borne a part himself. His other battles had been in smaller ships and there had been about the service the little taint of gain, which always attaches to the privateer, the soldier of fortune of the ocean. Now he was the commander of a perfectly appointed ship-of-war representing the dignity and power of the United States. The spirit which had defied blockades, laughed at odds, struggled with Paul Jones, was with him still, however, and he did not doubt the outcome of the combat; neither did his men, and in silence and confidence they approached the enemy.

When the *Constellation* had drawn well abreast her antagonist, at a distance of perhaps thirty feet, the Frenchman hailed. Captain Truxtun's answer was a terrific broadside, which was at once returned. As the shot of the enemy came crashing through the *Constellation*, one poor fellow flinched from his gun, on seeing his mate literally disembowelled by a solid shot, and started to run from his quarters. The man was at once shot dead by Lieutenant Sterrett, commanding the third division of guns. There was no more flinching in that battery—that was the kind of discipline on the ship. The French ship, which carried one hundred more men than the other, now immediately luffed up into the wind to board, firing fiercely the while; but the *Constellation* drew ahead.

Then Truxtun saw his chance; it was "up helm and square away again." He ran the *Constellation* sharply down across the bows of her enemy, and at short range poured a raking broad- side fairly into her face; then ranging along the other (the starboard) side of the French-man, he finally took position off the starboard bow, and for nearly an hour deliberately poured in a withering fire. At four o'clock Truxtun drew ahead once more, luffed up into the wind and crossed the French ship's bow, again repeating the raking, sailed along the larboard side, firing as he went, took up a position on the larboard bow, and soon dismounted every gun on the main deck, leaving the enemy only the light guns above with which to continue the fight—the French ship was as helpless as a chopping block. With masterly seamanship the American had literally sailed around the devoted Frenchman, de-stroying each battery in succession and raking him fore and aft again and again. The doomed French ship now drew ahead again and the *Constellation* crossed astern of her, and took position in preparation for another tremendous raking and pounding, when the Frenchman reluctantly struck his flag.

The prize was the splendid frigate *L'Insurgente,* forty guns and four hundred and nine men; Captain Barreaut, her commander, made a noble defence and only struck his flag when he had not a single gun in the main battery which could be used, and after seventy of his crew had been killed or wounded. The *Constellation* had two killed and only three wounded! The happy result of this brilliant action between the two ships was due mainly to the seamanship of the commander and the gun practice of the men, though the *Constellation* carrying long twenty-four pounders on her main deck as against *L'Insitrgente's* long eighteen pounders had a decided advantage of her.

Among the American officers in this engagement were two men, afterward justly celebrated in the War of 1812; Lieutenant John Rodgers and Midshipman David Porter; the latter, who was stationed in the foretop, seeing at one period of the action that the topmast had been seriously wounded and was tottering and about to fall, being unable to make any one hear him on deck, took the responsibility of lower-ing the foretop-sail yard on his own motion, thus relieving the strain on the mast and preventing a mishap which might have altered the fate of the battle.

Rodgers and Porter were placed in charge of the prize. During the night a fierce gale blew up, and in the morning the *Constellation* was nowhere to be seen by Rodgers, whose position was most critical. Thirteen Americans all told were to guard one hundred and seventy-three prisoners who had not been transferred to the *Constellation*, on a leaking, shattered, dismasted ship, wallowing in the trough of the sea, the dead and dying still tossed about on her heaving decks. There were no handcuffs or shackles aboard, the gratings which covered and secured the hatches had been thrown away. Rodgers was a man of splendid proportions and great strength. Porter was a determined second. They and their plucky companions put a bold front on the matter and resolutely drove the mutinous Frenchmen into the lower hold, where they were kept in check by a cannon loaded to the muzzle with grape and canister, and pointed down the hatchway over which bags of heavy shot were suspended by lashings which could easily be cut and the shot dropped down upon the heads of an attacking party below.

Every small arm on the ship was loaded and placed conveniently at hand, and the hatch was closely guarded by three men armed to the teeth. The others cleared the wreck, made sail, and after three days and two nights of the hardest labour and the greatest anxiety, during which every man of them remained continuously on deck, they finally reached St. Kitts, to the very great relief of Truxtun who had preceded them. This exploit was scarcely less notable than had been the battle itself. This was the stern school of the American navy, and the subsequent wars have showed that it developed men.

★★★★★★

One year after the capture of *L'Insurgente*, the *Constellation*, still under Truxtun's command, was cruising on her old grounds to the southward of St. Kitts, and about fifteen miles west of Basseterre. Early on the morning of February 1, 1800, a sail was sighted to the southward, standing to the west. Whereupon the Constellation immediately made sail and bore down in pursuit of the stranger, which was soon seen to be a large and heavily armed ship-of-war, evidently much stronger in force than the *Constellation* herself. Not in the least disquieted by this open disparity in favour of the enemy, Truxtun made every effort to close with her. The Frenchman apparently had no stomach for a fight and made equally determined efforts to get away.

The wind was light and baffling, with frequent intervals of calm, and the Americans could not get alongside in spite of the most persistent efforts. For over twenty-four hours the pursuit continued with no result whatever. About two o'clock on the afternoon of February second, being Sunday again (the frigate's lucky day it seemed), the breeze freshened and steadied; and by setting every cloth of canvas the swift sailing *Constellation* at last began to draw up to the rather deep laden chase. As the breeze held and there was every prospect of soon overhauling her, the men were sent to quarters and every preparation made for the fight, the yards were slung with chains, top-sail sheets, shrouds, and other rigging stoppered, preventer backstays reeved, boarding and splinter nettings triced up, the boats covered, decks sanded, magazines opened, arms distributed, etc.

The battle was to be a night one, however, as it was eight o'clock in the evening before the two ships were within gunshot distance. The candles in the battle-lanterns were lighted and each frigate presented a brilliant picture to the other as the light streamed far out over the tossing water. It was a bright moonlight night and the ships were as visible as if it were daytime. Seeing that escape was hopeless, the Frenchmen apparently made up their minds to a desperate contest and all hands, including a number of passengers, went to quarters, cheering loudly, the sound of their voices coming faintly up the wind to the silent *Constellation* sweeping toward them.

Before the battle was joined the stout commodore with his aides descended to the gun-deck and passed through the ship. The men had been as exuberant as children and had gone to the guns dancing and leaping, but as they drew near the enemy their exuberance subsided, and joyousness gave way to a feeling of calm deliberation and high resolve to repeat, if possible, the success of the year before. As he walked through the batteries Truxtun emphatically charged his men not to fire a gun until he gave the word, under pain of death; those who had been in the last battle knew what he meant. He knew as did other great American naval commanders the value of a close, well-delivered broadside at the right moment, and of that moment he himself would be the judge. His instructions were that the loading of the pieces was to be as rapid as possible and the fire deliberate, and only delivered when it would be effective; not a single charge was to be thrown away; the guns were to be loaded mainly with solid shot with the addition of a stand of grape now and then; and the object of their attack was to be the hull of the enemy; no attention was to be paid by the main battery to the spars or rigging.

The marines and small-arm men were to devote their efforts particularly to the officers and crew of the enemy. The officers were charged to allow no undue haste nor confusion among the men of the several divisions, and they were cautioned to set the men an example of steadiness by their own cool and determined bearing. Like a prudent commander. Commodore Truxtun wisely determined to throw away no chance of success by any carelessness on the part of himself or his men; as they neared their huge, overpowering antagonist, the necessity for making every shot tell was as apparent to them as to him. Again enjoining strict silence, the commodore regained the quarter-deck, and stepping to the lee side, for he had skilfully held the weather-gage of his big enemy, he seized a large trumpet and prepared to hail her.

At this moment a bright flash of light shot out into the night from the black side of the towering Frenchman, followed by the roar of the discharge of a stern chaser beginning the action, in which all of the after guns of the Frenchman immediately participated. The shot from the long eighteens and twelves, and the great bolts from the forty-two-pound carronades crashed into the American frigate sweeping steadily forward. Men began to fall here and there on the *Constellation's* decks; the wounded, groaning or shrieking or stupefied with pain, were carried below to the surgeon and his mates in the cockpit, while the dead were hastily ranged along the deck on the unengaged side. No one made a sound, however, except the wounded, and even they endeavoured to stifle their groans and rise superior to their anguish. But the punishment was exceedingly severe and it was almost more than the men could bear to stand patiently receiving such an attack, though Truxtun sent his aides forward again, sternly enforcing his command to the men to withhold their fire until directed. There was no flinching, however, on this occasion; the officers kept the men well in hand, but the situation was getting desperate, breaths came harder, hearts beat faster, the inaction was killing; was that imperturbable captain never going to give the order to fire?

Meanwhile the frigate was rapidly drawing nearer, now the bow of the *Constellation* lapped the larboard quarter of the French ship, the moment was coming, it was at hand. Truxtun swung his ship up into the wind a little and away from the other to bring the whole broadside to bear, and then leaping up on the taffrail and from thence into the mizzen-shrouds in plain view of both ships' crews and a target for a hundred rifles from the Frenchman, leaning far out over the black water, in his deep, powerful voice he gave the command to fire----a noble and heroic figure! With wild cheers for their gallant captain the men delivered the mighty broadside. Their own ship reeled and trembled from the recoil of the discharge of the heavy battery, and the effect on the enemy was fearful; his cheering stopped at once and a moment of silence broken by wild shrieks of pain and deep groans and curses supervened.

The conflict was soon resumed, however, and shot answered shot, cheer met cheer as the two ships, covered with smoke, fought it out through the long hours of the night. The men toiled and sweated at the guns, cheering and cursing; the grime and soil of the powder smoke covered their half naked bodies; here and there a bloody bandage bespoke a bleeding wound, dead men lay where they fell or were thrust hastily aside; the once white decks grew slippery with blood in spite of the sand poured upon them, as the raving, maddened crew continued the awful conflict. There was little opportunity for manoeuvring, and until midnight they maintained a yard-arm to yard-arm combat. The fire of the Frenchman was directed mainly at the spars and rigging of the *Constellation*, so that an unusually large part of her crew was employed in splicing rope and reeving new gear as fast as it was shot away. Nevertheless, the remainder of the crew served their artillery so rapidly and brilliantly that many of the guns became so heated as to be useless, until men crawled out of the ports, in the face of the open fire of the enemy, and dipping up buckets of water cooled them off.

About one bell in the mid-watch (half after twelve), Truxtun at last ranged ahead and, taking position on the bow of the French ship, finally succeeded in silencing completely her fire which had grown more and more feeble as the long hours wore away. After five hours of most desperate struggle, the stranger was defeated. Indeed, twice during the night she had struck her colours, but her action being unknown on the *Constellation*, the combat had continued. There was no doubt of the matter now, however; she was not only defeated but silenced. The last shot of the battle came from the *Constellation*.

The moon had set now for some time and, save for the lights on the ships, the sea was in total darkness. The shining stars in the quiet heavens above them looked down upon a scene of desolation and horror. Forty of the *Constellation's* men were dead or wounded out of her crew of three hundred and ten, and there were no less than one hundred and sixty casualties out of a crew of three hundred and thirty on the decks of the hapless Frenchman—a fearful proportion! The rigging and spars of the latter were more or less intact, but her hull was fearfully wrecked; she had received nearly two hundred solid shot therein, and she was almost in a sinking condition, her decks resem-

Resolved, by the Senate and house of Representatives, of the United States of America, in Congress assembled. That the President of the United States, be requested to present to Captain Thomas Truxtun, a Golden Medal, emblematical of the late action between the United States Frigate Constellation of thirty eight Guns, and the French Ship of war La Vengeance, of fifty four Guns. In testimony of the high sense entertained by Congress of his Gallantry and good conduct in the above engagement, wherein an example was exhibited by the Captain Officers Sailors and Marines, honourable to the American name and instructive to its rising Navy.

And it is further Resolved, that the conduct of James Jarvis a Midshipman in said Frigate, who Gloriously preferred certain death to an abandonment of his post, is deserving of the highest praise, and that the loss of so promising an Officer is a subject of national regret.

Theodore Sedgwick,

Speaker of the house of Representatives.

Thomas Jefferson,

Vice President of the United States and President of the Senate.

Approved March 29th 1800.

John Adams,

President of the United States.

Thomas Truxtun.

(The Medal and Congressional letter presented to him after the action between the
Constellation and La Vengeance.)

bling a slaughter-pen.

As the smoke drifted away, the *Constellation* was headed for the stranger, to range alongside and take possession, when it was discovered that every shroud and stay supporting her mainmast had been carried away, and the mast which had been badly wounded under the top was tottering with the swaying of the ship. The men in the top were under the command of Midshipman James Jarvis, a little reefer, only thirteen years old. The boy was worthy of his ship and captain. One of the older seamen in the top had warned him that the mast must certainly fall and had advised him to abandon his post while there was yet time. The lad heroically refused saying that they must remain at their stations, and if the mast went they would have to go with it. Before the crew, who were working desperately, could secure it or save it, it crashed over the side and carried with it to instant death little Jarvis and all the men with him in the top except one. The action of young Jarvis was as great an act of individual heroism as was ever recorded on the sea. Taken in connection with his extreme youth, it is even more remarkable than the more famous devotion of young Casablanca on the *Orient* at the Battle of the Nile.

Taking advantage of the delay and confusion thus caused, the surrendered French ship made sail and slowly faded away in the blackness of the night. By the time the wreck had been cleared, she was lost to sight, and in the morning could nowhere be seen. She turned up at Curaçoa a few days later in a sinking condition. The *Constellation* ran for Jamaica to repair damages and refit. The French ship proved to be the frigate *La Vengeance* of fifty-two guns, throwing one thousand one hundred and fifteen pounds of shot as against the Constellation's fifty guns, throwing only eight hundred and twenty-six pounds of shot! The difference in favor of *La Vengeance* over the *Constellation* was about the same as the difference in favour of the *Constellation* over *L'Insurgente*, but in spite of that the *Constellation* had proven the victor.

Truxtun received a medal from Congress, a magnificent piece of plate valued at six hundred guineas from Lloyds, in England, swords, prize money and other rewards.

Little Jarvis was not forgotten, as the following resolution of Congress will show.

Resolved, that the conduct of James Jarvis, a midshipman in said frigate, who gloriously preferred certain death to an abandonment of his post, is deserving of the highest praise, and that the loss of so promising an officer is a subject of national regret.

That is certainly honour enough for any one boy or man, and I believe he is the only youth so distinguished by Congress.

L'Insurgente had been taken into the service of the United States, and one summer morning in 1799 she sailed away into the ocean under command of Captain Patrick Fletcher, and never came back again. No tidings of her end after she left the Capes of Virginia were ever received and her fate is one of the untold secrets of the teeming sea.

Six months after her action with the *Constellation* the unfortunate *La Vengeance* was captured, after another desperate battle, in which she lost over a hundred men killed and wounded, by the British thirty-eight-gun frigate *Seine*. In both instances she was beaten by an inferior force. The *Constellation* still flies the American flag, and hundreds of future admirals (and some who are not, and never will be, admirals, including the writer) learned their seamanship upon her when she was the practise ship of the Naval Academy; playing at war upon those decks which had resounded with the roar of the guns in those half forgotten days when she so successfully fought the enemies of her country under the command of brave old Truxtun and his gallant men.

Decatur and the "Philadelphia"

The most romantic and brilliant figure in the naval annals of our country is Stephen Decatur. Born in 1779, while this country was in the throes of the Revolution, his ancestry French and Irish, always a brilliant combination, he early set the pace for daring and courage and consistently kept up to his own mark until the end. Most of our other naval heroes gained their immortality by a single fight. Decatur's name is associated during three wars with a half dozen exploits and encounters of the greatest brilliancy, any one of which would give him eternal fame.

Think of his dash and desperate courage in the hand to hand fighting with the gunboats at Tripoli, his decision and firmness in wringing a treaty of peace from the Dey of Algiers subsequently; the splendid battle in which he captured the *Macedonian* while in command of the frigate *United States* in the War of 1812; the bold way in which he dashed out of New York Harbor in the face of a heavy blockade later on in the *President*; his smashing fight with the frigate *Endymion*, and his persistent and desperate effort to escape in a disabled ship from a whole British squadron after that action; his intrepidity in several personal encounters in the shape of duels—unfortunately so prevalent at that time—in one of which he finally met his death.

Add to this catalogue his burning love of country, his unquenchable determination to stand up for his service and his flag on every occasion, at whatever cost; his famous sentiment, "*My country! may she always be right; but right or wrong, my country!*"—why, any one of these things is enough to have given him immortality, any one would put him upon a plane of equality with the other great captains of his time. But the event which, more than any of those cited, has endeared him to his countrymen, and to all who love the brave, is that exploit which Lord Nelson, than whom there could be no better judge, called "*the*

most bold and daring act of the age"—the cutting out of the *Philadelphia.*
This occurred in the year 1804, in the war with the Barbary pirates.

It is to the eternal glory of America that the United States, then
a young, weak, struggling country, should have been the first among
civilized powers to put down the frightful depredations of those brutal
pirates with an iron hand. The nascent navy followed Scipio's famous
maxim and carried the war into Africa, prosecuting it there with such
vigour and success that, when the conflict was over, the ships of our
country alone, among the nations of the world, sailed the Mediterranean untroubled by these ruthless *corsairs*; while merchant vessels of
other countries pursued their way before these licensed blackmailers
in fear and trembling, unless protected by ignoble tribute, until our
example of resistance was followed.

The war not only resulted in the protection of the merchant marine, but it proved the nursery of the navy as well, and in it were laid
those foundations of skill and ability which were so costly to Great
Britain, and so useful to our country in later days. The history of the
little war fairly bristles with glorious achievements, and the names of
stout old Commodore Preble and his efficient subordinates, Stewart, Hull, Bainbridge, Somers, Wadsworth, Trippe, Sterrett, Lawrence,
Macdonough, Morris, Jones, Israel, and many others, constitute a gal-
axy of heroes whom it would be hard to equal, much less surpass.
The brightest name among them all, however, was that of Stephen
Decatur. He had been but five years in the naval service, to which he
traditionally belonged, as his father had been a naval officer during
the Revolution, and his brother and other relatives were in the service
with him, when he was sent to Tripoli at the age of twenty-four as one
of Preble's "schoolboy captains."

The frigate *Philadelphia*, 38, one of the best of her class, had been
blockading the harbour of Tripoli in the fall of 1803. She was under
the command of William Bainbridge, an officer of great professional
skill and high merit, who subsequently distinguished himself in the
War of 1812 in the old *Constitution*, by his capture of the frigate *Java*.
One morning, while chasing a cruiser or blockade runner hard in
shore, she ran upon an hitherto unknown and uncharted reef. Her
guns were thrown overboard, the foremast cut away, the ship otherwise lightened, and every effort made to force her off, but with no
success, as she finally bilged. When in that helpless condition and unable to make any resistance she was captured by a swarm of Tripolitan
gunboats.

In spite of the efforts which had been made by Bainbridge to render her unseaworthy, the Tripolitans, unhampered by any American vessels of war, for none were present, succeeded in hauling her off the rocks, patching her up, and taking her into the harbour of Tripoli, where she was anchored under the guns of the Bashaw's castle. Her guns had been recovered and replaced in her ports. This capture materially altered the situation. The addition of this heavy frigate to the other defences of the place rendered it impossible for the small American squadron to attack with any degree of success. It might be said that the whole war depended, for the present at any rate, upon the *Philadelphia*.

Decatur conceived the idea of cutting her out, and applied to Commodore Preble for the privilege of doing so. The notion seems to have occurred to several other officers independently about the same time, one of whom was Stewart, and probably to Preble himself as well; but careful investigation inclines me to believe in the priority of Decatur's conception. At any rate his offer was accepted and arrangements were at once made to carry it out. The *Mastico*, a little *ketch* of about fifty tons burden was ready to hand. She was a vessel peculiar to the Mediterranean, with two masts, the forward one set well amidships, leaving a long, clear space forward upon which bombs were frequently mounted, and the after one, the smaller, both carrying fore and aft sails; the boat was provided with sweeps or enormous oars, used in fair or calm weather. She had been captured recently by the *Enterprise*, at that time under the command of Decatur himself.

The *ketch* had been built by the French and used as a bomb vessel in Egypt, where she had been captured by the English at the Battle of Aboukir, and by them presented to the Tripolitans—a Greek gift as it afterward turned out! When she was captured by Decatur she had just left the harbour with a lot of female slaves on board, a present to the Sultan of Turkey. When she returned she carried quite a different crew. She was small and in every way a miserable vessel, but the best for their purpose that could be had.

As soon as he had received his orders from Preble, to whose wise planning their success was largely due, Decatur mustered his crew on the *Enterprise*, explained the hazardous nature of the venture, and called for volunteers. Every officer and man at once clamoured to be taken. From the *Enterprise* Lieutenants James Lawrence, Joseph Bainbridge, Jonathan Thorn, Surgeon L. Heerman, and Midshipman Thomas Macdonough (late of the *Philadelphia*, and escaping capture on account of being on detached service when she was lost), with sixty-two of the more active men of the crew, were chosen. To these were added Midshipmen Izard, Rowe, Charles Morris, Lewis, and Davis from the *Constitution*, and a Sicilian pilot named Salvator Catalino. Charles Stewart, who commanded the war brig *Siren*, and who as Decatur's superior officer was nominally in command of the whole expedition, though the details and the execution of the matter were entirely left to Decatur, was ordered to accompany the *ketch*, which had been re-named, and most appropriately, the *Intrepid*, on her adventure.

One hour after receiving notice they left Syracuse, Italy, on February 3, 1804, and six days after, late in the afternoon, appeared off the mouth of the harbour of Tripoli. The wind was rising and the sea breaking over the bar off the mouth of the harbour with such force that Midshipman Morris and the pilot, who had been sent to recon-noitre in one of the cutters, reported that it would be difficult to get in with safety, and impossible to get out, so the two vessels reluctantly decided to wait for better weather. It came on to blow tremendously almost immediately thereafter, and for six days the two little boats beat up against an awful storm. The situation on the *ketch* was most criti-cal. No provision had been made for so extended a stay; there were no places in which the men could adequately shelter themselves from the fury of the storm and the cold wintry rain; the captain and three lieutenants occupied the small cabin, the midshipmen and marines slept upon a small platform, the sailors on the water and provision casks. The salt bacon, their only provision, spoiled, and as the ship was infested with vermin from her previous occupants, their situation was as uncomfortable as it was precarious. The men, like true Ameri-can jackies, kept their spirits up, however, and endured the hardships cheerfully.

After six days of labour the gale abated and the two ships deter-minedly made for the harbour once more to carry out their astonish-ing purpose. After getting as near as she dared, for fear of discovering her character to the enemy, the *Siren* hove to, about two miles from the harbour mouth, and the *Intrepid* went on alone. Before she parted with the *Siren* Midshipman Anderson and eight men were sent aboard her by Stewart to supplement the crew. It had been arranged that the attack of the ketch should be supported by the *Siren's* boats, but delay occurring, Decatur decided not to wait for them, remarking to his officers, "The fewer the number the greater the honour!" It was still early evening, and with beating hearts the men on the brig watched the little *ketch* speed into the harbour toward the *Philadelphia.*

The frigate lay swinging to the wind under the guns of the Bashaw's castle, and protected on every side by the powerful land batteries and forts, mounting over one hundred and fifteen heavy guns, beside numberless smaller pieces, and manned by twenty-five thousand men. On either side, reaching toward the entrance of the harbour, like the horns of a wide crescent, were arranged three smart cruisers, two large galleys and nineteen gunboats. The group of vessels resembled an open mouth, at the back of which was the *Philadelphia.* Into these jaws of death Decatur boldly sent the *Intrepid.* The breeze being still fresh, though dying, drags composed of buckets, spare spars and canvas were cast astern to diminish the speed of the vessel coming on too rapidly, as any attempt to take in sail would have been suspicious. As the hours of the evening wore away, the wind fell and she crept slowly up the harbour.

The evening was balmy and pleasant, the moon in that tropic land had flooded the heavens with mystic light, bathing the minarets and towers of the sleeping town upon the shores with silver splendour; lights twinkled here and there in the white walled city, and the *Philadelphia* herself was brilliantly illuminated by long rows of battle-lanterns which sent beams of yellow lustre to mingle with the soft moonlight upon the sparkling water. The frigate's foremast had been cut away in the effort to get her off the reef, her topmasts were housed and the lower yards lay athwart ship on the gunwales; the lower rigging was set up and as it was afterward learned, all her guns were shotted. A heavy crew, probably three hundred and fifty men, was on board.

What must have been the sensations of the men in that little *ketch* as they glided along? To what were they going? Destruction, victory, what would be the end of it? By Decatur's orders, the men had concealed themselves by lying flat upon the decks, behind the bulwarks, rails, masts, bitts, etc., and only a few of the seamen, dressed like Sicilian sailors, with Decatur and the pilot aft to con the ship, and an old battle-scarred veteran at the wheel, were visible. Eighty-three men in a little ramshackle boat, a cockle-shell, were going into a harbour defended by scientifically constructed and well-armed batteries, to attempt to take a thirty-eight-gun frigate full manned and armed and surrounded by a fleet of small boats carrying fifty to sixty more guns, all bearing upon the *Philadelphia* herself, in expectation of just such an attack; the attack itself to be delivered in the bright moonlight and in the early evening, about half after ten o'clock!

The very audacity of the conception strikes one with amazement, and to its boldness is largely due the immunity the attackers enjoyed; that anybody should attempt such a thing was absolutely incredible! The thoughts of the young men doubtless went back to home and friends, sweethearts and wives, but, with the determination of heroes, they schooled their beating hearts, nerved their resolution, and stifled any sensations of trepidation which might naturally possess them.

As they approached the *Philadelphia* Decatur ordered the seaman at the wheel to head the *ketch* for the bows of the latter ship, determining to lay his vessel athwart the hawse of the frigate and board from thence. As they drew near the Tripolitan hailed. By Decatur's direction the pilot answered that they were traders from Malta, who had lost their anchors in the recent storm and desired the privilege of riding by the Philadelphia for the night i. e., attaching their boat to the frigate's cables until morning.

This not unusual request was granted as a matter of course, and after assuring the watchful Tripolitan that the brig in the offing, about which he had made inquiry, was an English schooner, the *Transfer*, the *Siren's* boat, which was swinging astern, was manned by the sailors upon the deck and a line carried forward to the port-sheet cable. At this moment a sudden shift of wind took the *ketch* aback and she hung motionless, directly in line with the frigate's battery, and not forty yards away. The position was one fraught with the greatest danger. If they were discovered now they were lost. The pilot, however, by Decatur's orders, amused the enemy with descriptions of the cargo and sea gossip in his *lingua Franca*, the common language of the Mediterranean, until the boat got away, and the *ketch* feeling the breeze moved forward again.

The coolness and resource of their young commander had saved them. The Tripolitans with ready kindness—soon to be ill-requited—had sent a boat of their own with a cable leading from the port quarter off which they desired the *ketch* to lie. With great presence of mind the Americans intercepted the boat and took the cable back to the *ketch* themselves. The two lines were fastened together and then passed in board, where the men, lying down on the deck, grasped it in their hands without rising and lustily hauled away, breasting the *Intrepid* steadily in toward the frigate.

As the *ketch* gathered way, she shot into the moonlight between the shadows cast by the masts of the *Philadelphia*, when the Tripolitan commander at once discovered her anchors hanging over her bows in plain sight. Indignant at the deception which had been practised, but still unsuspicious of the true character of the stranger, he ordered the fasts immediately to be cut; at the same moment some of his crew discovered the men upon the decks of the *ketch*. The alarm was instantly given. The cry, "*Americanos, Americanos*," rang out over the water. The Americans sprang to their feet, and though the *ketch* at this time lay directly under the broadside of the *Philadelphia*, and could have been blown out of the water by her heavy guns, disregarding their peril in their wild desire for action after their long restraint, they gave such a pull upon the line that before it could be cut the ketch had sufficient way to strike the side of the *Philadelphia*, where eager hands at once made her fast. Not an order had been given nor a sound made.

Decatur now shouted the command "boarders away," and sprang at the main chains. Midshipmen Morris and Laws, who were beside him, leaped forward at the same instant. Laws dashed in through a port, but the pistols in his boarding belt caught between the gun and the port-sill, the foot of Decatur slipped, and Charles Morris was the first man to stand upon the deck of the *Philadelphia*. A second after, the other two men were with him, and the rest of the crew poured in over the rail, and with cutlasses or boarding pikes, charged down upon the astonished Tripolitans. The weapons were cold steel, the watchword "*Philadelphia*." No firearms were used, for Preble's strict orders had been to "carry all with the sword."

Without cheers and with desperate energy the little band dashed at the masses of astonished and terrified men before them, and the whistle of the cutlasses, the ring of steel against steel, the thud of the pike as it buried itself in some beating heart, alone gave evidence of the fell purpose of the stern boarders.

Their attack was pressed home with such vigour that the Americans could not be denied; forming a line from bulwark to bulwark they cleared the deck. After a short but fierce resistance, in which upward of twenty Tripolitans were killed, those remaining on the upper deck jumped overboard, where many of them were killed by Anderson and his boat crew, or were drowned; others concealed themselves below to meet a worse fate later, A similar scene was enacted upon the gun-deck by Lawrence, Bainbridge, Macdonough, and others, during and following the action above. Only the watchword in the darkness and excitement had prevented several of the Americans from attacking each other. In ten minutes the ship was captured. Not an American had been wounded, so far.

Decatur would have given half his life to have brought her out, and many naval officers have believed that he could have done so. It would have been a matter of extreme difficulty in face of the dangers, especially as there was not a yard crossed nor a sail bent; and as he had received positive orders not to attempt it, he had to obey. The ketch had been filled with combustibles, and they were immediately passed on board. The crew had been divided into several different parties, and each body of men, under the direction of an officer, had been carefully instructed just what was to be done. With remarkable speed and order each group proceeded to its appointed station and, speedily arranging the inflammable matter, applied the torch.

So rapidly was this done that those charged with the duty of starting the fires below were almost cut off from escape by the flames and smoke from the conflagration above. In less than thirty minutes the ship was on fire in every direction, and the Americans had regained the *ketch!* Decatur was the last man to leave the *Philadelphia*. The bow-fast and the grapnels on the *Intrepid* were hastily cut, the sweeps manned, and instant endeavour was made to get clear. For some unaccountable reason, however, the *ketch* clung to the frigate. Broad sheets of flame came rushing out from the latter's ports and played over the deck of the *Intrepid*.

The situation was serious. It was the most critical moment of the enterprise. All the powder on the *Intrepid*, in default of a magazine, was stored upon the deck, covered only by a tarpaulin, over which the flames were roaring. In another moment they would be blown up. They retained their presence of mind, however, and soon discovered that the stern-fast had not been cast off. Decatur and others sprang upon the taffrail in the midst of the flames, and as no axes were at hand, hacked the line asunder with their swords. The *Intrepid* was clear. After a few lusty strokes, which carried them a little distance away, the men stopped rowing and gave three hearty American cheers. They waited until success was achieved and then, in the midst of further danger, gave tongue to their emotions—a significant action!

At the same moment the startled Tripolitans awoke to life. The minutes of stupor with which they had witnessed the attack, which they hardly comprehended, gave place to energy. The rolling of the drums upon the shore mingled with the wild shouts and cries of the excited soldiery. Lights appeared upon the parapets and immediately the roar of a heavy gun, which sent a shell over the *ketch*, broke the silence. As if this had been a signal, every battery and every vessel in the harbour awoke to action and commenced a furious cannonade.

Solid shot, shells, canister and grape shrieked and screamed in the air about the devoted *Intrepid*, casting up beautiful *jets-d'eau* upon the surface of the bay, which the flames from the burning *Philadelphia* rendered as light as day. The Americans, having cheered to their hearts' content, bent to their oars, and with such energy as they probably never had used before, they speedily fled from the harbour.

The spectacle they were leaving was one of awe inspiring magnificence. The frigate, from her long cruise in the tropic latitude, was as dry as paper, and burned like tinder. The flames ran up the lofty spars in lambent columns and clustered about the broad tops in rosy capitals of wavering and mysterious beauty. As the fire spread, the guns of her battery became heated, and in sullen succession they poured forth their messengers of death upon the harbour and the affrighted town toward which the starboard broadside bore. It was a death song and a last salute, for, as the eager watchers gazed in melancholy triumph upon the results of their own destructive handiwork, she drifted ashore and with a frightful explosion, which seemed to rend the heavens and surface the sky with fire, she blew up! A moment of silence supervened, which was broken by the roar of the batteries resuming the cannonade.

Strange to say, the *Intrepid* passed through the fusillade unharmed, one man being slightly wounded, and a grape shot passing through a sail! The moon had set and the eager watchers on the *Siren* finally lost track of the vessel in the darkness. Their burning anxiety as to her fate was not relieved until a boat dashed alongside and a manly figure, clad in a sailor's rough jacket, and grimed with smoke, sprang on board, triumphantly announcing their safe arrival. It was Decatur!

The "Constitution's" Hardest Fight

On December 29, 1812, about nine o'clock in the morning, the United States ship *Constitution* was lazily tossing to and fro in the long swell of the Atlantic Ocean, about thirty miles off the northeast coast of Brazil. She was carrying all plain sail, from royals down, and under the influence of a light breeze was gently shoving her mighty prow through the tumbling waters. Almost a month before, in company with the sloop-of-war *Hornet*, she had started on a cruise for the Pacific Ocean in the hope that the ships might play havoc with the British East India trade. They were to be joined later at a certain rendezvous by the frigate *Essex*, Captain David Porter, and the little squadron was under the command of Commodore William Bainbridge, as fine a seaman and as bold a fighter as ever trod an American deck. The *Hornet* had been detached to blockade another British sloop-of-war, the *Bonne Citoyenne*, in the harbour of Bahia, and the *Constitution* was cruising off the coast while waiting for the *Essex*.

Bainbridge was a most distinguished officer, high in rank and held in great consideration in the service. He was a veteran of the French and Tripolitan wars, and it was due to his arguments, coupled with those of the famous Charles Stewart, that the American ships at the beginning of the War of 1812 were allowed to get to sea wherever possible. It had been the plan of the authorities to dismantle the ships, never dreaming that they could cope with the gigantic and successful English navy, and it was only after the most urgent representations that Bainbridge and Stewart succeeded in changing the plan. There is therefore due to these men, from all Americans, a deep debt of gratitude, for the War of 1812 would have turned out very differently had it not been for the exploits of our ships, which laid in that period the foundation of the future naval greatness of our country.

The successes of Manila and Santiago may be traced back to Bainbridge and Stewart. Bainbridge had been an able but not hitherto a very lucky captain. In the war with France his ship had been captured, though by his address he had saved two other vessels from being taken at the same time. Subsequently he made a brilliant cruise in the *Norfolk* and performed some remarkable feats of seamanship and skill in blockading. During the Tripolitan War he had the misfortune to lose the *Philadelphia*, as we have seen, though without the slightest reflection being attached to him in any way, his conduct having been characterized by a court-martial as exhibiting the highest degree of professional skill and courage.

He was a man of striking personality, six feet high, and of splendid proportion as well. His spirit was as great as his body. While in command of an armed merchantman, on one occasion he captured an English war vessel of twice the size and armament of his own. When master of the merchant ship *Hope*, an English ship-of-the-line took from him one of his men. He vowed that he would supply the place of the man from the next English ship he met and he did so. A bad man to tackle was Captain William Bainbridge on this bright, sunny morning, when at nine o'clock two sail were reported from the masthead. The larger of the two ships discovered to the windward at once set toward the *Constitution*, the other made sail to escape. As the ships drew nearer it was seen that the escaping ship was a large merchantman, afterward known as the American ship *William*, a prize to the British frigate *Java*, which was the name of the war vessel sweeping gracefully down to the *Constitution*. The *Java* was commanded by Captain Henry Lambert. He was one of the most thorough seamen who ever handled a ship, and in every other way a man of deservedly high reputation.

A brief catalogue of his exploits shows that he was an officer of the first quality. He was a man of proven courage and great hardihood as well, and he had under him one of the finest frigates in the British navy, originally the French frigate *Renonimèe*, which had been captured by the English almost as soon as she had been launched late in the previous year. She was a beautiful model and one of the swiftest vessels on the sea. Her destination was India, whither she was conveying a lieutenant-general, recently appointed Governor of Bombay, his staff, a naval captain, several other sea officers and a large number of supernumerary seamen, together with supplies to outfit a ship-of-the-line, the *Cornwallis*, and two sloops-of-war. The total number of persons on board of her, therefore, was about four hundred and fifty. She was slightly smaller and not quite so heavily armed as the *Consti-*

tution, the proportion between them in efficiency being represented by about ten to nine—not a very material difference.

The two ships sailed toward each other in the light breeze all the morning, each flying signals which the other was unable to comprehend. Bainbridge made his preparations for the expected battle with the greatest deliberation. He sent his men to dinner at the proper time, allowed them a comfortable smoke afterward, and then leisurely beat to quarters and luffed up to get into range. At two o'clock in the afternoon he plumped a shot from a long gun across the forefoot of the *Java*, whereupon the English ship showed colours from every masthead, and Bainbridge followed up his introduction with a broadside, most of the shot from which cut the water around the English ship and did no damage. The broadside was returned with effect by the *Java*, for, strange to say, it was better aimed than that of the *Constitution*, and several of the latter's men were killed and wounded. It must have been luck rather than skill, for after that the English gunnery was execrable!

The firing on both sides now became rapid and continuous, and both vessels sailed along in the light wind covered with clouds of smoke. The English had the weather-gage, and the *Java* was very much faster than the *Constitution* which, as she had been cruising without going into dry-dock for a long time, had a very foul bottom covered with weeds. Bainbridge, who had been watching the flame-pierced cloud of smoke off to port, noticed that the fire of the enemy seemed to draw forward, and he was not surprised when he saw the *Java* suddenly shoot out of the smoke, put her helm hard up, and make a broad sweep to cross his bows and rake. He followed her manoeuvres with the quickness of thought itself, and the *Constitution*, admirably handled, wore swiftly around on the other tack and escaped the threatened peril.

The *Java* still preserved the weather-gage and the two ships sailed together as before, only heading the other way and shifting their crews to the other battery. The superior speed of the *Java* enabled her to forereach on the *Constitution* a second time, and as soon as he had gained sufficient distance Lambert put his helm hard up again and tried once more to cross the *Constitution's* bows. As before, Bainbridge was too quick for him, and the two ships repeated their previous evolution, wearing and heading in the opposite direction again, shifting batteries and keeping up a hot and continuous fire. Lambert still maintained his weather-gage in spite of the skilful efforts of the *Constitution* to cut him out of it. During all this manoeuvring whenever the guns bore they were fought furiously, different batteries being engaged in alternation. Whenever the *Constitution* luffed up to close the *Java* attempted to rake her, but the aim of her men was now so poor that they made little use of the opportunities afforded them, and practically no damage was done the *Constitution*.

Finally, in desperation at his inability to get near the swift English ship, Bainbridge determined to set his foresail and mainsail, the action having been fought hitherto under the topsails and topgallant sails, and boldly headed for the English frigate to close and run her aboard. Necessarily in doing this he presented his bow fair and square to her broadside, thus deliberately taking a dangerous risk. It was a superb opportunity for the *Java* to deliver a smashing blow in the face of the *Constitution*, but the shot of her broadside, except one bullet from a nine-pounder, went wild. If the *Java* had led down on the *Constitution* that way she would have been cut to pieces.

The *Constitution* now drew to within pistol-shot distance of the *Java's* starboard quarter, and the fire of her heavy battery at close range was fearfully effective. Under the additional pressure of the fore and mainsails, Bainbridge in his turn now forged ahead, the *Java* at the same time losing her jib-boom and bowsprit at the cap. As the *Constitution* luffed again to lay the *Java* aboard, the latter put her helm down and tacked ship, when the *Constitution* immediately wore, the two ships thus circling away from each other. Owing to the loss of her headsail, the *Java* paid off very slowly and the *Constitution* crossed her stern at a distance of a cable's length, pouring in a tremendous raking broadside the while.

Both ships now ran off with the wind free, the *Java* being handled beautifully and still preserving the valuable weather-gage. Though exchanging broadsides continually, the firing of the American was at last proving much more disastrous than that of the Englishman. The *Java's* rigging was cut to pieces and her masts were seriously wounded. Unable to stand this exchange of shots in which his disadvantage was manifest, Lambert determined to board. It was, in this instance, the last resource of the British captain. Taking advantage of his weather-gage, he boldly put his helm up and came swooping down for the *Constitution*. His boarders swarmed forward ready to spring, Lambert himself preparing to lead the charge.

As he headed toward the American he was coolly raked again and again by the latter's guns. The carnage was fearful, but Lambert resolutely held on—he had to keep on or strike his flag. Before he reached the Constitution, by her fearful fire his main topmast was carried away at the cap and the fore-mast just below the cat-harpens. The wreck fell upon the deck and in the water, dragging the head of the *Java* away from the *Constitution*, which still kept up its merciless resistless fire. As the two ships neared each other the stump of the *Java's* bowsprit caught for a moment in the mizzen rigging of the American, but the frigates were not yet in contact and it was impossible for the English to board.

The American top-men and marines now poured a tremendous rifle fire into the ranks of the British grouped forward, while the carronades below kept smashing the English ship in the bows. It was an awful moment—for the *Java*—but the ships finally separated and the *Constitution* kept away to avoid being raked, as the bowsprit of the *Java* swung slowly across her taffrail, and the English ship headed for the south. The two vessels now ran off parallel to each other, the *Java*, marvellous to relate, still keeping the weather-gage! The ships again drew side by side, but the *Constitution*, having lost none of her sails or spars, was now the swifter and she ranged ahead of the *Java*.

Bainbridge then wore his ship, came up under the quarter, raking the helpless *Java* again, shot past her stern, wore a second time, and at a quarter past three came alongside and renewed the conflict. His seamanship was simply masterly. He had been wounded early in the action by a musket ball in the hip, but, though bleeding seriously, he had remained at his post. Leaning over the wheel, he continued the direction of the action. A little later a heavy shot from the *Java* carried away the *Constitution's* wheel and drove one of the copper bolts with which it was fastened deep into the thigh of the commander. It was an excruciatingly painful wound, but he still persistently refused to go below, so he had the wound dressed on deck and continued to direct the manoeuvers of this wonderful battle while in the hands of the surgeon! It was an exhibition of supreme courage and resolution. The *Constitution* thereafter, for the greater part of the action, was steered by relieving tackles, word being passed below by a line of midshipmen!

About this time Captain Lambert was dreadfully and mortally wounded by a ball from the American maintop which shattered his breastbone and passed through his lung. The first lieutenant, Chads, took command and, assisted by the supernumerary naval officers, continued the combat with unabated resolution. The wreck of the masts of the *Java*, which had not yet been cut away, hung over her starboard

162

side and caught fire with almost every discharge of the battery. Chads himself was severely wounded, but remained in command. The British fought on with desperate courage and heroically continued their now hapless battle. The vessels were almost in contact and the Americans deliberately knocked the remaining spars out of the helpless English frigate. The mizzenmast was cut away, the stump of the foremast cut down further still, and all her guns were silenced.

At five minutes after four the *Constitution*, under the impression that the *Java* had struck, as no flag was flying, concluded that the battle was ended. Bainbridge drew off, therefore, in accordance with the common practice of the Americans after action when alone on seas swarming with British cruisers, to re-reeve the cut gear and make necessary repairs. An hour after, fit for another battle, she stood toward the old enemy. The English had pluckily hoisted an ensign, but as the *Constitution*, in grim silence, crossed the forefoot of the helpless, rolling, dismasted hulk of the *Java*, deliberately taking a position in which she could have raked her to pieces, the flag of the latter was struck.

There was not a single spar left standing except the stump of the mainmast and the stump of the bowsprit. At 5.25 p.m. Lieutenant Parker boarded the frigate and received the surrender. The actual fighting time, including the manoeuvring, had been about an hour and forty minutes, the action having been protracted by the brilliant seamanship of both captains. Lambert had never lost the weather-gage until the end of the battle, he had made the best possible use of his superior speed and handiness, and it was only the most consummate ability on the part of Bainbridge which had saved the *Constitution* from being raked again and again. The loss on the *Java* was sixty killed and one hundred and two wounded, on the *Constitution* twelve were killed and twenty-two wounded, the heaviest loss she ever sustained in action. The *Constitution* went into the action with her royal yards across, and came out of it with everything standing, while the *Java* had been cut to pieces!

Some little incidents of the battle are worth recording. Two brothers named Cheever were among the crew of the *Constitution*. One of them was killed early in the fight, the other mortally wounded at the close. He was lying upon the deck when he was told that the other ship had struck. In spite of his desperate wound he immediately lifted himself up and gave three cheers, expiring with the last cheer. On the *Java* were two boys, twin brothers, midshipmen on their first cruise. They were both killed, the last one begging that he might die under

THE CONSTITUTION AND JAVA

the English flag, which was spread over him by his kind-hearted conquerors.

Bainbridge's treatment of his prisoners was everything which could be expected from so high-minded and courteous a gentleman, and Lieutenant-General Hislop, the captured governor aforesaid, presented him with a sword in token of gratitude for his kindness. Owing to the shattered condition of the *Java* and their great distance from the United States, Bainbridge determined to blow her up. The unfortunate Lambert, who had been delirious most of the time since receiving his frightful wound, muttering and moaning over the loss of his ship, which evidently preyed upon his mind, was removed with the greatest care in the midst of a heavy sea to the *Constitution*, the whole ship's company looking on in strained anxiety till the removal was affected. Bainbridge, being informed that the English captain was enjoying a lucid moment or two, immediately caused himself to be carried by two of his officers, his wound preventing him from walking, to the cot of the dying Lambert which had been placed upon the quarter-deck.

When he reached his whilom enemy he gave his sword back to Lambert, laying it on the cot with the hilt by the dying man's nerveless hand. Lambert was so weak that he could only look his gratitude. The wounded American supported in the arms of his officers, and the dying Englishman on the cot on the grim, blood-stained deck of the war-ship, make one of the sweet pictures of American history, and the mind loves to dwell upon this tender action of the great-hearted and heroic Bainbridge. It seems to me, that in such little occasions as this, we may found our hope that war and its horrors will someday vanish from among the children of men. After the war was over some English nautical experts were inspecting the *Constitution*. "Well," said one them at the close of his visit, "your ship seems to be absolutely perfect, but as I must make some criticism, I will say that you have a very ugly wheel for so beautiful a vessel."

"Yes," said the American officer to whom he was speaking, "it is ugly. We lost our wheel in the action with the *Java* and, after the battle was over, we replaced it with hers, and somehow we have never cared to change it!"

From the point of view of seamanship, tactics and gunnery, this battle was one of the finest ever fought. Lambert, however, handled his ship quite as brilliantly as Bainbridge had done, and the action was decided by the superior gunnery of the American. I do not suppose that the Americans were any better gunners naturally than the British. Both ships had been out about the same time, but during five weeks the *Java's* men had never engaged in a single target practice, while the Americans were frequently given an opportunity for perfecting themselves in that necessary requisite of a successful man-o'-war's-man; in fact the English had only fired six blank broadsides in the whole of their cruise, had little or no drill, other than the ordinary routine of the ship, while the Americans were exercised and drilled morning, noon and night! Drill, discipline, gun practice told then as it told in our recent war, and as it will tell in other wars in the future; aye, as it tells even in the daily affairs of so-called peaceful life.

No man should stand higher than Bainbridge in our naval history. I look upon him possibly more than any other man as the "father" of the American navy. Without his determined pleading there would have been no naval war in 1812 and England would still be the undisputed mistress of the sea.

The Niagara Campaign

1. CHIPPEWA

For fierce, hard, desperate fighting, no army which has ever upheld the prestige of American arms, was ever more distinguished than that commanded by Major-General Jacob Brown, in the year 1814, when he made his famous campaign on the Canadian side of the Niagara River, sometimes called the Niagara campaign. Nothing particular eventuated from that campaign—it had no result except to discourage the British, give them a more healthy respect for the American regular and to encourage the Americans correspondingly—but while it was in progress it was marked by several sanguinary and desperate battles, in which were displayed as cool courage, as pretty fighting and as brilliant tactics, as were ever exhibited upon a battlefield. General Brown seems to have been a very capable and determined fighter; although his glory has been almost obscured by the more brilliant reputation gained by Winfield Scott, his principal brigadier, he deserves to be held in high remembrance by his countrymen as a sturdy, courageous and successful soldier. The land engagements during the war prior to this campaign had not reflected any great credit upon either British or American combatants. The armies on both sides were inferior in quality, and the leadership was poor; it anything the honours were with the British.

General Scott, who had shown his daring and capacity on several occasions, in conjunction with General Brown, who had also exhibited great gallantry and skill, had seen that the pressing needs of their countrymen were more thorough drill, more rigid discipline and some adequate teaching in military tactics, of which they were mainly ignorant. During the winter and spring of 1814 they had instructed the men of the little army of regulars they commanded in the most thorough manner; the drills occupying long hours daily, the men grumbled and rebelled as usual, as much as they dared, until they got in action and saw the value of it all. It is said that there was but one book on military tactics, a copy of a French work, in the army; they made good use of it, however, for Scott translated it and established a regular school of instruction for the higher officers, who communicated what they learned to their subordinates, and they in turn to the men. The labours of them all were arduous and unceasing and, as the summer dawned, the painstaking and hard working commanders were conscious that they had an army under their direction at last. They needed one; the British had also waked up to the situation and larger and better forces, veterans of Wellington's command, had at last been despatched to this country to end matters.

General Brown planned a campaign on the west bank of the Niagara River which he hoped would result in the seizure of all the British posts in the peninsula between Lakes Ontario and Erie, after which he trusted that, with the cooperation of Commodore Chauncey, who commanded the naval forces on the lakes, he might successfully possess himself of Canada, which was the dream of the American soldier in this war. His little force consisted of two small brigades of regular soldiers of three regiments each, under the command of Brigadier-Generals Winfield Scott and Eleazer W. Ripley, each numbering about fifteen hundred men; in addition he had another brigade of about one thou- sand Pennsylvania and New York militia under Brigadier-General Peter B. Porter. There was also a small train of artillery comprising Ritchie's and Towson's batteries under Major Hindman, and a squadron of cavalry, in all but little more than four thousand men of all arms. It was a compact, handy, well-officered, well-drilled, little force. Early in the morning of July 3, 1814, the army which had assembled at Buffalo and Black Rock, began to cross the Niagara River.

The English had begun the erection of a small work called Fort Erie opposite Buffalo; it was then garrisoned by one hundred and fifty men. Scott's brigade crossed above, and Ripley's below it, and the fort, which was immediately invested, surrendered in the afternoon of the same day without making much of a defence. The main body of the British forces in the peninsula, numbering then about three thousand men, was encamped at Chippewa, a village situated near the great falls, about sixteen miles above Fort Erie. Major-General Riall, who commanded it, was an Irishman of no great ability and of slender military capacity, but of very large means, who had attained his rank mainly through the pernicious purchase system. He was a man of undoubted courage, but as a commander he was decidedly inferior—another wooden pole in a cocked hat!

On the morning of the fourth of July, the American array was put in motion. During the advance of fifteen miles up the river, which was led by Scott's brigade, there was constant and heavy skirmishing with Pearson's brigade which Riall had sent down to relieve the fort, and which had arrived too late. The English were astonished at the skill and the courage of the American advance until, as they said, they remembered what day it was—they were to find out soon that all days were alike to that little army when it came to fighting! Late in the evening Scott's brigade had reached a little stream called the Chippewa River, behind which Riall's camp had been previously established. Brown, with Ripley's brigade and Porter's volunteers and the Indian auxiliaries under Red Jacket, was some miles in the rear. To attack the strong works of the camp would be impossible, so the pursuit was given over and Scott's brigade moved back to the south bank of a little brook called Street's Creek, where it pitched its tents for the night. Ripley's brigade was some miles further back, and Porter's militia lay refused on Scott's left flank.

On the morning of July fifth Porter was instructed to advance on the enemy's right, with orders to push through the wood beyond Scott's position to try to drive back parties of English scouts and Indians who would harass the American advance. The duty was gallantly performed until early in the afternoon, when the skirmishers were met by the enemy advancing in force. Brown, who had been carefully observing the scene from a distant and commanding hill, saw an immense cloud of dust rising over the plain between the Chippewa River and Street's Creek. Rapid firing apprised him that Porter was heavily engaged. He at once sent orders to Ripley to advance to the support of the first brigade and then galloped forward to Scott's position. That gallant officer was entirely ignorant of the close proximity of the British, and had just made arrangements to lead his men across the bridge over the creek in order to have a dress parade on the open plain before them! He could hardly believe Brown's statement that his parade bade fair to become a battle. However, he welcomed the opportunity with alacrity, and made all speed to cross the creek.

Porter, after making a gallant defence against the whole British army led by Riall in person, had at last fallen back. As the British came out of the wood they discovered Scott's brigade marching across the bridge. The American army was uniformed in gray. There had been a great scarcity of blue cloth and the quartermaster at Buffalo offered to provide gray, of which he had a large supply on hand; Brown and Scott had accepted his offer and consequently the usual blue uniform was mainly conspicuous by its absence. In honour of this campaign, by the way, the memory of the gray uniform has been perpetuated in the dress of the West Point Cadets, which has since that time been of the same gray colour. Scott was a great stickler for the pomp and circumstance of glorious war—he used to be called "Old Fuss and Feathers" by the rank and file—and, in fact, he and his officers had agreed to make this campaign in full, fig—cocked hat, rosettes, epaulets, sashes, and so on! Consequently when the red-coated British veterans saw the gray-coated, full dressed American regulars advancing, Riall remarked that they were nothing but Buffalo militia, and that they would have an easy victory! He opened fire upon the Americans at once from his battery of nine guns posted on the high road; Towson, opposite him on the right, returned the fire with his small battery of three guns, which he used with great effect. The Americans in the face of the British fire crossed the bridge and deployed with the steadiness of veterans, undeceiving Riall at once as to their character.

Scott detached Major Jessup in command of the Twenty-fifth regiment, to make a flank movement through the woods, while he sent the rest of his men straight for the enemy. Jessup executed his movement with alacrity and skill, and while the engagement was being hotly contested in the front, he fell upon the right flank of the British. Meanwhile Colonel Leavenworth had massed upon the left flank of the enemy, and assisted by Towson executed a furious charge upon it. These attacks were stubbornly resisted for a time, especially on the right flank where Jessup was. The men of the Twenty-fifth regiment had become somewhat disorganized through the dash and impetuosity of their wild charge, and as the British advanced to deliver a countercharge, Jessup deliberately re-formed the regiment under fire, bringing them to a support arms the while. The discipline of his detachment was very fine, and their gallantry and steadiness remarkable. When he had perfected his alignment to his entire satisfaction, he sent them forward again with the bayonet.

The right of the British was completely shattered, and separated from the centre by a wide gap. At this juncture the quick eye of Scott saw his opportunity; riding down to his remaining regiment, the Eleventh, under the gallant McNeill—the other two being hotly engaged on either flank—he shouted in a voice heard plainly by the men above

BATTLE OF CHIPPEWA

the roar of the battle: "The enemy say we are good at long shot but cannot stand the cold iron! I call upon the Eleventh instantly to give the lie to that slander! *Charge!*" Officers in action do not usually make speeches of that kind, but it was intensely like Scott to have done so. At any rate, the Eleventh, led by Scott and McNeill in person, rushed forward into the gap with fixed bayonets, and that charge practically ended the fight. The British were routed on every hand and fled with all speed back to their encampment and entrenchments across the Chippewa. Scott moved up to attack but found the position too strong to be carried by his shattered regiments. Ripley's brigade did not reach the field in time to take any effective part in the battle. While Scott waited for the rest of the army to assemble, the British abandoned their position during the night, leaving a large portion of their stores and equipage, and fled precipitately to the northwest, to Burlington Heights at the western end of Lake Ontario.

In this sharp action, known as the Battle of Chippewa, the number of British engaged was about twenty-two hundred, as opposed to an American force numbering nineteen hundred. The American loss in killed, wounded and missing, was three hundred and twenty-seven, that of the British five hundred and seven. Scott had attacked and defeated a superior force upon whom he had inflicted much greater loss than his own. The battle had been fought on an open plain and the brilliant tactics of the Americans assured the British that there was a soldier in command. Brown now pushed forward for Lake George at the head of the river, intending to capture it, and then move on Burlington and thence to Upper Canada, but Chauncey, who was the most inefficient of all the American naval commanders in this war, was ill, and it never seemed to have occurred to him that anybody else could have commanded his fleet, so he did nothing. Meanwhile, the British were reinforced by Lieutenant-General Sir Gordon Drummond, with a large body of men, bringing the total of their army up to nearly five thousand men, including some of the best regiments in their service, the One Hundredth, the Royal Scots, the King's Own, etc.; some, at least, of which had been with the redoubtable Wellington.

2. LUNDY'S LANE

Brown thereupon moved back to Chippewa, and Drummond and Riall advanced down the river. Scouts had reported that a large body of British had been detached to cross the river at Queenstown and menace the American supply depot on the other side. Brown was in a quandary on the receipt of this news. He dared not divide his force in the face of an enemy who already outnumbered him, neither could he afford to lose his supplies, and to retreat across the river would be to give up the whole campaign. He determined wisely, therefore, in the face of these three possibilities, to move up to attack the main force of the British in front of him. If they had detached an expedition, they would be weakened thereby and he might defeat them, or cause the recall of the expedition, or prevent it—if it had not started—anyway, it was good, bold tactics to attack. On the twenty-fifth of July, therefore, he ordered his plucky little army to advance. The first brigade under Scott, now comprising the regiments of Colonel Hugh Brady, the Twenty-second; Majors Jessup, the Twenty-fifth; Leavenworth, the Ninth; and McNeill, the Eleventh; Towson's artillery and Harris' cavalry, numbering in all about thirteen hundred men, took the lead. About five o'clock in the evening, the advance under Colonel Brady with the Twenty-second infantry, discovered the forward division of the enemy drawn up in force at a place called Lundy's Lane.

The rumours which had reached Brown had not been correct. The whole British army was still on the same side of the river. The position they had taken was an exceedingly strong one; this portion of the army, numbering about two thousand men, had been drawn up in a crescent shaped line with a heavy battery of artillery in the centre, upon a little hill, which commanded the whole field. To retreat was to be defeated, to stand still would mean destruction, there was but one thing to be done. Scott despatched messengers post-haste to Brown imploring reinforcements and with the instinct of a true soldier, at once boldly moved his little force forward to the attack. Repeating his tactics of Chippewa, he sent a flanking party under the command of Brady (after Scott the ranking officer of the brigade) and Jessup, to the open ground on the British left, and forming up the remainder of his brigade in the thick woods, desperately charged the centre. It was an amazing manoeuvre; over two thousand men in a chosen position, defended with artillery, were charged in the open by less than one thousand, while three hundred were detached for a flank attack!

The shock of the battle was terrific. The roar of the mighty falls nearby mingled in deep undertones with the crash of the artillery and the rattle of the small arms. Again and again the Americans were led forward; Brady and Jessup finally established themselves on the flank and Jessup actually got in the rear of the enemy, where he had the good fortune to capture General Riall himself, who was in command of the defence. The bold detachment made good its retreat thereafter in the face of reinforcements, and rejoined Scott's thin straggling line. When they reached the centre they were immediately sent forward in the charge. Colonel Brady, Majors Jessup and McNeill were desperately wounded, Brady twice. All the officers of the three regiments which they commanded, the Twenty-second, the Twenty-fifth and the Eleventh, except two or three, were killed or wounded. There was not a horse left in the brigade, two had been killed under Colonel Brady, before he was wounded.[1] These regiments, somewhat disorganized by the hot firing they had received, and the large numbers killed and wounded, rallied in the rear of Leavenworth's battalion of the Ninth, which still preserved its integrity, and the whole mass actually moved forward for another charge!

Fortunately Brown, with the head of Ripley's brigade, now galloped on the field. It was high time for him to appear, he was sorely needed. As fast as the men of Ripley's brigade, who had been marching desperately for the last hour upon the dead run, arrived, they were deployed for attack. Scott's exhausted, decimated men were collected to form a reserve. Porter soon joined Ripley. With first-class military instinct Brown at once discovered that the battery in the centre of the British line was the key to their position. He lost no time in reflection; calling up Colonel Miller, of the famous Twenty-first, he pointed it out and asked him if he would storm the hill and take the battery with his regiment. "I will try, sir," replied the intrepid soldier. The First Regiment, under Colonel Nicholas, was ordered to support him. It was now eight o'clock at night and quite dark, the waning moon, veiled under heavy clouds of smoke from the continuous discharges, giving but little light and the armies were actually fighting in thick darkness.

Miller and his men crept up the hill on their hands and knees until, about twenty yards from the battery, they reached a rail fence undiscovered. They could see the British guns plainly by the light of the burning linstocks which the cannoneers held in their hands ready to discharge the loaded pieces. Thrusting their muskets through the fence rails the Americans took careful aim and poured in a volley which killed or wounded many of the surprised gunners. They then rushed up the hill, cleared its top with the bayonet and found themselves in possession! The loaded guns were swung about instantly and

---

1. Colonel, afterward Major-General, Hugh Brady was a great-great-uncle of the writer.

poured forth their murderous discharges upon the retreating British. The First Regiment, which had been met by a smart fire and had wavered, now recovered its ground and reinforced the Twenty-first on the hill. The men of Miller's regiment after that wore upon the buttons of their coats his famous words, "*I will try, sir!*"

Lieutenant-General Drummond now arrived with heavy reinforcements for the British and assumed command. He immediately formed his fresh men in the thick darkness in the valley below and advanced to attack the hill, which Brown had meanwhile strongly reinforced. Five separate assaults were delivered upon this hill, the attacks being made with the greatest determination. They were repulsed in each instance with equal courage. Men aimed at the flashes of light from the opposing line, and when their pieces were discharged, fought in the night, hand to hand, with the bayonet and the sword. Late that night Scott's brigade, which he had rapidly got into shape again, not yet having had enough of it, executed a bayonet charge up Lundy's Lane. In the height of the charge Scott was desperately wounded in two places, his shoulder being shattered by a grape shot. At the same moment Brown had ordered an advance down the hill, and while leading it received also a second wound. In spite of a severe wound which he had received early in the fight, he had persisted in continuing the command of the field. Faint from the loss of blood he had to retire and the command now devolved upon General Ripley.

It was now about midnight. The British had completely abandoned the field. The Americans were fatigued and exhausted by their desperate struggle. There was no water to be had on the top of the hill, and so Ripley, most unaccountably, ordered a retreat. The Americans withdrew, leaving the British guns which they had captured and so gallantly defended to remain alone upon the hill because there were no horses, all of them having been killed, with which to bring them off! Miller's men, who had captured the hill, dragged away one gun by hand—the only trophy of their exploit. In the morning when Brown, the wounded commander, heard of the withdrawal of the army and the abandonment of the hard-won position, he was furious with indignation. He at once ordered an advance, but the British had re-occupied their lines in greater force, and as Ripley was no great offensive fighter, though a man of high personal courage, the victorious army reluctantly withdrew.

The Americans had, with twenty-five hundred men, engaged over three thousand five hundred British. They had taken a strong position,

BATTLE OF LUNDY'S LANE

held it and driven the enemy from the field. Scott's dashing tactics and the desperate resolution of his men who had attacked immediately under his leadership, and had held the enemy in play until Brown could bring up his supports, awakened admiration on every hand. The attacks of the Americans had been so determined that the English artillerists had been bayoneted while loading their guns. The American batteries were advanced within a few yards of the British. Even the English historians acknowledge the superior gallantry and courage of their foes, saying that it would have done honour to any service. Each side lost about nine hundred men, or about thirty *per cent*, of the total force engaged, or three times as great a proportion as has usually obtained in the greater battles of later wars.

3. THE SIEGE OF FORT ERIE

After the battle the Americans withdrew in good order to Fort Erie, followed leisurely at a safe distance by the superior forces of the British. General Gaines, in the absence of Scott and Brown—the life of the former being despaired of, and the latter seriously wounded—now was ordered to the command of the American position. Entrenchments were at once thrown up, forming a long, narrow enclosure, with Fort Erie, a star-pointed, bastioned fort at the right upper corner, Fort Douglass near the lake to the right, and a long line of entrenchments terminating in Fort Towson on the lake to the left. The works were well-constructed, provided with ditches and abattis. Both armies were soon reinforced, bringing the British numbers to over four thousand, the American to little less than three thousand.

Drummond regularly laid siege to the fort, meanwhile sending Colonel Tucker with five hundred British regulars across the river to destroy the batteries at Black Rock. The expedition was badly defeated by three hundred American regulars fighting behind strong entrenchments thrown up on the bank of a creek, and withdrew to the main army again. On the thirteenth of August, the British batteries being then completed, a furious cannonade of the American works was begun which continued without intermission until the night of the fifteenth, when an attack in force was delivered upon the works.

The British came forward in three heavy columns of one thousand men each. One column attacked Towson's battery on Snake Hill on the left. The American guns there were so well served that they poured out a continuous sheet of flame and shot through the black night. The men called the place "Towson's light-house." Though they finally reached the parapet there and crossed bayonets, the assailants were ultimately repulsed with great slaughter. The attack on Fort Douglass on the right, which was met with equal determination, was equally unfortunate. The second column, however, under Lieutenant-Colonel Drummond, brother of the general-in-chief, had succeeded in entering the northeast bastion of Fort Erie. The men struggled through the ditch, some men from the defeated column from Fort Douglass reinforced them, and they planted their scaling ladders on the fort and drove out the Americans at the point of the bayonet—indeed, during the whole of this desperate assault, the English did not once fire their muskets; by the specific orders of their commander, the flints had been removed from the guns, and they relied entirely upon the secret and sudden use of the bayonet, the watchword was "cold steel" and they used it effectively.

Lieutenant-Colonel Drummond was the first man to enter the fort. The Americans in the bastion made a heroic resistance, but they were all immediately killed or wounded. No captures were made or allowed. Lieutenant Macdonough, in command of the position, being wounded and helpless, asked for quarter. Drummond ruthlessly shot him down. His word had been "Give no quarter to the damned Yankees!" and he was distinctly heard to pass that order. One of the American soldiers who had himself asked for quarter, seeing Macdonough's fate, shot the British commander, and immediately followed the discharge of his rifle by savagely thrusting him through the heart with the bayonet. The steel passed through a paper in Drummond's breast pocket, on which was written the order to attack containing these significant words:

The Lieutenant-General most strongly recommends the free use of the bayonet!

The blood-stained paper is still preserved by the New York Historical Society; Drummond, of course, was instantly killed, his slayer also. His party, however, held the bastion with the most tenacious courage until morning.

The Americans brought up party after party to effect its capture, without success. As the day dawned the broken assaulting columns which had been rallied after their repulse at Forts Towson and Douglass, accompanied by the British reserves, were seen deploying in the open, preparing to support the column which had not yet been dislodged from the bastion. The American artillery at once began playing upon them, doing great execution; still they came on. Gaines was making ready for another desperate attempt to recapture the coveted bastion, when there was a violent explosion inside the work which killed or wounded most of the British, and the position was at once recaptured, whereupon the British columns withdrew precipitately and the battle was over. It is reported that Lieutenant Macdonough, wounded and dying, incensed at his brutal treatment, saw an opportunity and exploded an artillery caisson by the flash of his pistol, Samson-like destroying himself and his foes. The total loss of the British in this attack in killed and wounded was one thousand men, the American rather less than one hundred! The bastion was repaired under fire, and the cannonading was renewed with spirit on both sides.

Sometime after, General Gaines was badly wounded by a solid shot, and General Brown, though still weak from his wound, came over to take command in person. He immediately resolved upon a sortie. On the seventeenth of September, at half after two o'clock in the afternoon, the carefully arranged sortie was delivered. The assaulting forces were divided into two columns of one thousand men each. One under General Porter marched over a road which had been opened through the woods and fell upon the flank of the British camp and entrenchments. The other, under Colonel Miller, marched up a ravine and interposed between the left and the centre of the enemy's line. The attack, brilliantly delivered under cover of a thick fog, was a great surprise and was followed up successfully. Batteries number three and four were stormed and after a furious action of thirty minutes, were captured by Porter's men.

This success was followed by the capture of the blockhouse in the rear of battery number three. The garrison were made prisoners, cannon and carriages destroyed and the blockhouse and magazine blown up. All three of Porter's regimental commander's were killed or wounded, with many of his men. Miller, equally successful with his column, captured two more batteries and another blockhouse. Within forty minutes the whole forward line of the British entrenchments was in possession of the Americans. General Ripley, who had supported the attack, now brought up his reserve, and, in the new action which ensued received a severe wound. The cannon having been destroyed and the batteries rendered useless, the Americans having affected their purpose withdrew in good order, their loss in killed and wounded being five hundred as against one thousand of the British; the whole affair was considered most creditable to the Americans.

Hastily collecting his shattered forces, on the night of the twenty-first, Drummond broke up his camp and retreated behind the Chippewa, leaving large stores and munitions of war in the hands of the Americans. The brave Brown being unable to continue in command any longer, his wound breaking out afresh, the charge of the army was given to General Izard, who, after a futile engagement with the British, mainly carried on by skirmish and advance parties, destroyed Fort Erie and recrossed the river to the American side late in the fall. General Drummond withdrew his force at the same time to Burlington Heights, so the peninsula was abandoned by both armies. The British loss in killed and wounded in the whole campaign, in which they always had the superior force and never once gained the victory, was over three thousand, and the American loss less than eighteen hundred. The quality of the fighting, and the way the Americans had developed their army, went a long way toward convincing the English of the futility of continuing the struggle, and was largely instrumental in bringing about the peace treaty which was signed on the twenty-fourth of December in the same year.

The American "Wasps"
and Their Victims

1. THE FROLIC

The most famous name among the smaller ships of the early American navy is that of the *Wasp*. It was borne in succession by two similar vessels, which in each instance sustained the high reputation of the American arms with an equal degree of fortune and success. The first, which was a small *corvette* of four hundred and fifty tons burden, was built shortly after the close of the Tripolitan War. She was armed with sixteen short thirty-two-pounders, and two long twelves, giving a total weight of about two hundred and fifty pounds to the broadside. Just before the beginning of the War of 1812, she was in England with despatches under the command of Captain Jacob Jones. He was the third eminent man of the same name who distinguished himself in the service.

As soon as he reached home Captain Jones refitted and started out on a cruise with his ship to see what he could devour. On his second cruise, about the middle of October, 1812, he was making for the track between England and the West Indies for the purpose of picking up prizes, when he was overtaken by a violent gale during which the jib-boom carried away, taking with it two men who were on it at the time; and his ship was otherwise damaged in the severe weather. The gale had abated somewhat, though the sea was still running high, when a little before midnight on the seventeenth of October, in latitude thirty-seven degrees North, longitude sixty-five degrees West, or about five hundred miles east of Albemarle Sound, North Carolina, he raised several lights, which he at once suspected to be a convoy. Uncertain, however, as to the character of the force which might be guarding the supposed merchant vessels. Captain Jones prudently refrained from making a closer inspection until the morning.

When the sun rose, he saw that the convoy consisted of five merchant ships, several of them armed, under the charge of a heavy brig-of-war. Jones was to windward of the squadron and he immediately bore down in chase. The war-brig appeared nothing loath for action, and signalling her convoy to make sail and run before the wind, she interposed between them and the *Wasp*, and dropped astern to reconnoitre, clearing for action at the same time. As the *Wasp* drew nearer, Jones saw that the brig, which had hoisted a Spanish flag, had her main-yard on deck; it had been damaged in the gale of the day before. However, as the wind was very heavy, the brig was manoeuvring easily under a boom mainsail and the foretopsail and, in fact, had been converted into a brigantine, a very handy and convenient rig for her under the circumstances. The *Wasp* was under short fighting canvas also.

At half after eleven o'clock in the morning, when the two vessels were within fifty yards of each other, Jones hailed and demanded the stranger's name. The brig hauled down the Spanish flag—which had deceived no one, by the way, for the Spaniard never lived who would come down upon a foe and carry sail as she had done—hoisted the English colours and poured in a broadside followed by a rattling volley of musketry. The *Wasp* responded in kind immediately, and the two vessels sailed side by side nearing each other with every passing moment. The firing was rapid and severe on both sides, although the English delivered three broadsides to the American two. The sea was still running very heavy and the roll of the ships was tremendous, the decks were flooded from time to time and the gun muzzles went under with every roll. After a few minutes of combat, the main topmast of the *Wasp* was shot away, and together with its yards fell across the fore-braces, rendering it impossible to swing the head yards for the rest of the action. A few moments after this misfortune, the gaff and the mizzen topgallant mast were shot away, which rendered the *Wasp* almost unmanageable.

At 11.52 a.m. the vessels had worked to within half pistol-shot distance of each other. The *Wasp* had been cut up fearfully aloft, every brace and most of her running rigging had been carried away, and, so far as the Americans could see, but little damage had as yet been done to their antagonist. They could not account for it; their fire had been deliberate and it was believed accurate, the crew had been carefully trained and exercised in frequent target practice, they were going about their work coolly enough, and why no damage appeared on their enemy was difficult to understand. There had been very few casualties on the American vessel and the fire was still kept up unremittingly, though it was perceived that the English return was gradually decreasing in violence and force. At this juncture the head braces of the brig were carried away, and as she was unable to trim her yards, the pressure of the wind upon her after sails threw her bows up toward the broadside of the *Wasp* which was forging ahead slowly.

The two vessels came together with a tremendous crash, the brig's bowsprit was thrust violently between the main and mizzenmasts of the American and jammed tightly in the main-shrouds. The Americans loaded their port guns with grape and canister and actually fired through the English bridle ports and raked the enemy with terrible effect. No reply of any kind came from the brig. The ships were so close together that the American ramrods struck the sides of the British brig. The bowsprit of the enemy having been fouled, so that she could not extricate herself, Jones, in view of his shattered spars, desired to rake her again before he attempted to board, but in spite of his peremptory orders, the impetuosity of his crew could no longer be restrained.

After the first rake, Jack Lang, an American sailor, who had a bitter score to pay against the British government for impressment, jumped on his gun and reaching for the brig's bowsprit clambered to her deck. Lieutenant James Biddle had stepped up on the rail in readiness to jump as soon as the roll of the vessels should bring them close enough together; at a nod from Jones he at once leaped for the enemy's rail, which he caught with his hands; little Midshipman Baker, utterly unable to reach the deck of the other ship, now caught hold of Biddle's coat-tails and endeavoured to swarm up his back, whereupon both of them fell back upon the deck of the *Wasp*, narrowly escaping a fall into the water between the two ships. Biddle picked up the plucky little midshipman, threw him on the rail of the silent brig, and scrambled up afterward, to support the intrepid Lang, who had been alone on the enemy's deck for nearly a minute. The other boarders immediately followed and gained the brig's forecastle.

Lang, who had been in no danger whatever, was standing on the forecastle, with his arms folded about his cutlass, surveying in great awe the English ship, the like of which neither he nor any other man had ever seen before. The deck was covered thick with dead and wounded men, many of the latter groaning and shrieking in horrible agony. Aft

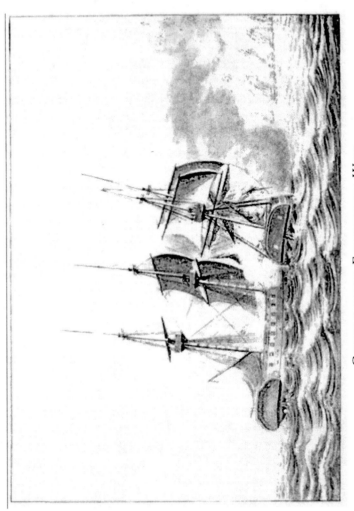

Capture of the *Frolic* by the *Wasp*

on the quarter-deck were three officers, two of them unable to stand alone, and all of them badly wounded. At the wheel and clinging resolutely to its spokes, was a grim, blood-stained old sailor, an heroic example of devotion to duty, who still kept his station and that was all. The guns were dismounted on every hand; ports had been beaten into each other, rails smashed, not a boat left at the davits. The decks were washed about with water brightly coloured with the blood of the dead and dying.

The American boarders were simply appalled at the sight of the slaughter. They stood in silence for a few moments, until Biddle, followed by Lieutenant Rogers and Midshipman Baker, after directing the other men to remain where they were, picked his way over the bodies to the quarter-deck. As he approached them, the three officers flung down their swords at his feet, and one of them, burying his face in his hands, leaned upon the rail and burst into tears. The grim old sailor still kept his place at the helm. Biddle sprang into the rigging and with his own hands lowered the flag. After forty-nine minutes of struggle the battle was over. Almost as he did so, the masts of the prize fell, the mainmast breaking off close to the deck, the foremast ten feet above it.

Out of a crew of one hundred and ten, between ten and twenty only were unscathed, and had fled below to escape the awful punishment of the American shot. The actual loss in killed and wounded was over ninety. The prize proved to be the British brig *Frolic*, Captain Thomas Whinyates. She was of four hundred and seventy tons burden and carried twenty-two guns, sixteen short thirty-twos and four twelves on the main deck, and two twelve-pound carronades on the forecastle, which gave her two hundred and ninety pounds to the broadside. She was larger, better armed and in every way superior to the *Wasp*, and she had been absolutely beaten to pieces. She had been desperately defended and her gun fire had been exceedingly accurate.

The English, however, had fired on the upward roll of the ship on the waves and most of their shot had gone into the rigging and braces. The Americans had fired on the downward roll and their shot had hulled the *Frolic* repeatedly, though, of course, they had not been aware of its destructive force until after the action. Captain Whinyates was much censured for his defeat by an inferior force and was never afterward employed in active service. The loss on the *Wasp* was only five killed and five wounded. Immediately after the battle another

English vessel, the *Poictiers*, a seventy-four, hove in sight and captured both vessels. The *Wasp* made an effort to escape, but when her men shook her sails out of the gaskets they found they had been cut to ribbons by the enemy's fire and she was helpless.

2. THE REINDEER

Eighteen months after the capture, a new and improved edition of the former ship bearing the same name, which had been built at Washington after her loss, got to sea from Portsmouth, New Hampshire, on May 1, 1814, under the command of Captain Johnston Blakely, of North Carolina. The new vessel carried twenty short thirty-two-pound carronades and two long twelves, a total of twenty-two guns with about three hundred and nine pounds to the broadside. She was larger and better built than the old ship, and of a beautiful model, upon which her designer and ship- builders had lavished all their inventive capacity and skill, until they had produced one of the swiftest and handiest vessels upon the sea. Her crew had been selected with especial care and she was very heavily manned. Blakely was already a distinguished young officer and he was destined to add greatly to his reputation by this cruise. He made for the crowded waters of the European coast, and by his captures of merchant vessels spread consternation in the narrow seas.

At four o'clock in the morning of June 28, 1814, in latitude forty-eight degrees thirty-six minutes North, longitude eleven degrees fifteen minutes West, the weather being cloudy with a light breeze from the northeast, two sail were raised to windward. As the *Wasp* made for the stranger, three other vessels appeared close at hand off the weather beam. Blakely changed his course for the nearest ship, and at 12.30 p.m., as the American had not recognized signals thrown out by the strangers, Blakely cleared for action. He vainly endeavoured to get the weather-gage, for the English ship was beautifully handled, and the *Wasp* finally fired a lee gun and ran off free with the wind a little forward the port beam. The English ship, a brig-of-war, accepted the bold challenge at once and hoisted sail to close. She slowly crept up on the weather quarter of the American, and at 3.17 p.m. opened fire, at a range of about sixty yards, from a shifting twelve-pound carronade upon her forecastle, which was loaded with grape. To this discharge the Americans could make no reply and they had perforce to endure patiently the fire of the gun which was discharged five times with the utmost deliberation, inflicting much damage to the ship and causing some loss among the men for nine minutes, or until 3.26 p.m., when, finding that the enemy did not draw abreast of him, Blakely put his helm a-lee and luffed up, firing his carronades from aft forward as they bore.

For ten minutes the two vessels, lying side by side about as far from each other as the width of an ordinary city street, kept up an unremitting fire. The cannonade was terrific. The concussions of the explosions deadened the little wind prevailing, so that the ships lost way and the smoke hung over them in heavy clouds. Both crews worked at the guns with desperate energy but the odds were too great for the English vessel, the *Reindeer*, Captain William Manners, her commander, one of the finest officers in the service, saw that his only hope lay in employing that last resource which has been so often successfully tried by British seamen, the steel of their cutlasses and their good right arms. The ships were now almost touching. Suddenly putting his helm hard up, the captain of the *Reindeer* ran the *Wasp* aboard on her port quarter. Manners had been slightly wounded several times and, though bleeding, still stuck to his post. At this moment a grape shot passed through his thighs, bringing him to the deck, but with unparalleled resolution he dragged himself to his feet, and clinging to a stay, cheered his men as they sprang to board. Blakely was ready for them.

As the ships came together, he called his boarders aft and massed them behind the rail. As the two vessels lay side by side, their boarders hacked and thrust at each other through the ports in the shrouding smoke. As it blew away from the now silent guns, the English sprang to the rail. But a little chasm separated them, caused by the bends of the ships, and there commenced a deadly hand to hand conflict. The top-men and marines on either ship poured in a withering fire. Presently the English gave back. Then it was that Manners sprang into the breach sword in hand, and wounded and dying though he was, he summoned the last vestige of his strength and leaped to the rail to lead his men again. They followed him gallantly, like the brave fellows they were.

At this instant, a bullet from the American maintop crushed into his skull. He clapped his left hand to his face, shrieked out "My God!" and still brandishing his sword in his right hand fell back upon the deck he had defended so desperately. No one ever died better. As the British hesitated in the face of this loss, Blakely sprang to the *Reindeer's* rail and gave the order to board, and with wild cheers the Americans followed their leader to the British deck. There was a furious struggle for a few minutes, when the British were either killed or driven below, and the captain's clerk, the highest surviving officer, surrendered the ship!

The time of the conflict had been twenty-seven minutes from the time the *Reindeer* fired her shifting carronade, and only eighteen minutes from the time the *Wasp* had first responded. The *Reindeer* was smaller than the *Wasp*, her broadside was only two hundred and ten pounds as against three hundred and fifteen; her crew numbered one hundred and eighteen as against one hundred and seventy-three. The *Wasp* had twenty-six killed and wounded and had been rather severely handled. The *Reindeer* had sixty-seven killed and wounded and had been cut to pieces. She fought under greater disadvantage than any other of the British sloops which had been captured in a single action during the whole war, yet she had made incomparably the best fight of them all! There were no mistakes made on either side. Manners had fought his ship in the most brilliant way, and no human man could have done better.

On the other hand, the difference in execution on the two vessels in favour of the American was fully proportioned to the latter's preponderance in force. It is impossible to see how Blakely could have ended the fight more quickly and thoroughly than he did. As Roosevelt remarks, "*We may take great pride in the prowess and courage and skill exhibited on both ships.*" Manners illustrated in his death the glorious traditions of his service as few men have done. The day after the conflict it was found impossible to save the *Reindeer*, and by Blakely's orders she was burned.

3. The Avon

After the battle the *Wasp* went into l'Orient to refit. On the twenty-seventh of August Blakely sailed again, taking several prizes. On September first he overhauled a convoy bound for Gibraltar under the protection of a line-of-battle ship, the *Armada*, 74. The brave American, in spite of the fact that he was several times chased away by the line-of-battle ship, finally succeeded in cutting out one of the convoy, laden with guns and military stores of great value, which he deliberately proceeded to burn and destroy under the nose of the infuriated captain of the liner. It was a part of Blakely's bold daring that he should have accomplished this audacious feat without harm to his ship. At half past six in the evening of the same day, being in latitude forty-seven degrees thirty minutes North, longitude eleven degrees

West, having run the convoy out of sight, he discovered four sail, two to starboard and two to port; he at once determined to have a nearer look at them—that they might all be ships-of-war made no difference to him. It soon appeared that they were three English war vessels chasing an American privateer.

At seven o'clock the nearest one, which had lagged far behind the others, and which was afterward found to be the British brig *Avon*, Captain John Arbuthnot, made night signals, to which the *Wasp* paid no attention. At 8.38 p.m. the *Avon* began firing her stern chaser. At twenty minutes after nine the *Wasp* weathered on the *Avon* off the port quarter. Hails were exchanged and the brig was ordered to heave to. She declined and set her foretopmast studding sail to escape. At 9.29 p.m. the *Wasp* began firing with a twelve-pound carronade which had been mounted forward after the action with the *Reindeer*. The *Avon* replied briskly with her stern guns. Blakely, then fearing that the enemy would square away before the wind and escape in the darkness, shifted his helm and ran to leeward of her and ranged alongside after pouring a semi-raking broadside into her starboard quarter as he passed.

A furious engagement began immediately at very close range. The night was a black one and all the men on the *Wasp* could see was a great shadow rushing rapidly through the water by their side. They could aim at the flashes of their enemy's guns or at the white foam on her water-line, and as usual their practice was excellent. The *Avon* was hulled again and again, her guns were dismounted, the mainmast was carried away, and after thirty minutes of conflict she was completely silenced. When Blakely, suspending his fire, asked if she had struck, she returned with a few scattered discharges and the battle was commenced. For ten minutes the Wasp again poured her broadsides into the *Avon*, which was hailed at the end of that time, and this time answered that she surrendered.

Before Blakely could take possession of his prize, another sail, the British brig-of-war *Castillian*, 18, Captain Brainer, which had abandoned the chase, was seen astern. The men sprang to quarters again, and in a few minutes two more sail hove in sight, one of which was the English sloop *Tartarus*, 20. The braces of the *Wasp* being much cut up, she ran off before the wind while re-reeving new ones. The *Castillian* made after her until she came within range, when she poured in a broadside which went over the American and did no damage at all. When her fire was returned with promptness, she immediately tacked and edged away in the darkness. The ship with which the *Wasp* had been engaged and whose name the crew never learned, was now making a signal of distress. The three British ships left the *Wasp* to pursue her course unimpeded and the *Castillian* made for the *Avon*. The *Castillian* reached her at twelve o'clock, midnight, when Captain Brainer was informed by Captain Arbuthnot that she was sinking fast, and by one o'clock, just as the last boat load of men had been taken from her, the *Avon* went down bow foremost. The *Avon* mounted eighteen guns, carrying two hundred and sixty-two pounds to the broadside; out of her crew of one hundred and seventeen men, forty-two had been killed and wounded. The loss on the *Wasp* was two killed and one wounded.

The *Wasp* continued on her course, capturing and destroying several merchantmen and letters-of-marque, one of which, the *Atlanta*, proving of great value, was sent home. The prize reached Savannah safely on November fourth, bringing Blakely's report of his cruise to the Secretary of the Navy. On October ninth the Swedish brig *Adonis*, carrying two American lieutenants paroled from the captured frigate *Essex*, was overhauled by a ship-of-war in latitude eighteen degrees thirty-five minutes North, longitude thirty degrees ten minutes West. Upon being informed that the man-of-war was the American sloop *Wasp*, Messrs. McKnight and Lyman, the two lieutenants, went aboard her, and she sailed away upon her cruise. From that day to this she disappeared from the ken of humanity. Not a sight nor a sign of her has ever come up from the great deep to say whatever became of Blakely and his gallant crew.

Sometime afterward, it is stated, a large British frigate put into Lisbon very badly damaged and cut up, and related that she had suffered in a night action with a small American sloop, at the close of which the latter suddenly disappeared. James Barnes surmises that this might have been the *Wasp*. It is certainly possible of course, though there is no proof of it, and who could wish for a better end for that little terror of the sea than for her to go down with her colours flying, after a bitter battle against overwhelming odds? But there is nothing certain about the surmise, and we shall not really know what became of them until that long deferred day when the earth and the sea shall give up their dead.

It is singular also that the first *Wasp*, which was captured by the *Poictiers* and was taken into the British service, sailed away on a cruise in this same year and, like her younger American namesake, never came back again. Perhaps in some mighty ocean Valhalla, in amity and friendship, these heroes of the deep meet together and tell tales of the old days when they battled stoutly for the honour of their flags upon the sea.

Macdonough at Lake Champlain

The greatest figure In the naval annals of our country from Paul Jones to David Farragut is Thomas Macdonough. Prior to the Civil War, the naval battle which he fought and won, was certainly the most important of any in which the American navy has participated. From the point of strategy, tactics, seamanship, and hard, desperate fighting, it stands in the first rank. Singularly enough, it has never been a popular battle, and Macdonough does not hold that place in the affections of his countrymen to which his merits entitle him. Two of the largest and most popular encyclopedias in my library do not even mention his name. Without in the least minimizing the service nor disparaging the greatness of Perry, at Lake Erie, as a tactician, as a fighter, as a man, he is not to be mentioned in the same breath as Macdonough.

As might be surmised from his name, the tall, slender, blue-eyed, red-headed young fighter (twenty-eight when he fought his great battle) was of Scotch descent. His great-great-grandfather emigrated to Ireland and from thence his grandfather came early to America, so that if any one falls within the disputed category of "Scotch-Irish," it is certainly he. His brother had been a midshipman with Truxtun, and when the *Constellation* captured *L'Insurgente*, one of the three men wounded on the American was James Macdonough, who lost a leg and retired from the service. Inspired by his brother's glorious example, and I doubt not by the memory of the sacrifice of his father, a successful physician who had given up his practice to go into the line of the army of the Revolution, where he rose to a high rank, Thomas Macdonough at the late age of seventeen gladly received a midshipman's warrant. He took a distinguished part in the operations around Tripoli, and was one of the officers who accompanied Decatur when he cut out the *Philadelphia*.

A year or two after, while he was first lieutenant of the brig *Siren* and in command in the absence of the captain, a British man-of-war sent an eight-oared boat to an American merchantman lying near the *Siren* and took from her a sailor. On his own responsibility Macdonough called away his boat, manned by four stout oarsmen, pursued the Britisher until he caught up with him, and peremptorily demanded the return of the man. When he was refused he boldly reached over the gunwale of the English boat and hauled the captive into his own boat, right under the guns of the frigate, and made his way back to the *Siren*. The English captain followed hot foot and furious with rage, but Macdonough, entirely equal to the occasion, stood his ground and declared he would sink alongside rather than give up the man. The man was not given up.

There is a family tradition to the effect that while in command of a merchant vessel during a leave of absence. he was actually seized himself, by a press gang, and in spite of his protestations, was sent aboard a British frigate, where his name was duly entered upon the ship's books. The night of the capture his hammock was swung next to that of the corporal of the marine guard. The story goes, that when the corporal turned in, Macdonough dressed himself in the marine's uniform, went up on deck, and boldly got permission from the officer in charge to go into the cutter alongside at the swinging boom, to search for spirits. As he went forward to drop into the boat, the real corporal awakening and missing his clothes, came up on deck to give the alarm. The bold American knocked him senseless with his fist, ran out on the boom, dropped into the boat, cut the lashing, drifted away, and in spite of pursuit, regained his own ship and got under way. He paid back the score fully later on.

When he was sent, a young lieutenant, to take command on Lake Champlain, like Perry, he had to improvise a navy, ships, guns, officers and nearly everything else. By herculean exertions he finally built or assembled a small squadron: a sloop-of-war, the *Saratoga*, which he commanded himself; a brig, the *Eagle*, Lieutenant Robert Henly, an old friend from the *Constellation*; the schooner *Ticonderoga* (converted into a war vessel from a broken down steamboat, by the way) commanded by Stephen Cassin; the sloop *Preble*, and ten galleys or gunboats, small affairs, mainly propelled by oars, carrying one or two rather heavy guns and manned by from twenty-five to forty men each.

The British, under Commodore Downie, an experienced officer, with equal skill and exertion had secured or built a similar squadron, comprising a heavy frigate, the *Confiance*, about twice as large as the *Saratoga* and three times as efficient, and which should have been a match for any three of Macdonough's vessels; a brig, the *Linnet*, of slightly less force than the *Eagle*; two sloops, the *Chubb* and the *Finch*, each about half again as large as the *Preble* and correspondingly smaller than the *Ticonderoga*, and twelve gun boats similar to the American vessels of the same class.

Except for their light draft the large vessels of both squadrons were built, rigged, and equipped as if for sea. A reference to the table following this chapter shows the force, etc., of the two squadrons. It will be seen that the British had a great superiority in the number and size of their long guns and in the arrangement of them. The more force that is concentrated in one ship in such circumstances, the greater the advantage. This advantage, however, the tactical disposition and sea-manlike prevision of Macdonough largely neutralized.

The little bay near Plattsburg between Cumberland Head and Crab Island looks toward the south, and the American position had been so skilfully chosen that the attacking force would be compelled to come up bows on, whatever the state of the wind, and thus subject themselves to a raking fire. This did not matter much to the ordinary English seaman, for he had been accustomed by years of success to swoop down upon his continental enemies in any sort of a way, his only object being to get alongside, when the end was certain. It may be remarked in passing, if Nelson had led down upon an American fleet as he did on the French and Spanish at Trafalgar, his vessels would have been beaten to pieces in succession, and the result of the battle would have been the other way. This is no disrespect to Nelson, the greatest admiral of all history, for he knew upon whom he was leading down!

Macdonough had drawn up his fleet in line ahead, the *Eagle* in the lead close to the shore, her nose fairly poking into a shoal, so that it was impossible for an enemy to turn that flank so long as she stayed there. Next to the *Eagle* was the flagship *Saratoga*, following her the *Ticonderoga*, and at the rear of the line resting on Crab Island, which carried a one-gun battery, a six-pounder, manned by invalids and con-valescents from the hospital thereon, was the little *Preble*. The inter-spaces between the large ships were filled by the gun-boats which were withdrawn somewhat to form a second line, and the larger part of the gunboats were ordered to support the more vulnerable part of the line where the *Preble* and *Ticonderoga* lay (which they mainly failed to do).

Every one of the American ships had sent anchors down with ropes leading to different parts of the ship, by hauling in or slacking off which the vessels could be turned in any direction. Technically, they had springs on their cables, with which to wind ship, and stream and kedge anchors out, in case any of the sheet or other cables were shot away. It was this precaution which finally gained the victory for Macdonough.

The morning of Sunday, September 11, 1814—singular how many of our naval battles have been on Sunday—was as fair a day in which to worship God as ever comes to these beautiful regions in the early autumn. The gentle breeze from the north slightly ruffled the surface of the lake as the enemy slowly made their way with the wind aft round Cumberland Head, and then hove to out of range below the American line, until the vessels were all assembled and in place, when they deliberately began to beat up toward the waiting squadron. It was not the first time that the besom of war had swept the waters of the lake, nor the clamour of battle re-echoed from the crags which fringed its shores. Every silent hill was eloquent with the war-cry of the terrible savage and the shriek of his terrified victim; the valleys were reminiscent with the prayers of the heroic Jesuit priests; the air was filled with memories of the French, the German and the English soldiers and woodsmen; in every rocky cavern lurked the echo of ringing steel and roaring cannon.

Now a powerful army of veterans of the peninsula, than whom, as their own officers testified, there never was a braver soldiery nor a more bloody, brutal, and ferocious, were making ready to strike down the old war-path, in order to cut the struggling young United States in two and dictate terms of peace and surrender in the chief city of the conquered. General Macomb, with a small body of regulars and a few thousand militia, his total force not a third as great as that which menaced him, was yet resolutely preparing to dispute the advance to the bitter end, but the fate of the enterprise depended upon the strength of the naval forces on the lake. When they had brushed aside Macdonough the valley of the Hudson would be clear and their way to New York open. As long as the Americans held the lake the movement was impossible. Downie came on in full confidence of his own ability to do the necessary brushing aside.

As the rolling echo of the drums beating to quarters softly melted away among the surrounding hills, and the busy note of preparation subsided into an expectant silence, Macdonough bade his waiting crews to prayer. There at their stations with bowed heads they knelt down upon the white decks, soon to be stained with their own blood, while with his own lips, in. the familiar words of the *Book of Common Prayer,* the young, commander invoked the protection of the God of Battles for the coming conflict—a rare and memorable scene indeed!

As the British in grim silence slowly drew near, their plan of attack developed itself. The brig *Linnet* and the sloop *Chubb* luffed up toward the head of Macdonough's line, where the *Eagle* lay. The sloop *Finch* and all of the galleys kept away toward the rear of the line, while the *Confiance* prepared to smash in through the centre, between the *Eagle* and the *Saratoga.* The plan was simple but good. Macdonough was a disorganizing factor in carrying it out, however; with his own hands he aimed and fired the first gun (a previous broadside from the *Eagle,* which fell far short, not being counted); the twenty-four-pound shot from the *Saratoga* struck the English flagship squarely in the bow, passed through the hawse pipe and, ranging aft, dismounted a gun, killed several men, and carried away the wheel; she had been fairly raked. It was a little after eight in the morning.

The American ships now opened, as their guns bore, and the *Confiance,* which came on steadily and imperturbably, was raked again and again. All hope of breaking through the line had to be abandoned in the face of that smashing fire, and the battle necessarily resolved itself into an artillery duel at long range. Therefore, when Downie reached a position in which he judged he could use his preponderating force of long guns to the best advantage, the *Confiance* dropped anchor, deliberately and with splendid courage took in sail, swung calmly round until her battery bore, and within the distance of two hundred and fifty yards poured into the *Saratoga* a shattering broadside from her long twenty-fours. The effect was fearful.

On the American over a hundred men were knocked down by the force of the concussion. The ship shivered and reeled from stem to stern, from truck to keelson, under the fearful impact. More than forty poor fellows lay weltering in their blood. First Lieutenant Gamble, in the act of sighting a gun, was killed by a piece of a quoin which was driven against him, though the blow did not break the skin. With great courage Macdonough rallied his men, and the broadside was returned with effect.

For two long hours the two anchored ships poured into each other a tremendous and continuous fire, Macdonough toiling at the guns

BATTLE OF PLATTSBURG

like a common seaman with the rest, and by his personal gallantry sustaining his men. It has been fondly noted by various writers that the terrible first broadside of the *Confiance* smashed a chicken-coop on one of the American vessels, thus liberating a game cock, which sprang into the rigging and with lusty crowing encouraged the cheering crews. Inasmuch as nearly every writer puts the chicken in a different ship, it is safe to conclude that there must have been one chicken there, and the incident probably did occur. At any rate, if it was an American chicken, it would certainly crow upon being made free.

Meanwhile, up at the head of the line, which they unsuccessfully endeavored to turn, the *Linnet* and the *Chubb* were heavily engaged with the *Eagle*. After an hour's combat the *Chubb* was completely disabled by a severe raking from the *Eagle*, about one half of her crew were killed and wounded, and, with reeking decks and shattered spars, she drifted helplessly down the line. As she came opposite the *Saratoga*, a twenty four-pound shot brought down her colours, and she was gallantly taken possession of by Midshipman Pratt, and removed from the combat to the rear of the American line.

During this episode the *Linnet* had at last secured a raking position off the starboard bow of the *Eagle*, and the springs of the latter's cables being unfortunately shot away, Henly was unable to make any effective defence, so he finally cut his cable, sheeted home his topsails, and sailed down in the rear of the *Saratoga*, where he brought to between her and the *Ticonderoga*, and opened a brisk fire from his port guns upon the big *Confiance* and the gunboats. This left the head of Macdonough's line entirely exposed, and that flank was at once turned. The *Linnet*, admirably handled, took a position squarely across the bows of the *Saratoga*, and deliberately raked her again and again. Macdonough, hotly engaged with the *Confiance*, had to grin and bear it as best he might. It was now about eleven o'clock.

While the head is being turned and the fierce attack is being made on the centre, let us look to the other end of the line. The little *Preble* had almost immediately been driven out of the combat by the onslaught of the flotilla of British galleys, and she took no further part in the action. The *Finch* was so roughly handled by the larger *Ticonderoga* that she drifted down under the lee of the Crab Island battery and the invalids fired their little gun at her, which caused her to surrender, and they took possession of the sloop, finding her full of dead and wounded.

This left the *Ticonderoga* and four of the American gunboats to sustain the attack of the heavier, better manned, and more efficient British gunboats. Some of the American gunboats did not behave well, and for a time the *Ticonderoga* was practically alone. The English gunboats attacked with the greatest spirit, driving up to the *Ticonderoga* again and again, pouring a perfect stream of grape and solid shot upon the schooner, getting so near her on several occasions that the oarsmen sprang to their feet and handled cutlass and pistol, preparing to board, but time and again they were beaten off with great slaughter.

The brave Cassin throughout the whole of the fierce little battle walked the taffrail of his ship as calmly as if he had been in a drawing-room, unmindful of the stream of bullets which screamed past him, encouraging his gallant crew, and, with the greatest possible resolution, holding his ground against these overwhelming odds, until succoured by some more of the American gunboats and a portion of the fire from the *Eagle*. His conduct was simply heroic, his services invaluable—yet there are few people who have even heard of his name. During this part of the action the matches gave out on the *Ticonderoga*, and Mid-shipman (after Rear Admiral) Paulding fired the guns by snapping his pistol at the touch holes. The executive officer, Stansbury, was struck by a round shot, cut in two, and his body carried overboard. His dis-appearance had not been observed, and the mystery of it was not explained until his body rose two days after the battle. The schooner was riddled with bullets. It is not too much to say that if she had been driven from her post the battle would have been irretrievably lost. So much for Cassin and his men.

It was almost lost anyhow. To return to the centre, the raking of the *Linnet* and the steady fire for nearly two hours from the enor-mous battery of the *Confiance* had at last silenced the overmatched *Saratoga*. Twice she had been set on fire by hot shot. All the offic-ers, except Macdonough, had been killed or wounded. He himself had been knocked senseless three times. The first time a shot cut the spanker boom above his head, and one of the broken pieces fell upon him; a splinter struck him on the second occasion; and the third time he was actually struck in the breast by a human head, which belonged to the captain of his favourite gun, who had just been decapitated by a round shot. Macdonough was like Jones, however, in that he never knew when he was beaten.

The slaughter had been fearful. Many of the men had their clothes literally torn from them by the splinters, the master being a striking example. He fought the latter part of the action in a breech-clout alone, though he had not been otherwise damaged by the splinters which had stripped him of his raiment. On the *Confiance* the loss had been extremely severe also, and in one sense irreparable. About fifteen minutes after the battle began, a shot from the *Saratoga* had struck one of the guns of the *Confiance*, torn it from its carriage, and hurled it against Commodore Downie, who had been instantly killed, though the skin of his body, as was the case with Lieutenant Gamble, was not even broken. English seamen who had been at Trafalgar said afterward that this little battle was infinitely more fierce and bloody than that great one. The fight was going on all along the line at the same time, and the lake was covered with smoke. The light breeze had died away entirely.

At this moment Macdonough, finding that every gun in his starboard battery had been dismounted and silenced, determined to wind ship and thus bring his new and hitherto unengaged port battery into play. His forethought had provided him with the means to do this, and as the undaunted men strained at the hawsers the gallant little corvette swung slowly about until presently the after gun of the port battery bore upon the *Confiance*. When it sent its missile of death crashing through the side of the doomed frigate, the end of the battle began.

Robertson, who had succeeded Downie in command of the *Confiance*, finding his own battery almost dismounted, attempted to emulate Macdonough's manoeuvre, but for lack of proper prevision could not complete the evolution. His bower anchors had been shot away early in the fight, and his vessel only turned so that her bows faced the Saratoga as she swept about, and there she hung, absolutely helpless and immovable. Manning the port battery with eager avidity, the Americans on the *Saratoga*, heartily seconded by the *Eagle*, poured a tremendous raking fire into the *Confiance*. It was more than humanity could stand, and in a short time her colours were hauled down.

She was a wreck. Her masts looked like bunches of match wood, and her sails like bundles of rags. Over one half of her crew had been killed or severely wounded. By the testimony of one of her own officers, there were not five men left on her who had not some mark of the combat on them. The *Saratoga* was now swung again until her broadside bore upon the plucky *Linnet*, which had enjoyed immunity heretofore on account of weightier matters, and for fifteen minutes she had made a chopping-block out of that devoted vessel.

Pring, with a resolution so great that it cannot be too highly commended, fought his little brig to the last, in the hope that the gunboats might come up and assist him, or something might happen, until she was a total wreck in fact, when, not getting the desired help, he reluctantly struck her colours. The battle was over. It was a little before twelve o'clock. The shattered British gunboats now surrendered to the *Eagle* and the *Ticonderoga*, but as the Americans were in no condition to take possession or to pursue, the English boats slowly drifted away and finally escaped, many of them in a sinking condition.

Practically the whole British fleet had been captured. I only know of three other instances when a whole fleet of ships was captured or destroyed—one was by Nelson at Aboukir, the second by Dewey at Manila, the third by Sampson at Santiago. The combat had lasted over two hours and a half without intermission, and had been fierce and bloody in the extreme. The attacks on Plattsburg by Wellington's veterans under Prevost—rather feebly delivered, to be sure—had been stoutly repulsed by Macomb's levies, who had made a most gallant defence, and when the news of the victory of Macdonough was carried ashore, Prevost withdrew incontinently, leaving a large part of his stores and munitions of war behind. New York was free from invasion and capture, and the stupendous victory of Macdonough played a great part in the treaty of peace which soon after ensued.

Medals, swords, honours, prize money, grants of land, were poured upon the great seaman, who announced his victory in this modest despatch:

> The Almighty has been pleased to grant us a signal victory on Lake Champlain in the capture of one frigate, one brig, and two sloops-of-war of the enemy.

Spears, the naval historian, says, with all due respect to religion (he reminds me of George Sampson in this), that for the purpose of rousing the seamen a rooster in the rigging is worth more than a dozen prayers on the quarter-deck; but, without any undue piety, we may question his decision as to the relative value, even upon the sailor's mind, of the prayers to God of the humble-minded but high-spirited Christian commander and the shrill cry of the game cock in the shrouds.

Macdonough died at sea, in 1825, while returning from the command of the European squadron. An anonymous writer in the *National Portrait Gallery* well sums him up in these words:

"The great charm of his character was in the refinement of his taste, the purity of his principles, and the sincerity of his religion. These gave a perfume to his name which the partial page of history seldom can retain for departed warriors, however brilliant their deeds."

American	Tons	Crew	Guns		Total	Killed and ser. wd.
			Long	Short		
Saratoga	750	240	8	18	26	57
Eagle	500	150	8	12	20	33
Ticonderoga	350	112	12	5	17	12
Preble	80	30	7	0	7	2
6 Gunboats	420	246	6	6	12	3
4 Gunboats	160	104	4	0	4	3
Total	2260	882	45	41	86	110
British						
Confiance	1300	325	31	6	37	180
Linnet	350	125	16	0	16	50
Chubb	110	50	1	10	11	20
Finch	110	50	4	7	11	20
5 Gunboats	350	205	5	5	10	} 80
7 Gunboats	280	182	3	4	7	
Total	2520	937	60	32	92	350
British Excess over American	260	55	15	....	6	240

Reid and the "General Armstrong"

Way for the bold men of the privateers—the freelances of the sea! The sails of their saucy clippers gleamed in the sunlight of every horizon, their stanch keels parted the waters of every ocean in their dashing pursuit of British merchantmen. With a valour which often equalled that of their better-trained naval brethren, they upheld the honour of the flag in all quarters of the globe. When resistance was made to their attacks they generally fought with credit and success, even, in many instances, against regularly commissioned war ships of the foe. With a persistency which was the despair of the British ship masters and owners, they flaunted their flags in the English Channel in the face of the fleets and squadrons of English men-of-war, and displayed their skill and courage in the distant China seas as well. They searched the hidden recesses of the world for their prey, and no route of trade was so remote as to be safe from their ravages.

The damage they inflicted and the part they played in bringing the War of 1812 to a close can hardly be overestimated. Their adventures are as romantic as the inventions of the novelist. The story of their naval ruses, subterfuges, pursuits, fights, and flights, makes most brilliant history—history which, save in rare instances, has only been recorded in the most meagre way. They had no inconsiderable share in laying the foundation of the naval greatness of the United States, and though it cannot be denied that their first aim was plunder, yet their conduct in many a desperate little fight shows that patriotism and courage were, after all, master motives of their souls. There will be no more of them hereafter—international agreement has abolished them now— but the country should never forget their services in the two great wars we have fought with England.

The most conspicuous of them all, for he fought the greatest fight in their records and the most important, was Captain Samuel Chester

Reid. It gives one who has an idea that there has been a great gulf fixed from time immemorial between England and the United States, something of a shock to find that he was the son of an English naval officer. This officer, while in charge of a boat expedition in the war of the Revolution, was captured by the rebellious colonists, and when he had been sufficiently persuaded of the justice of their cause, he resigned his commission in the British navy and entered the American service. It may be that Miss Rebecca Chester, whose people were brave soldiers and stanch supporters of the Revolution, had something to do with the decision at which he arrived; at any rate, he married her in 1781, and to them, in 1783, the year of the peace, was born the great privateer.

He came of distinguished ancestry on both sides of the house, his father being a direct descendant of the Lord High Admiral of Scotland in the great days of Bruce; while the Chesters were of old colonial and English stock, none better, counting lords and earls galore among them. Young Reid was therefore brought up like a gentleman to adorn that station in life unto which it had pleased God to call him, and in every way he proved worthy of his sires. His first choice of a profession was the navy—following in the footsteps of the Lord High Admiral aforesaid—and he learned some good lessons while still a young boy from that past master of seamanship, discipline, and hard, close fighting, Thomas Truxtun, in whose squadron he served as a midshipman in the frigate *Baltimore* in the French war. For various reasons, however, at the close of that little war he entered the mercantile marine, and, rising rapidly to command rank, became widely known as a bold and successful navigator and captain.

About the middle of the year 1814 he was given command, by her owners, of the *General Armstrong*, a small New York privateer, brigantine rigged, and one of the smartest, most noted, and successful of her class. She had already proved, under her other gallant commanders, that she could not only prey but fight. She had just returned from her fifth lucky cruise. I suppose her to have been of about two hundred tons burden, one hundred and twenty feet long over all, and about thirty feet in beam. Her armament consisted of seven guns—three long nines in each broadside and a long twenty-four pounder on a pivot amidships, in sea parlance a "Long Tom." Her crew and officers numbered ninety men. They had been selected, by Reid himself, with especial care, and were probably quite up to the high standard which obtained on that most gallant frigate, the United States ship *Constitu-*

tion herself. On account of the high wages paid and the liberal prize money accruing from the captures in a successful cruise, in which the men were all interested, it was not difficult to secure desirable men for a crew. Indeed, with the exception of some of the more famous frigates, the pick of the seamen of the nation were on the privateers and letters-of-marque.

The twenty-sixth of September, 1814, found Reid and the *Armstrong* at the island of Fayal, in the Azores. He had run the blockade off New York about the middle of the month, distancing all pursuers by his great speed, and had stopped at the island on his voyage to the English Channel for food and water. The bay of Da Horta, the principal town and seaport of the island of Fayal, is crescent shaped and is surrounded by a sea wall, with the old castle of Santa Cruz, even then an obsolete fortification, at the base of the crescent. Opposite to the entrance of the bay, on a neighbouring island, boldly rises the splendid mountain called Pico, to a height of nearly eight thousand feet, and on all sides are lofty mountains and hills which descend in beetling crags and wild ravines to the water's edge.

Having speedily fulfilled his errand, the American skipper had gone ashore to call upon and dine with the United States Consul, Mr. Dabney, and after dinner had brought him, and a party of gentlemen with him, off to inspect his vessel. Just about sunset the spars of a large brig-of-war, flying English colours, were discovered making around the rocky headlands which bound the entrance to the harbour. The brig, it was soon discovered, was followed by two other large ships, still some distance away. It was the first time any English war vessels had been in the harbour for months. The Portuguese pilot had told the English commodore of the arrival of the privateer, and he came into the harbour with his squadron with the deliberate purpose of effecting her capture.

In spite of Consul Dabney's assurances, it instantly occurred to the wary and experienced Reid that the neutrality of the place would not be respected by the English. It seems to be a general practice among nations to disregard the so-called laws of neutrality with perfect equanimity, provided they feel themselves able and willing to abide the consequences. England has done it on several occasions, and the United States has not hesitated to follow her example as late as in the Civil War, so we can cast no stones in this case. So Reid sent his guests post-haste ashore, and began to warp his vessel closer into the harbour. The English brig, which proved to be the *Carnation*, eighteen guns, Commander George Bentham, did not waste any time. She had hardly dropped anchor in the harbour before she exchanged signals with the other ships, and then put out four boats, crowded with about a hundred and twenty armed men, who, with the usual British intrepidity, made straight for the *Armstrong*.

Reid left the business of warping in to a more convenient season, dropped anchor temporarily, called his men to quarters, and, as the menacing boats rapidly drew near, he repeatedly hailed them, to discover their purpose, warning them to desist from their approach or come on at their peril. There was not the least doubt as to the character of the movement in any rational mind. The armed men were in plain sight, as the moon flooded the placid waters of the bay with a soft, autumnal splendour. The English disdaining to make any reply to his hails and urging their boats persistently onward, Reid opened the fight with a severe, well-directed fire from the great guns of his battery and his small arms, to which the enemy replied with boat guns and an ineffective musketry fire.

A very few minutes were sufficient to determine this event; only one boat touched the American, and most of those in her were killed or wounded. The other boats stopped rowing, and the officers called for quarter; then, while Reid, who might have sunk the whole business without difficulty, mercifully held his fire, the boats turned tail, and, with a large number of killed and wounded on board, made their way back to the brig. They had hoped to carry the *Armstrong* by a *coup-de-main*, but had met with a most discouraging and costly repulse instead. The privateer had only one man killed, and her first lieutenant, a brother of the noted General Worth, of the United States Army, severely wounded. Two more masterful players entered the game at this juncture, however, in the shape of His Britannic Majesty's frigate *Rota*, 38, Captain Philip Somerville, followed by his Britannic Majesty's huge ship-of-the-line *Plantagenet*, 74, Commodore Robert Lloyd, who commanded the squadron. This raised the effective force of the enemy to nearly two hundred guns and twelve hundred men.

It was soon evident that Commodore Lloyd intended to take up the frustrated attempt of the Carnation, for boats were called away from all three ships to the number of twelve. This statement is made upon the testimony of unimpeachable witnesses, among them Captain Reid and Consul Dabney, a fine old gentleman of the highest reputation, who stood upon shore in full sight of the battle, with many other observers, some of whom go so far as to say there were fourteen boats, though the British allow there were but seven. These boats were loaded with nearly four hundred and fifty men. They were towed in by the brig, and then rendezvoused in three divisions under the lee of the little reef just beyond gunshot range from the *Armstrong*, while they matured their plans for the contemplated attack.

Meanwhile Reid and his gallant crew, not in the least alarmed by this display of overwhelming force, had completed their preparations to receive and repel the expected onslaught. The *Armstrong* had been warped within a short distance of the shore, where she lay under the useless and silent guns of the Portuguese castle. Two of the guns on the unengaged side of her had been shifted over to face the enemy, through ports cut in the rail for them. All the small arms in the brigantine—of which she had a great many, the pistols actually being in bucketsful—had been charged and placed close at hand. Boarding nettings, made of heavily tarred rope, had been triced up from one end of the ship to the other. The cutlasses, boarding axes, and pikes were distributed to the men, who were all provided with steel and leather boarding caps. Reid commanded upon the quarter-deck, his lieutenants in the waist and forward.

Pending any movement of the British, the men were allowed to rest beside the guns, while the officers and a few of the older and more experienced seamen kept watch. It was a strange picture the stars looked down upon that calm September night. That little vessel was surrounded by grim and threatening antagonists. Her crew was menaced by an overwhelming force, which outnumbered them five to one; yet we are told the hardy men slept on the white deck of the privateer, under the shadow of the great peaks and mountains of the island, as soundly and peacefully as though they had been at home. There was something notable, too, in the spirit which their quiet slumber betokened, of their confidence and trust in the officers, to whom they looked up as the American sailor has ever looked up to those who led him. More notable still was their willingness to fight an absolutely hopeless battle, in which they had everything to lose and nothing whatever to gain, except the consciousness of having upheld the honour of the American flag against tremendous odds.

About twelve o'clock, under the lead of Lieutenant William Matterface, the first lieutenant of the *Plantagenet*, the flotilla of boats moved out around the reef, and in line ahead—*i. e.*, a long, single column—swept down upon the *Armstrong*. The midshipmen and other junior officers ran along the decks of the privateer and awakened the sleeping men, who sprang quietly to their stations. The stillness of the night was broken only by the rustle of the oars in the row-locks and the splash of the dark water parted by the bows of the boats or tossed up in the air by the feathering blades of the oars, to sparkle in the moonlight. The men on the *Armstrong*, so far as the attacking party could see, might have been asleep or dead.

The shore was fairly crowded with spectators now, who held their breath while watching the advance and awaiting the denouement. Out in the harbour the men left upon the ships swarmed in black clusters in the rigging at eager gaze. The officers of the English men-of-war were closely grouped on the different quarter-decks eagerly scanning the *Armstrong* through their night-glasses. With what apprehension Dabney and his son and the few Americans on shore watched the British draw near! It was a moment fraught with the most intense anxiety. Would the *Armstrong* never fire? Was Reid asleep or dead? Had she been abandoned by her crew? Ah, what was that!

A flash of light tore through the gray darkness. A cloud of smoke broke out amidships on the privateer, and a roar like thunder echoed and re-echoed among the surrounding hills. "Long Tom" had spoken! The battle was on. Before the echo had died away the other guns in the starboard battery, which had been trained upon the advancing line, spoke in quick succession, and sent their messengers of death out over the dark waters. The head of the column was smashed to pieces by the discharge. The first boat was completely disabled, and the shower of American grape shot did great execution all along the line. With the courage of their race, the stalwart English broke into loud cheers, and, manfully tugging at the oars, swept around the wrecked boat and dashed into close action at once. The boat carronnades in the bows of the launches now rang out, adding their sharp notes to the confusion of the exciting moment, as they returned the *Armstrong's* fire. The men of the privateer remained grimly silent, for Reid's command had been:

No cheering, lads, till we have beat them off and gained the victory!

There was no time for either side to load its artillery again before the first boat crashed against the side of the privateer, and the leading man sprang up on her low rail. He clutched the netting, which barred his passage, and shortening his sword hacked frantically at it. He was a fair and easy mark to an old man-of-war's man on the brigantine, who buried a half-pike deep in his bosom. He had scarcely fallen back before others, undaunted by his fate, gallantly sprang to the rail and took his place. Encouraged and led by their officers, the English strove to board on every hand, and the action at once became general. The boats ranged themselves about the engaged side of the *Armstrong* as hounds surround a wild boar at bay. One division attacked forward, the other in the waist, and the last and strongest endeavoured to gain the quarter.

For a few moments the roar of the great guns was succeeded by the sharp crackle of the small arms, the pistols and muskets of the marines; and the darkness was punctured by vivid flashes of fire, in lurid contrast to the moon's pale light. But these ringing reports gradually died away, and as there was no time to recharge the guns the conflict resolved itself into an old-fashioned hand to hand encounter. There was displayed the old knightly courage on both sides, which had left a glorious record of many a bloody fray in centuries of history.

The cheers, shouts, curses, and groans of the desperate men, mad with the blood lust of the fight, the ringing of steel on steel, as sword gritted against sword, or axe crashed on boarding cap, or bayonet crossed half-pike in the dreadful fray, filled the hearts of the spectators nearby on the shore with horror. The British, in overwhelming numbers, though at a disadvantage as regards position, striving determinedly to make good a footing on the deck, fought with the same indomitable courage as their American brethren. Most gallantly led, again and again they sprang at the rail, officer after officer fell, man after man was cut down; the stout arms of the privateersmen grew weary with hacking, and hewing, and slaughtering men. The boarding netting was at last nearly cut to pieces, and the way was clear for an entrance. Although the slight success came too late to be of much service, a lodgement was finally effected forward in the forecastle by way of the bowsprit; one of the American lieutenants in command there had been killed, the other wounded.

At this moment Reid himself, the only officer of rank now left on deck, after a brief rally with swords between them, in which he was slightly wounded, succeeded in cutting down Matterface, the English leader, who had been engaged in a last desperate endeavour to effect a lodgement on the quarter-deck. All danger from further attack there was over. Some of the boats of this division were sheering off slowly, manned by a few oarsmen; others, full of silent dead and shrieking wounded, were aimlessly drifting about. The party attacking the waist had fared little better. Alarmed by the cries in the bows, and seeing

209

that the enemy near him had been effectively disposed of, the captain led a dashing charge forward, and speedily cleared the forecastle. It was all over. That was the expiring effort of the British. They hurried away as they were able, in full retreat. They had been totally beaten.

Two of the boats were captured, two of them had been sunk, two others drifted ashore and were abandoned by the remainder of their crews—all but three of the sixty or seventy men they originally contained being killed or wounded! In one of the boats all were killed but four. Most of the boats which escaped regained their respective ships, with the greatest difficulty, in a sinking condition, not only from the fire of the American heavy guns, but on account of having been stove in by solid shot hurled into them by the Americans. The total loss was at least two hundred and fifty men on the part of the British, nearly half of whom were killed and the others severely wounded. The Americans had two killed and only seven wounded! It seems incredible, but it is true, though the British admit only about half of the losses ascribed to them.

This desperate and bloody action had lasted forty minutes, and in its sanguinary results is unparalleled. Victory had a second time crowned the efforts of Reid and his undaunted men. I picture them, some pale as death from their exhausting labours, others with faces engorged with Blood and trembling still with the passion generated in the fight, grouped about their heroic captain on those bloody decks, looking wildly out upon the drifting, shattered, sinking boats, with their dreadful cargoes. It was time now and they began cheering madly in triumph in the still night. They had a right to cheer. Such a fight as they had fought and such a victory as they had won it has been given to but few on this earth to participate in.

Not much damage had been done to the privateer either. The boarding netting had been cut to pieces, some of the guns, including the "Long Tom," had been dismounted by the shots from the boat carronades, but a few hours sufficed to put everything to rights again. Sending his dead and wounded ashore, and with the remaining men asleep in sheer exhaustion at their quarters again, Reid waited for the next move. At daybreak the *Carnation* weighed anchor, sheeted home her topsails, and got under way. When she came within range she opened a fierce cannonade from her heavy guns upon the privateer, which did much damage to the vessel, though producing no casualties among the crew. Reid and his men met and returned the attack with the same splendid spirit they had all along exhibited, discharging the guns of their smaller battery with a calm deliberation which enabled them to do great execution. After a short and fierce engagement the *Carnation* prudently withdrew from the combat, her foretopmast having been shot away and her other head-gear much damaged, with several more of her crew killed and wounded, mainly by shot from "Long Tom," which, carefully and skilfully served, had again saved the day. This was victory number three.

The Portuguese governor meanwhile was protesting against the violation of neutrality, and requesting Commodore Lloyd to desist from the fighting. He was informed in reply that the English intended to capture the privateer if they had to bring the ship-of-the-line in and bombard the town to do it. Seeing the uselessness of further resistance, and having maintained the honour of the American flag, as few men have been able to do, after fighting a battle which is without parallel in naval annals, and having acquired glory sufficient to satisfy any reasonable man, Reid determined, upon the advice of Dabney and others to sink his ship, so the "Long Tom" which had done such splendid execution was swung in board and pointed down the hatchway and discharged. The *Armstrong* went down from the shot from her own guns. Reid and his men, after spiking the great guns, throwing overboard the powder and small arms and removing their private belongings, escaped to the shore. A boat party from the British boarded the sinking ship, and set what remained of her above the water on fire.

The loss in the first and third attack probably raised the British total to nearly three hundred, though it had not increased that of the Americans. There are several fleet actions on record in which the British won glorious victories without inflicting or receiving so much damage as they got in the combat with this little insignificant privateer. The English commander-in-chief was furious with rage at the results of the action, so much so that he never made proper report of it to the home authorities, but the statements here given are supported by unimpeachable evidence. Lloyd was so angered that he insisted that there were British deserters among the escaped American crew on shore, and actually compelled the Portuguese commander of the island to have the seamen mustered, that he might inspect them. He didn't find any deserters, or at least he did not try to take any, which showed a late discretion on his part. One of two ships-of-war which soon joined Lloyd's squadron was finally sent back to England with the wounded.

The action had an importance far beyond its immediate results in this way: The three English ships were destined to form a part of the fleet rendezvousing at Jamaica to convey Pakenham's army of Wellington's veterans to the attack on New Orleans. A delay of ten days was caused by the necessity of burying the dead, attending the wounded, and repairing the brig and boats at Fayal, consequently the fleet at Jamaica, which this squadron finally joined, was also delayed ten days in its departure, to the great indignation of its admiral. This was just the time that was required to permit the doughty Andrew Jackson to assemble that army and make those preparations by which he was enabled to win one of the most astonishing victories that was ever achieved upon the land, so that the stout and hard fighting of Reid and the men of the *General Armstrong* proved of incalculable service to their country. Moral: It is always best for the fighter to fight to the end, whatever the odds; for upon the action of the moment the whole future may depend.

Reid himself was received with the greatest honour on his return to America, and the usual rewards in the way of swords, pieces of plate, banquets, etc., were showered upon him. It is a noteworthy fact in his subsequent history that he made the design for the present American flag; heretofore a star and a stripe had been added for every new State, and it was due to his suggestion that the flag took its present shape. For this he was thanked by Congress. Later in his life he was placed upon the navy list and retired. After this he lived a long life of eminent usefulness in New York, where he was held in the highest respect and honour. His funeral, in 1861, was a national affair, and some of his immediate descendants are still living. As a specimen of a bold, daring seaman, a magnificent fighter, a true patriot, and a high-toned gentleman, he ranks with the very best, and no one should stand higher in the affections of the people of the land than he.

Since writing the above I have received word from a creditable source that in the first attack one of the boats had its bottom stove by the fall of a grindstone which had been balanced on the rail, and rolled into the boat by a sailor named Granniss.

The Defence of Louisiana—The Last Battle With England

At half after one o'clock on the afternoon of December 23, 1814, a little party of officers in the parlour of a dwelling house used as headquarters, on Royal Street, New Orleans, Louisiana, who were earnestly engaged in conversation, were interrupted by the entrance of three gentlemen, who had galloped post-haste to the door. One of them wore the brilliant uniform of the Louisiana Creole Light Infantry. The other two were older men, evidently planters. The young officer was Major Gabriel Villeré. He bore startling news, which he proceeded to tell in French, as he was unable to speak English, one of the planters interpreting for him.

He said that the little outpost guarding Bayou Bienvenu had been surprised that morning, and subsequently he himself and all his people had been captured on the Villeré plantation, his father's home; but that, being negligently guarded, he had seized a horse, galloped away under a shower of balls, and escaped. The British were out in full force about ten miles away, and were marching up the dry ground between the river and the morasses inland. If they continued their march they might probably reach the city of New Orleans that night.

"By the Eternal!" said the chief of the officers in the room, Andrew Jackson, of Tennessee, a very tall and very thin man, with reddish-gray hair brushed straight up from his high forehead, his piercing blue eyes sparkling with fire and determination—"by the Eternal," he repeated, bringing his hand down upon the table, "they shall not sleep upon our soil this night!"

The man was dreadfully emaciated, worn to a skeleton by wasting disease, utterly broken in health, and at that moment suffering from a dreadful wound in the shoulder, which had been inflicted months

213

before in a duel and which prevented him from ever wearing the heavy bullion epaulet of his rank, which was that of Major-General in the Regular Army of the United States. But such greatness of spirit looked out of his eyes, such indomitable resolution was evidenced by the straight, tense lines of his mouth and his square jaws that it was easy to see that here was a man who would exercise command, sickness or no sickness, until he was laid in his grave.

He had enjoyed no opportunity for perfecting himself in the technical art of soldiering; true, as a boy, he had fought in the partisan warfare which devastated the Carolinas in the Revolution, during which he had been wounded, captured, starved—he knew all about that part of it. He had learned to look into the cold barrel of a pistol without flinching, too, through many duels, some of them dreadful in character, in which he had been a principal. He had been a Member of Congress, a Senator, and United States District Attorney, when to be a district attorney on the frontiers was to invite destruction. He had just terminated successfully, after unheard-of hardships and the exhibition of the most heroic resolution and courage, one of the most famous campaigns ever carried on against the Indians, and for this had been made the junior Major-General in the Regular Army.

He had come to New Orleans, on the second of December, fresh from the conquest of Pensacola, which he had taken by storm from the Spaniards because the place had been used by the British as a base from which to make forays and incursions into the American territory. Incidentally, also, the troops under his command had repulsed a British attack on Mobile, Major Lawrence, at Fort Bowyer, having beaten off four British ships-of-war and a landing party of six hundred men, one of the British ships being burned and sunk after heavy loss in men.

The spirit of the people of New Orleans was very high, but they were without a head, and they welcomed the advent of the general from Tennessee with the greatest joy, seconding his efforts for the raising and equipment of an army for the defence of the city in every possible way. Jackson was a natural leader, popular with his men, and knew instinctively the best disposition to make of the motley forces under his command. When Villeré brought the news all the available troops, amounting to but three or four thousand men, including the militia, were in camp north of the city. Messengers were sent galloping in every direction, bidding them take up the line of march. They responded to their orders with alacrity, and the roads were soon covered with armed men marching gaily through the city toward the south.

On the river there were two armed vessels, a sloop-of-war, the *Louisiana*, commanded by Commodore Patterson, and the schooner *Carolina*, Captain Henly, whom we saw at Lake Champlain. Word was despatched to the ships, and they immediately cleared for action and dropped down the river. They were important factors in Jackson's brilliant plan of attack. The news brought by Major Villeré was alarming in the last degree. The troops he had seen were an advance guard of two thousand men of a powerful British army five times as great. They had appeared in their ships a few days before off the Passes in the Delta, through which the Mississippi gains the sea. There were over fifty vessels in the convoy, including the powerful fleet of Admiral Cockburn's ships-of-the-line. They had sailed from Jamaica a month before bearing a large army of Wellington's veterans which had been transported thither from their successful maraud in Virginia and Maryland, which had resulted in the capture and destruction of Washington, to which point they had come straight from the Garonne. Ross, their commander, had been killed before Baltimore, and Brigadier-General Keane, a younger soldier, was in charge. Reinforcements and other generals were even then speeding across the water as fast as wind could drive them.

There was no way to take the ships-of-the-line, or even the frigates and transports, up the river, and if the city was to be captured by the troops their only mode of access to it would be by Lakes Borgne and Ponchartrain. To prevent this, there was a little American force on Lake Borgne consisting of five gun-boats, each carrying one heavy gun and several smaller ones, and manned by from twenty to thirty men, under the command of Lieutenant Thomas ap-Catesby Jones, the third officer of that name to distinguish himself in the early service. His total force amounted to less than two hundred men and fourteen available guns in broadside.

The British attacked him with forty-two boats, carrying as many guns and over one thousand men. There was absolutely no hope of successful resistance, yet no one thought of surrender or flight, and there was a hotly contested battle on the lake, in which several of the British boats were sunk with heavy loss, but which finally resulted in the capture of the entire American flotilla, after a series of desperate hand to hand conflicts, in which the Americans were overpowered by force of numbers and only gave way when nearly one fourth of them had been killed or wounded, among the latter being their gallant commander.

The British then surprised the picket post on Bayou Bienvenu, and marched up the river on the only firm ground in that part of the country. If Keane had pushed on vigorously after the escape of Major Villeré, instead of halting to entrench and reconnoitre, it is more than probable that he would have effected the capture of the unprepared city at once. Jackson's quick decision to attack him without delay, which usually receives but little attention in the consideration exacted by the greater battle which followed, was more of an indication of the high natural military instinct which he possessed than anything else in his life.

The land upon which the British were encamped, was somewhat lower than the level of the great Mississippi, which was here confined by immense retaining walls of earth called levees. About half after seven in the evening the British pickets on the levee noticed a schooner dropping silently down the river, grim and ghostlike in the night. The boat was hailed, and one or two muskets were fired at her, but no answer was elicited. She came to anchor opposite the camp, deliberately made her preparations, and then the astonished sentries heard a stout voice cry, "Give them this, lads, for the honour of the United States!"

The sides of the schooner burst into flame, and a whole broadside of grape at short range was poured into the crowded British camp. Numbers clustered about the campfires were killed or wounded. The eager men tramped out the fires as if by magic, and sought instant shelter from the deadly rain of shot which came from the *Carolina's* guns by crouching under the lee of the river embankment. There were but two guns in the camp, little three-pounders, and about as efficient as popguns under the circumstances. There was nothing for the English to do but to hide away and bide their time. So long as they remained under the cover of the levee they were reasonably safe, though they could get nothing to eat and could not occupy their tents. They were good soldiers, however, and made the best of their situation, philosophically disposing themselves to pass the night in their uncomfortable position as best they could.

Their rest, if they got any, was interrupted by a rifle shot from the landward flank of their position about eight o'clock at night. The shot was succeeded by another and another, and then by a perfect fusillade of small arms from all sides. It was Jackson delivering his attack. He had skilfully disposed his men so as to surround the enemy. Though his total force was no greater than the British, the latter were cornered. Necessarily, since the Americans had arrived on the scene, the fire of the *Carolina* was stopped. The British soon found this out, and rushed to meet their midnight assailants with their usual dogged courage. Then ensued in that darkness a demoniacal struggle, utterly unlike any battle that had occurred heretofore on the continent. Rain fell in torrents. Firearms became useless, and the bayonets of the English crossed the long hunting knives of the Kentuckians in a deadly death grapple in the black air, in the series of bitter hand to hand conflicts.

The general and his staff were in the thick of it all, and he was personally engaged. After continuing the struggle for several hours, Jackson drew off his troops, in fairly good order, about ten o'clock in the evening, and retreated a few miles up the river behind the Rodriguez Canal, an abandoned watercourse, and entrenched himself at the narrowest pass, where the distance between the river bank and the impassable morass was the shortest. The *Carolina*, now seconded by the *Louisiana*, opened fire again, and once more dominated the situation. Jackson had effected his object. With a loss of about three hundred men he had paralyzed the advance of the British army. They would remain where they were, he felt certain, and make no offensive movement whatever until reinforcements were brought up, and that would give him what he most earnestly desired, and what is of vital importance to every military commander—time.

The British had lost over five hundred in killed and wounded in this audacious attack, and were so thoroughly and completely astonished by their rough handling that they dreamed of nothing but holding their position and sending for reinforcements; all idea of advance was abandoned. It was no use even to consider it; for the American ships made a direct target out of every individual who ventured to show himself for a moment behind the levee.

The British soldiers were the best on earth and Jackson knew that his troops—with the possible exception of the Tennesseans—who were all of them without bayonets, could never have met them in the open with any prospect of success; therefore he contented himself with strengthening his entrenchments, assiduously drilling his men constantly in such military tactics as he was familiar with himself, and in sending expresses and requisitions for help and supplies in every direction.

The militia of Louisiana turned out nobly. So, by the way, did La Fitte, the last of the *buccaneers* and his pirate crew. The citizens were fighting in defence of their homes. It was well understood that if New Orleans, which was then a populous and wealthy city of some thirty thousand people, and a place of the greatest commercial importance, for the whole trade of the Mississippi valley passed through it, were captured, that it was to be sacked by the soldiery. If one wishes to know to what excesses the British soldiery could descend in the sacking of a town he need only read the descriptions of similar affairs by Lord Napier in his great *Peninsula Campaign*. The soldiers of Tilly, at the famous storming of Magdeburg, could not have been more lustful, brutal, wanton and ferocious. Said British soldiery at that time could almost have given pointers to a Geronimo Apache. (*Geronimo* by Geronimo, also published by Leonaur).

The main reliance of Jackson, however, was upon the famous Riflemen from Kentucky and Tennessee under Coffey and Carroll. They knew little about manoeuvres or tactics. The school of the soldier was a thing of which they had heard little, and about which they cared less; but they could shoot and shoot straight and shoot fast and keep it up. Nothing could exceed their courage. They had fought under their general before and knew what manner of man he was. They loved him even for his faults and the enemies he had made, and most excellently officered, could be depended upon to the last gasp. There was also a small but efficient contingent of regular troops.

Matters remained in *statu quo* for two days, until Christmas, when Sir Edward Pakenham, a brother-in-law to the Iron Duke, arrived from England to take command of the army. He was accompanied by General Samuel Gibbs, and was followed soon after by General John Lambert, with several regiments of men who, with the officers named, were all veterans and had been taught in the splendid school of Wellington.

Pakenham had especially distinguished himself in the Peninsula. He was a man of the highest personal gallantry and much military skill and experience. At the Battle of Salamanca, the charge which he led at the head of his division had saved the day. He expected to make an easy conquest of the "backwoods general" and add new laurels to his wreath by the capture of New Orleans. A peerage would probably reward his success.

He found Keane's army still clinging desperately to the lee side of the levee. Under his orders a battery of heavy guns was landed from the ships, and on the evening of the 26th they set fire to the *Carolina* with red hot shot. She was windbound at the time and after making a gallant defence with the single long gun which would bear, she blew up. The *Louisiana*, further away, managed to tow out of range and escape.

Pakenham then determined upon a reconnoissance in force. There were some plantation buildings in front of the American line, and as his troops came marching along the level ground on the morning of the twenty-eighth of December they were concealed until they advanced beyond the buildings. As soon as they passed them they were met by such a discharge of artillery as convinced Pakenham that the works were far stronger than he had anticipated. The buildings were set on fire by the American shot. After marching his men up to the old canal in front of the American fortifications, losing many of them by the way, the troops withdrew, having effected nothing beyond informing themselves of the strength of the American position. This affair is sometimes called the Battle of Chalmette's plantation.

On the other side of the river the navy had erected a formidable water battery by landing some of the *Louisiana's* heavy guns, which enfiladed and thus protected the front of Jackson's entrenchments. Jackson himself had a motley lot of artillery mounted between embrasures made of cotton bales, the heaviest gun being an old thirty-two-pounder. Pakenham now resolved to begin a regular siege of the American position. Consequently very early in the morning of January 1, 1815, his troops advanced silently to within three hundred yards of the American entrenchments, and cautiously opened a parallel. Their fortifications were made of barrels of sugar, of which there were a great number in the various plantations.

When the fog lifted about ten o'clock the Americans, who were holding dress parade in front of their entrenchments in honour of New Year's Day, were astonished to see the frowning batteries of the British. They scampered back in hot haste to their positions, and a cannonade immediately began, which lasted the greater part of the morning. The British guns were silenced, the sugar barrels were knocked to pieces, and proved no protection whatever. The *Louisiana* and the water battery on the other side had done dreadful execution with their raking fire. Pakenham withdrew his troops at once, and succeeded, through the gallantry of some of the seamen of the ships, in saving all his guns. On the American side the cotton bales forming the embrasures were set on fire or knocked out of place, and were afterward supplanted by the soft, muddy earth of the Delta.

The American Mounted Riflemen now harassed the British camp continually on every side. The life of a sentry on the picket line was always in jeopardy. Foraging was decidedly unsafe. The *Louisiana* and the water batteries sent balls from their long guns toward the British camp at regular intervals day and night, so that the men got neither sleep nor rest. Pakenham and his lieutenants chafed under the annoying position, and, irritated by the taunts of that valiant house-burner. Admiral Cockburn, who threatened to land his marines and do up the job himself, they at last resolved upon a final attempt.

Pakenham's plan was an excellent one—indeed, the only possible one under the circumstances. He determined to detach a large body of men under Colonel Thornton, one of his most efficient officers, and send them across the river to capture the water battery and the *Louisiana*, which were defended by about a thousand inefficient militiamen, then turn their guns upon Jackson's line, upon which, with the balance of his army, he would deliver a direct assault in force. In order to get the boats of the ships into the Mississippi to ferry over the troops, a canal was cut through from Lake Borgne, with great labour, by the soldiers.

The morning of January 8, 1815 (Sunday), was selected for the attack. When Thornton reached the canal, however, he found that instead of boats for fifteen hundred men he only had transportation for about four hundred. He was delayed in getting even those in motion by the caving in of the banks of the canal, and when he reached the Mississippi he was swept down for two miles below his projected landing place by the swift current. Pakenham, meanwhile, ignorant of all these mishaps, had put his army in motion, and had crept slowly up toward the American works in the gray of the morning. It was four o'clock when the British columns reached their designated positions. They waited and waited in vain for the signal from Thornton to begin the attack.

Three thousand men, under Generals Gibbs and Keane, were to assault the left of the American line; one thousand men, led by Colonel Rennie, were to attack the right; the Ninety-third Highlanders, eight hundred strong, a splendid regiment of hard-praying and hard-fighting Caledonians, just in from the Cape of Good Hope, under Colonel Dale, were to attack the centre; and a reserve of two regiments, about fifteen hundred strong, under General Lambert, were to follow up whichever one of the attacks was the most successful. Pakenham had been told by a deserter that the left of the American line was the weakest point, which was true at the time. Jackson, however, had fortunately reinforced it on the day before the battle with a strong body of the Tennessee riflemen.

As the mists rolled away the Americans saw the vivid scarlet lines of the British advancing upon them. It was six o'clock in the morning. Pakenham had to attack now. He was already within range, and a retreat was not to be thought of. Besides, the idea of defeat never entered his head. What, the finest soldiers in the world to be stopped or defeated by a lot of volunteers, militiamen, backwoodsmen? Nonsense! Forward was the word!

The head of Gibbs' column was led by the Forty-fourth regiment, under Colonel Mullens, who had been ordered to provide the fascines and scaling ladders, to enable them to cross the ditch and mount the walls. The regiment, badly commanded, passed by the place of storage in the darkness, and had failed to bring up the ladders; and General Gibbs, promising to hang Colonel Mullens after the action, had sent them back at the double quick to procure them. They now came straggling back in great disorder, with only a few ladders. The troops meanwhile were steadily advancing in the face of such a hellish fire as few troops have ever attempted to withstand. The great thirty-two-pounder, charged with musket balls to the very muzzle, actually tore up the head of the column.

The continuous crackle of the small arms and the deep roar of the great guns filled the air with stunning sound. The cloud of smoke over the American lines was lined and seamed with streaks of fire, and the lightning itself was not more swift and deadly than the leaden messengers which leaped from it. Grape and solid shot ripped long lanes through the advancing soldiery, but they still came on! It was magnificent! Reaching the edge of the ditch, they were in point-blank range of the deadly American riflemen. Mullens and his men were nowhere to be seen. There were no ladders, no fascines, no anything. No troops that lived could stand the steady, awful fire of the Tennesseans. In the face of that blasting storm of death they stopped, faltered, broke, and ran.

The officers recklessly and heroically strove to reform them and lead them on. They were shot down like sheep in their brave efforts. Gibbs came up to Pakenham weeping and crying.

"The men will not follow me," he said brokenly. "I can't get them to come on."

"Here comes the Ninety-third," said Pakenham, looking at the splendid regiment of Highlanders advancing coolly in the awful confusion. "Rally on the Ninety-third!" he cried, darting in among the retreat- ing men, followed by the officers of his staff. They finally succeeded in checking the backward movement, the brave men fell into line once more, faced the other way slowly, and began another desperate advance.

On the other flank a small redoubt in front of Jackson's lines was captured by Rennie's men after a furious little combat, but not until every one of the few defenders was killed or wounded. The guns were then turned upon the American line. Rennie and a few of his men made for the ditch in spite of the fact that the black regiment from the West Indies, which was to lead, failed miserably at this juncture, behaving quite as badly as the Forty-fourth. There were no ladders, no fascines here either. Nevertheless, Rennie and a few men struggled across the ditch, and the colonel, the major, and one other officer mounted the works crying, "Surrender!" They were shot dead the instant their heads appeared over the parapets, and their bodies fell inward. The attack was broken, the regiments were actually crumpled up by the fierce, rapid firing of the Americans until they too fled—all who were able, that is.

Thornton, on the other bank of the river, had at last come up and had captured the American position with the loss of about one hundred of his men, mainly inflicted by the American naval contingent. Most of the militia behaved disgracefully, and fled without firing a shot. On that side the river only six Americans were killed. Thornton's success came too late to be of service.

Meanwhile, Pakenham, Gibbs and Keane led the new attack forward, with the magnificent Scotsmen in the advance—a forlorn hope, a desperate venture. They had seen hot, hard fighting in Spain; never had they met anything like this. There was no lack of Anglo-Saxon courage there. Valour teemed upon the field, but the trouble was that it was on both sides of the redoubt. The men came slowly, with fixed bayonets, grim determination in their white faces. They were waited for by the cool American commander. Again the word was given. Again the low, black, muddy redoubt of the Americans was tipped with vivid, death-dealing flame. The advancing troops were mowed down in sheets.

"Shame, shame!" cried Pakenham, intercepting those who would fain retreat. "This is the way. Forward! Forward!" he cried, beating the reluctant men with his sword. "Order up the reserve !" he said to his aide, who galloped madly away.

When the officer delivered the order to Lambert, who was watching the dreadful carnage with feelings of sickening horror, he ordered

BATTLE OF NEW ORLEANS

the bugler to sound the advance. The men sprang to their feet, waiting the signal, when a solid shot tore the trumpet from the bugler's lips before he had made a note. Ere he could procure another bugle the battle was over, and to put in the reserve would be only to devote more men to destruction.

Pakenham's arm was shattered, his horse was killed under him, but, forgetful of everything but the battle, he mounted another and, waving his sword, rode on, encouraging his troops until he was hurled from his saddle and instantly killed by another bullet. Keane fell desperately hurt. Gibbs was mortally wounded, and carried reluctantly from the field. Colonel Dale, at the head of the Highlanders, was shot dead. Officer after officer was killed. The splendid Ninety-third marched up to the edge of the ditch and stood there, unable to go forward, too proud to retreat—an heroic example of veteran soldiery. They won a deathless name on that field. Finally, with less than one hundred and twenty men out of nearly eight hundred, the Highlanders slowly retired. The rest of the army had long since fled. Less than half an hour had ended it all. Half the American force had not been engaged.

Jackson immediately despatched a large body of troops across the river to oust Thornton, but before the Americans could deliver their attack Thornton, under orders from Lambert, who succeeded to the command of the beaten army, abandoned the position. The British retreated precipitately to their ships a few days later, leaving behind those of their wounded unable to be moved, and many guns and supplies. Lambert conducted the retreat so skilfully that he was rewarded by a baronetcy when he returned to England.

The British loss in this battle was seven hundred killed, fourteen hundred wounded, and five hundred prisoners; a total loss of twenty-six hundred in twenty-five minutes—over one and a half per second! Incredible? True! The American loss was but eight killed and fourteen wounded, mostly in the redoubt captured by Rennie! These figures take no account of Thornton's attack. The British loss in the whole campaign was over thirty-five hundred men, the American about three hundred, the number engaged in the campaign being about ten thousand for the British and about seven thousand for the Americans, although in the decisive battle Jackson had in action less than three thousand to six thousand of the British.

It was the most astonishing battle ever fought, and the most stupendous victory ever achieved in this hemisphere prior to Dewey and Sampson, and the misery of it all was that peace had been declared some time before the battle was fought! Oh, for some earth-girdling "Puck" to have carried the news! The lives of all the brave men had been sacrificed in vain.

The English soldiers had fought with the utmost determination and valour. Pakenham's plans were good ones, in fact they were the only ones which could have been put in operation at all; no blame attaches to him, unless for haste in not waiting for Thornton, but the honour of the campaign must rest with Jackson. Nobody could have done better; few so well.

While the battle was unnecessary, the victory was very useful in creating among the British nation and the nations of the world generally a healthy respect for American arms, which has never entirely left them. We have kept it fresh from time to time. The battle of New Orleans was a great, glorious, and dreadful victory, and the most conspicuous military figure in the history of our country between the Revolution and the Civil War is undoubtedly that of the backwoods fighter—Andrew Jackson of Tennessee!

The "Constitution's" Last Battle

The last survivor of the great captains of the War of 1812, who indeed lived until four years after the close of the Civil War, having been previously retired in 1862 as rear admiral, was Charles Stewart. Though it does not appertain to this story, it is interesting to note that the daughter of this splendid American fighter became the mother of that equally brilliant fighter in other fields, Charles Stewart Parnell, the great Irish agitator. Stewart was born of Irish parentage, in Pennsylvania, in 1776, He entered the merchant service at thirteen, and was captain of a ship at nineteen, an age at which, at present and under modern conditions, our prospective naval officers cannot possibly have attained the rank of midshipman even! In 1798 Stewart was appointed a lieutenant in the navy, where he served with distinction in all the subsequent wars.

In the French War, while in command of the schooner *Experiment*, he captured a French armed schooner of much greater force than his own after a brilliant little combat. He was the second in command to stout old Commodore Preble in the Tripolitan War, and offered to cut out the *Philadelphia*; but Decatur had made the proposition before Stewart, who had command of the *Siren*, which had been away from the station, had learned of the disaster, and so he had to content himself with supporting Decatur's attack, as we have seen.

At the beginning of the War of 1812 he had command of the famous frigate *Constellation*. It was through his address that she escaped from a heavy British squadron into the Elizabeth River at Norfolk, where she was unfortunately so closely blockaded during the entire war that it was impossible for her to get to sea. It was his precaution and wise prevision which prevented the capture of that ship by several cutting-out expeditions which attempted it. At the close of 1813 he was given command of the more famous ship *Constitution*, 44, in which Hull and Bainbridge had won their notable victories over the *Guerrière* and the *Java*. Stewart at once put to sea, as usual escaping the blockaders off Boston. He had a rather successful cruise, capturing a heavily armed British schooner of war, an armed privateer of large size, a letter of marque, several merchant vessels, and chasing the frigate *Pique*, 36, which escaped at night, after a hard pursuit, through the Windward Passage. On his way back the *Constitution* was chased hard by the frigates *Junon* and *Nymphe*, either of which was a match for her. She escaped with difficulty, and finally made the harbour of Marblehead; thence, shortly after, she got into Boston, passing the blockade again.

The ship was in bad shape, nothing having been done to her in the way of refitting or repairing since her two hard battles. She was therefore entirely overhauled, under Stewart's direction—a long and tedious job. Her crew having been sent to the Lakes, where they gave good account of themselves, a new crew was shipped—the pick of the country—and on December 30, 1814, she got to sea, eluding the blockaders before Boston for the seventh time during the war! She was as fine and fit for every emergency as any frigate that ever sailed the ocean. It is quite within the bounds of truth to say that there never was a ship so dreaded by the whilom masters of the sea as the United States ship *Constitution*. Under previous instructions from the British Admiralty, as soon as she got away every vessel of whatever class which spoke another on the high seas was instructed to announce the escape of the *Constitution* from the blockade; thus, almost with the quickness of the wind itself, from ocean to ocean was carried the ominous news. Frigates cruising alone were instructed to avoid action with anything that looked like the great American. Other vessels were directed to hunt her in couples!

Perhaps Captain Stewart had this fact in mind, for when his young wife, to whom he had been recently married, in answer to the natural question of departing husbands—especially youthful ones—"What shall I bring you as a present?" patriotically answered, "A British frigate," he replied, smiling, "I will bring you two!"

However, his expectations did not seem in the way of being realized, for the cruise was more or less an uneventful one at first, and the officers and men began to feel that the usual luck of the *Constitution* had failed them. On February 18, 1815, long after peace had been declared, by the way, Stewart chased an English line-of-battle ship, the *Elizabeth*, off the Portuguese coast near Lisbon; before her character

227

was discovered he left the chase and captured a merchant vessel. When the *Elizabeth* reached Lisbon and learned that the *Constitution* was in the vicinity, without stopping for any purpose she at once squared away in pursuit.

It happened that the frigate *Tiber*, 36, under the command of Richard Dacres, who had been so badly beaten on the *Guerrière*, was in port also. Dacres had been especially preparing his vessel for the purpose of meeting the *Constitution*, or one of her sister ships, and he followed the *Elizabeth* close on the heels of the American. It was lucky for him he never caught sight of her. About the same time the *Leander*, the *Newcastle*, and the *Acasta*, two fifty- and one forty-gun frigates, which the *Constitution* had eluded before at Boston, were booming along toward the eastward in pursuit of her, deluded by a rumour which said that she had been joined by the *Congress* and the *President*. In addition, the seas swarmed with British cruisers in couples seeking her. Stewart, who had changed his course without any explicable reason, had sailed the *Constitution* down to within eighty leagues of the Madeiras, which then bore about southwest by west. She was sailing along serenely in the midst of all this commotion when, early in the afternoon of February 20th, a large sail was discovered, through a rift in the fog, bearing two points off the port bow. It was a raw, nasty day, the fresh wet breeze raising a choppy, uncomfortable sea.

The *Constitution* at once edged away in chase. At two o'clock another sail was raised, right ahead of the former and apparently in company with her. Signals were exchanged between the two vessels which had been sighted, and they made every effort to close with each other. A double row of painted ports on the nearest led the Americans to think that they were in the presence of two frigates, a large one of at least fifty guns and a smaller, but Stewart had promised his officers a fight, and he was quite in the mood to have tackled a line-of-battle ship rather than disappoint all hands, so the *Constitution* was soon covered with every strip of canvas, including studding sails, which she could carry alow and aloft, and bore down upon the strangers, which she soon began to overhaul. The two ships, which were gradually working nearer to each other, set all sail, hoisted the English flag, and endeavoured to escape.

About half past four in the afternoon the *Constitution* carried away her main royal mast in the freshening breeze, which so far delayed her that it gave her enemies time to close with each other. By smart seamanship, by five o'clock the damage was repaired, another spar replaced the broken one, sail was set, and the *Constitution* quickly regained her speed, and began to overhaul the chase again as before. There was some little manoeuvring on the part of the English, who had flung out their battle flags, to get the weather-gage, but they were unable to out-point the *Constitution*, and indeed had hardly time to settle back on the old starboard tack again when she came booming down upon them. Action was now inevitable. Seeing this they deliberately stripped themselves to fighting canvas, and Stewart did the same. At six o'clock in the evening the three vessels lay at the points of an equilateral angle, the two English vessels in a line ahead, the smaller in the lead, forming the base, and the *Constitution* midway between them at the apex; all were heading west, with the wind over the starboard quarter, the *Constitution* being to windward.

Stewart now saw that his antagonists were a small frigate and a large sloop-of-war—a very tidy couple indeed. At six o'clock the battle began at a range within two hundred and fifty yards, a little more than the length of an ordinary city block. It was a brilliant moonlight night, the clouds and the fog had disappeared, and all of the vessels were now plainly visible. Every gun on the engaged sides of the three ships was at once in action, and the firing for fifteen minutes was rapid and fierce. The British cheered loudly, while the men on the *Constitution* maintained a grim silence—they could cheer later on. A cloud of smoke drifted down between the *Constitution* and her antagonists, whose fire, by the way, materially decreased, and at 6.15 p.m. Stewart ceased firing.

As the smoke blew away he saw that he had forged ahead, and was now abreast of and very near the foremost ship, afterward found to be the sloop-of-war *Levant*, Captain Douglass. Stewart also discovered that the rear ship, the frigate *Cyane*, had lufted up into the wind and was endeavouring to go about on the other tack to cross his stern and rake him. He acted with the quickness of thought itself to meet this new danger, first pouring a tremendous broadside from double-shotted guns into the *Levant* at close range, which nearly smashed the life out of her; he laid his main and mizzen topsails to the mast, let fly the jib-sheet, braced the head-yards around until the sails shivered in the wind, and with astonishing rapidity actually backed the *Constitution* down upon her other enemy.

Instead of being able to cross the stern of the American, what was the surprise of Captain Falcon, of the frigate *Cyane*, to see her huge bulk come shoving through the smoke across his own bows. At this juncture, the two ships being almost in contact, the *Constitution* poured in a full broadside from her port battery, which raked the *Cyane* terribly fore and aft. She shivered from truck to keelson under this terrific smashing as if she had struck a rock. Beaten off from the wind by the Constitution's manoeuvres, the *Cyane* fell away, of course, and the two ships sailed side by side for perhaps five minutes, exchanging broadsides, until the lighter *Cyane* was silenced.

Leaving the helpless frigate for the moment, Stewart turned his attention to the *Levant*, which had been firing aimlessly into the smoke and had at last found out that the *Constitution* had dropped astern. Now, therefore, Captain Douglass attempted to come by the wind to cross the bows of the *Constitution* and rake her, in the hope of delivering his helpless consort. As soon as Stewart saw the manoeuvres he put his helm up, filled away, and, the ship being handled with wonderful smartness, ran down off the wind and crossed astern of the *Levant*, into whom he poured two raking broadsides at close range from his starboard battery, which almost completely disabled her. The *Levant* drifted far away and remained out of action for a long time, while her men worked desperately to re-reeve the gear and refit, so that they could once more engage in the fight.

Meanwhile the *Cyane* had pluckily followed the *Constitution*, and now attempted to wear to cross her stern and rake, but the *Constitution* was much better handled. She emulated the manoeuvre of the enemy, and actually succeeded in swinging around under the stern of the devoted *Cyane*, into which she poured another terrible raking broadside; then she rounded to on her port quarter, and for ten minutes she made a chopping-block of her gallant enemy. At 6.50 p.m. the *Cyane* struck her colours. She was immediately taken possession of by a prize crew, an operation which consumed some little time.

Meanwhile the *Levant*, having finished refitting, instead of trying to escape, now sailed boldly down to meet the *Constitution* again. Captain Douglass must have known that the *Cyane* had been captured, and that he, in his smaller ship, had no further chance in the fight, especially in view of the punishment he had already received, therefore his action was foolhardy, but gallant. At 8.50 p.m. the two ships passed each other on different tacks, exchanging broadsides, then the *Levant* spread everything to get away. The *Constitution* wore in chase, and by 9.30 in the evening had drawn so close to that ship that the shot from her bow-chasers could be distinctly heard splintering the timbers on board of the *Levant*. The situation of the latter was perfectly helpless, and she struck her colours. The *Constitution's* last and greatest battle was over.

As an exhibition of the highest seamanship this action has never even been paralleled. It is almost hopeless to attempt to prevent one ship engaged with two others from being frequently raked. In this instance the *Constitution*, by her masterly handling, raked both ships opposed to her repeatedly, manning her port or starboard battery at will. One of the opposing ships tried two times to cross her stern, the other to cross her bows, she frustrated both attempts with ease. In all her manoeuvres she never lost the weather-gage; she went backward, or forward, or turned about on her heel, attacking either ship apparently at pleasure. Stewart handled her like a yacht or a catboat. It was astonishing! Stewart's exploit excited the greatest admiration among nautical critics all over the world—and does to this day—and, with Hull's wonderful escape on the same ship from the pursuing British squadron, stands at the very high-water mark of consummate seamanship and skill.

The number of guns on the *Constitution* was fifty-one. Out of her crew of four hundred and fifty-six she lost four killed and ten wounded. The combined armament of the *Cyane* and the *Levant* amounted to fifty-five guns. Out of their crews of three hundred and fifteen they lost thirty-five killed and forty-two wounded. Both ships were terribly cut up.

The *Constitution* had sustained but little damage to her rigging, but she had been hulled thirteen times by solid shot. Only three shot had hulled her when she fought the *Guerrière*, and four when she had fought the *Java*, therefore the English had done better than usual. The *Cyane* had lost twelve killed and twenty-six wounded. Every brace and bowline had been cut, most of her standing and running rigging was carried away, her main and mizzenmasts were tottering, many important spars were badly wounded, she had been hulled many times, and five of her guns were disabled. The *Levant* lost twenty-three killed and sixteen wounded. She was smashed up as badly as her consort.

One or two little anecdotes in connection with the fight are of interest. The two British captains were discussing, over their wine after dinner in Stewart's cabin, the reason of their defeat, each accusing the other of being the cause of it. Stewart listened to their acrimonious debate for some time, and finally suggested, as a method of solving the problem, that he would put them and their crews back upon their respective ships and try it over! The solution was declined in silence.

Just before the battle grog was served out as usual to the crew of the *Constitution*. Some of the men claimed that they should have a double portion, as they had two ships to fight. This so filled the mind of a veteran seaman aboard with disgust that he kicked over the grog tub, amid the cheers of the men, remarking "that they didn't need no Dutch courage to fight them ships."

A sailor named John Lancey, from Cape Ann, was carried below to the cockpit, horribly mutilated by a solid shot and writhing in death agony, just as the *Cyane* struck her colours. The surgeon, after a hasty examination, told him that he could do nothing for him and that his end was approaching. "I know it," replied the heroic man; "I only want to know that the other ship has struck." When the shouts of the men above announced to him that the *Levant* had surrendered he actually lifted himself from his cot, waved his blood-stained, shattered arm stump in the air, and joined in the cheering, and immediately thereafter expired.

After a very gallant action many years before, by which Stewart saved the lives of some sixty Spanish people escaping from an outbreak at San Domingo, he had been presented with a superb Toledo blade by the King of Spain, his naval and official rank not permitting him to receive a completed sword from a foreign government. This blade had been beautifully mounted, and he wore the sword during this battle with the *Cyane* and the *Levant*. A solid shot, which grazed his side during the action, had carried away the hilt. The armourer of the *Constitution*, after the battle, fitted a rudely forged iron guard to the exquisite blade, and ever after, on state occasions, Stewart wore this rough, iron-hilted sword.

The prize crews from the *Constitution* made all haste to get the ships in shape again. By one o'clock in the morning of February 21st, or three hours after the surrender of the *Cyane* and the *Levant*, the *Constitution* was ready for another action. On the following day they headed for the nearest neutral port, and on the fifteenth of March anchored in Porta Praya, in the Cape Verde Islands. There Stewart found one of his prizes, which he determined to use as a *cartel* to send the prisoners back to England. The day after their arrival, as they were busily engaged in their preparations, an English midshipman on the *Constitution* called the attention of Captain Falcon of the *Cyane*, who was a prisoner there, to the sails of a large ship seen above the fog, coming toward the harbour. The air was filled with a dense mist, which hung low and prevented anything below the topgallant yards from being visible. The English captain angrily silenced the imprudent midshipman, but the attention of Shubrick, acting first of the *Constitution*, had been called to the stranger.

He hastily informed Captain Stewart, who was shaving in his cabin, and received orders to get under way and go out to engage. Immediately thereafter the sails of two other ships were detected towering above the fog. At this news the half-shaved, but fully alert Stewart came running on deck, ordered the cables cut, and signalled the two prizes to get under way at once. It was quite evident from the look of the sails that the force approaching was too great for him to cope with, with any chance of success. It is on a par with the rest of the seamanship of this remarkable cruise to note that ten minutes after the strange sails had been sighted the *Constitution* and her prizes, the latter naturally greatly undermanned with their small prize crews, had cut cables, got under way, and under their topsails alone, which rendered them invisible as the fog rose above them, they were stretching swiftly for the mouth of the harbour. Some of the English prisoners, who had been landed, took possession of a Portuguese battery and began firing at the escaping ships, which caused the English outside to get on the alert at once.

The fog gradually lowered as the three ships made the harbour entrance and, crossing their topgallant yards in gallant style, stretched away for the open sea. The various ships were plainly visible to each other down to the tops. The three English vessels were Sir George Collier's squadron, before mentioned—the *Leander*, 50, the *Newcastle*, 50, and the *Acasta*, 40. To oppose this formidable squadron Stewart had the *Constitution*, 44, the *Cyane*, 32, the *Levant*, 18, the two latter badly disabled still and with only small prize crews, insufficient in number to work the guns aboard. The English forces counted one hundred and sixty- three heavy guns and twelve hundred men. The Americans one hundred and six guns, most of them light, and four hundred and fifty men. The fifty-gun ships were especially large and heavy, and designed particularly to overmatch ships of the *Constitution's* class. To run was Stewart's only chance; he was as good at running as he was at fighting.

The chase that ensued was as exciting as any the *Constitution* ever participated in. The fog still held, though it gradually settled down so that the officers standing on the hammock cloths of the pursuing ships were easily seen from the American ships, though the hulls of the English ships still remained concealed. About 1 p.m., finding that the

Cyane was lagging behind and in danger of being overhauled, Stewart signalled her to tack, supposing that one of the chasing ships would be detached to pursue. If he could divide the enemy he determined to engage the nearest ship himself.

The three pursuers, however, paid no attention to the last ship—which, by the way, succeeded in reaching New York in safety a month later—but held on after the other two. At 2.30 p.m. the foremost English ship opened on the *Constitution*, firing by division, but the shot fell short by an hundred yards. Stewart gained a little more definite idea of the size and quality of his pursuer from the heavy fire of the divisions of her battery.

At 3 p.m., the *Levant* being now almost within range of the nearest pursuer, Stewart signalled her to tack, which she immediately did, when, to the surprise of the officers on board the *Constitution*, the whole of the formidable English squadron tacked and stood on in the wake of the little sloop *Levant*. The old *Constitution* at this time was skipping through the water at about twelve knots an hour. There was nothing on the seas to catch her, and she soon ran the enemy out of sight. She reached Boston in safety early in May. Ballard, the prize master of the *Levant*, seeing escape was hopeless, made for Porta Praya again. He anchored immediately under the guns of the battery, but the English commodore, as usual paying no attention to the neutrality of the port, sent the *Newcastle* and the *Acasta* into the harbour, and, after enduring the fire of these two heavy ships for some fifteen minutes, Lieutenant Ballard struck his colours.

"I believe, sir," said the English boarding officer, in great exultation, coming to take charge of the prize, "that I have the honour to receive the sword of Captain Blakeley of the *Wasp*."

"No, sir," said Ballard grimly, "you have the honour to receive the sword of Captain Ballard, prize master of His Britannic Majesty's sloop-of-war *Levant!*"

Why Sir George Collier's squadron acted in this extraordinary manner in this pursuit has never been definitely ascertained, though various explanations of it, all equally unsatisfactory, have been put forth. Sir George was so chagrined over the matter that, on being reproached with it some years later, he committed suicide.

The brilliant way in which Stewart had escaped from the harbour and succeeded in preserving two of his ships from the tremendously overwhelming force of his enemy added new laurels to the wreath which his grateful countrymen had twined about the head of the splendid sailor. He received the usual rewards from Congress and his countrymen, and, by graceful compliment, the popular name of the gallant ship he had so ably commanded was soon applied to him, and to the end of his days he was known as "Old Ironsides!"

LEONAUR

ALSO FROM LEONAUR
AVAILABLE IN SOFTCOVER OR HARDCOVER WITH DUST JACKET

IRON TIMES WITH THE GUARDS *by An O. E. (G. P. A. Fildes)*—The Experiences of an Officer of the Coldstream Guards on the Western Front During the First World War.

THE GREAT WAR IN THE MIDDLE EAST: 1 *by W. T. Massey*—The Desert Campaigns & How Jerusalem Was Won---two classic accounts in one volume.

THE GREAT WAR IN THE MIDDLE EAST: 2 *by W. T. Massey*—Allenby's Final Triumph.

SMITH-DORRIEN *by Horace Smith-Dorrien*—Isandlwhana to the Great War.

1914 *by Sir John French*—The Early Campaigns of the Great War by the British Commander.

GRENADIER *by E. R. M. Fryer*—The Recollections of an Officer of the Grenadier Guards throughout the Great War on the Western Front.

BATTLE, CAPTURE & ESCAPE *by George Pearson*—The Experiences of a Canadian Light Infantryman During the Great War.

DIGGERS AT WAR *by R. Hugh Knyvett & G. P. Cuttriss*—"Over There" With the Australians by R. Hugh Knyvett and Over the Top With the Third Australian Division by G. P. Cuttriss. Accounts of Australians During the Great War in the Middle East, at Gallipoli and on the Western Front.

HEAVY FIGHTING BEFORE US *by George Brenton Laurie*—The Letters of an Officer of the Royal Irish Rifles on the Western Front During the Great War.

THE CAMELIERS *by Oliver Hogue*—A Classic Account of the Australians of the Imperial Camel Corps During the First World War in the Middle East.

RED DUST *by Donald Black*—A Classic Account of Australian Light Horsemen in Palestine During the First World War.

THE LEAN, BROWN MEN *by Angus Buchanan*—Experiences in East Africa During the Great War with the 25th Royal Fusiliers—the Legion of Frontiersmen.

THE NIGERIAN REGIMENT IN EAST AFRICA *by W. D. Downes*—On Campaign During the Great War 1916-1918.

THE 'DIE-HARDS' IN SIBERIA *by John Ward*—With the Middlesex Regiment Against the Bolsheviks 1918-19.

LEONAUR

ALSO FROM LEONAUR
AVAILABLE IN SOFTCOVER OR HARDCOVER WITH DUST JACKET

FARAWAY CAMPAIGN *by F. James*—Experiences of an Indian Army Cavalry Officer in Persia & Russia During the Great War.

REVOLT IN THE DESERT *by T. E. Lawrence*—An account of the experiences of one remarkable British officer's war from his own perspective.

MACHINE-GUN SQUADRON *by A. M. G.*—The 20th Machine Gunners from British Yeomanry Regiments in the Middle East Campaign of the First World War.

A GUNNER'S CRUSADE *by Antony Bluett*—The Campaign in the Desert, Palestine & Syria as Experienced by the Honourable Artillery Company During the Great War .

DESPATCH RIDER *by W. H. L. Watson*—The Experiences of a British Army Motorcycle Despatch Rider During the Opening Battles of the Great War in Europe.

TIGERS ALONG THE TIGRIS *by E. J. Thompson*—The Leicestershire Regiment in Mesopotamia During the First World War.

HEARTS & DRAGONS *by Charles R. M. F. Crutwell*—The 4th Royal Berkshire Regiment in France and Italy During the Great War, 1914-1918.

INFANTRY BRIGADE: 1914 *by John Ward*—The Diary of a Commander of the 15th Infantry Brigade, 5th Division, British Army, During the Retreat from Mons.

DOING OUR 'BIT' *by Ian Hay*—Two Classic Accounts of the Men of Kitchener's 'New Army' During the Great War including *The First 100,000 & All In It.*

AN EYE IN THE STORM *by Arthur Ruhl*—An American War Correspondent's Experiences of the First World War from the Western Front to Gallipoli-and Beyond.

STAND & FALL *by Joe Cassells*—With the Middlesex Regiment Against the Bolsheviks 1918-19.

RIFLEMAN MACGILL'S WAR *by Patrick MacGill*—A Soldier of the London Irish During the Great War in Europe including *The Amateur Army, The Red Horizon & The Great Push.*

WITH THE GUNS *by C. A. Rose & Hugh Dalton*—Two First Hand Accounts of British Gunners at War in Europe During World War 1- Three Years in France with the Guns and With the British Guns in Italy.

THE BUSH WAR DOCTOR *by Robert V. Dolbey*—The Experiences of a British Army Doctor During the East African Campaign of the First World War.

LEONAUR

ALSO FROM LEONAUR
AVAILABLE IN SOFTCOVER OR HARDCOVER WITH DUST JACKET

THE 9TH—THE KING'S (LIVERPOOL REGIMENT) IN THE GREAT WAR 1914 - 1918 *by Enos H. G. Roberts*—Mersey to mud—war and Liverpool men.

THE GAMBARDIER *by Mark Severn*—The experiences of a battery of Heavy artillery on the Western Front during the First World War.

FROM MESSINES TO THIRD YPRES *by Thomas Floyd*—A personal account of the First World War on the Western front by a 2/5th Lancashire Fusilier.

THE IRISH GUARDS IN THE GREAT WAR - VOLUME 1 *by Rudyard Kipling*—Edited and Compiled from Their Diaries and Papers—The First Battalion.

THE IRISH GUARDS IN THE GREAT WAR - VOLUME 1 *by Rudyard Kipling*—Edited and Compiled from Their Diaries and Papers—The Second Battalion.

ARMOURED CARS IN EDEN *by K. Roosevelt*—An American President's son serving in Rolls Royce armoured cars with the British in Mesopatamia & with the American Artillery in France during the First World War.

CHASSEUR OF 1914 *by Marcel Dupont*—Experiences of the twilight of the French Light Cavalry by a young officer during the early battles of the great war in Europe.

TROOP HORSE & TRENCH *by R.A. Lloyd*—The experiences of a British Lifeguardsman of the household cavalry fighting on the western front during the First World War 1914-18.

THE EAST AFRICAN MOUNTED RIFLES *by C.J. Wilson*—Experiences of the campaign in the East African bush during the First World War.

THE LONG PATROL *by George Berrie*—A Novel of Light Horsemen from Gallipoli to the Palestine campaign of the First World War.

THE FIGHTING CAMELIERS *by Frank Reid*—The exploits of the Imperial Camel Corps in the desert and Palestine campaigns of the First World War.

STEEL CHARIOTS IN THE DESERT *by S. C. Rolls*—The first world war experiences of a Rolls Royce armoured car driver with the Duke of Westminster in Libya and in Arabia with T.E. Lawrence.

WITH THE IMPERIAL CAMEL CORPS IN THE GREAT WAR *by Geoffrey Inchbald*—The story of a serving officer with the British 2nd battalion against the Senussi and during the Palestine campaign.

CPSIA information can be obtained
at www.ICGtesting.com
Printed in the USA
FFOW02n2140290418
46376097-48074FF